MARC ELLIS' Good Fullas

MARC ELLIS' Good Fullas

A GUIDE TO KIWI BLOKES

MARC ELLIS AND CHARLIE HADDRELL

Hodder Moa

Dedicated to the original Good Fullas: Chris Ellis and Dave Haddrell

A catalogue record for this book is available from the National Library of New Zealand

Ellis, Marc, 1971-

Marc Ellis' good fullas : a guide to kiwi blokes / Marc Ellis,

Charlie Haddrell.

ISBN 978-1-86971-193-1

1. Men—New Zealand—Humour. 2. New Zealand wit and humour—

21st century. I. Haddrell, Charlie. II. Title.

NZ828.302—dc 22

A Hodder Moa Book

Published in 2010 by Hachette New Zealand Ltd

4 Whetu Place, Mairangi Bay

Auckland, New Zealand

Text © MCG Marketing Ltd 2010

The moral rights of the author have been asserted.

Design and format © Hachette New Zealand Ltd 2010

Designed, produced and typeset by Hachette New Zealand Ltd

Cover design and illustrations by Donovan Bixley, Magma Design

Printed by Printlink, Wellington, New Zealand

CONTENTS

ABOUT MARC

Known for his love of telling a few stories over a couple of triple star 'Prides of the South', Marc is a Funny Fulla who likes to compete, even if it's just walking with a mate or his wife to the dairy. Life is supposed to be fun. Competition is fun. Life is competition. Life is fun. Marc is probably best known for eating the hottest vindaloo in New Zealand, being a two-time Opito Bay gumboot-throwing champion and achieving other remarkable feats over the last few decades, including his crowning glory: victory in the world cheese-rolling championships in England in 2004.

ABOUT CHARLIE

Charlie Haddrell is an odd Fulla, who knows the botanical names of most of New Zealand's native trees and absolutely everything there is to know about the Chrysler Valiant. He loves beer but will always drink four at a time (with no two being the same), giving rise to the nickname Hadge the Simple Sampler. The same goes for cheese. He was the breast stroking champion at his school for two years running and it is rumoured he has swum naked in the Zambesi, Danube, Mississippi, Rio Grande, Duero, Waikato and countless other rivers. He cuts his hair once a year, but washes it more often than that.

Charlie and Marc, Dubai 2006.

ACKNOWLEDGEMENTS

Thanks to all these Good Fullas who helped make the book happen, especially: 'Mad Brad' Devlin, 'Crazy Tim' Schneideman, Dr. Matt Lines, 'Bird' Haddrell, Andy 'Hurricane' Higgs, Murray Higgs, John Kelt, Darren Caulton, Tim Harris, John O'Neill, Lou Thompson, Benjamin 'Chicken' Hickey, David Lavulo Edwards, Shaun Davies, Matt Harte, Mobeen Bhikoo, Duncan Anderson, Semih Kayikçi, Donovan Bixley, Kevin Chapman and Warren Adler. Also, a special thanks to Landreth & Co and Cafe Karadeniz.

The Fullas would like to thank their wives for their support in this project, and for putting up with their constant shenanigans. Marc confesses that occasionally getting together with Charlie to work on the *Good Fullas* was really just an excuse to have a few ales and a stinking hot tikka masala.

Charlie thanks Julia for leaving everything she had to come and live in New Zealand with a Kiwi Battler like him.

Finally, the Fullas hope their children, Sofia, Cristina and Harry, enjoy the stories they have told in this book . . . but never repeat them.

FOREWORD

I will start by conceding that when overseas I miss New Zealand terribly. We are very fortunate to have such a wonderful country and I for one greatly look forward to any contact with home, as a little reminder of what makes New Zealand so unique.

It was a great thrill to receive a courier parcel to my office containing this manuscript and to be asked to write this foreword. I have known Marc for a number of years now and have recently had the pleasure of meeting Charles on a recent return trip to Auckland.

Both of these gentlemen have done a remarkable job creating what I predict will become a Kiwi literary must-have. What you hold in your hand is a laugh a minute. Every single Kiwi will recognise the characters contained in this book and will laugh out loud reading about the great diversity of 'Fullas' we have in New Zealand.

I loved the book so much I gave a personalised copy to my husband and have a dozen copies to give to my staff at Christmas.

Love to all.

H.
Helen Clarke

INTRODUCING

THE GOOD FULLAS

For the record, this book is about Good Fullas. The very Good Fullas that we all come across every day. Bloody Good Fullas, in fact. It's a book based on Fullas the two of us have met and experiences we have enjoyed — although Fullas' real names have been changed to not reveal true identities or blow decent Fullas' cover.

Growing up in Wellington, studying in Dunedin and now living and working in Auckland, Marc knows New Zealand and New Zealanders as well as most, having encountered the full spectrum through sport, entertainment and commercial endeavours. Charlie has spent the last 12 years working closely with small and large New Zealand firms from the primary sectors through to leading-edge technology developers. Growing up in Papatoetoe, and most recently working as New Zealand Consul-General in Italy, he too knows how New Zealanders tick.

We have both interacted with New Zealand Jokers through every level, nook and cranny of society, and love nothing better than mixing it up with Good Fullas from all walks of life.

While sipping on a couple of Speight's ales (brewed not far from where we met and studied in Dunedin) we agreed there was no descriptive guide to all the differing types of colourful characters that we had come across in our travels throughout the country. We decided we'd best put one together in bound form. This is a light-hearted look at what makes these Fullas quirky, and why we should love them all, highlighting the traits, habits, mannerisms, attributes, vagaries and peculiarities that cubby-hole them within their particular pigeon-hole. The book is written to serve as a strong reminder not to take life too seriously and is a true celebration of Kiwi Manhood.

Neither of us have any respect for political correctness. But we have plenty of regard for the Fullas in this book. What this book is designed to celebrate are 25 stereotypical New Zealand blokes, through a humorous account of their eccentricities, idiosyncrasies, preferences and character. Simply put, the 25 are all just damn Good Fullas. Any urine that we have extracted from the characters in this book is purely so that Fullas are able to have a good old-fashioned giggle at themselves. We want to give every Fulla a chance to identify with a character or two, recognise other characters, learn more about themselves and realise that being slightly peculiar and particular is actually quite normal and natural, and in fact to be encouraged.

Every New Zealand household would do well to have a copy of this guide so that: the male members of the home can feel an association with one or more of the protagonists; foreign guests can finger through it to better or further appreciate New Zealand men; marketers can best identify, understand and target certain demographics; and anyone can pick it up when they need a bloody good guffaw or — as the 'Finkle' might describe it — a boisterous cachinnation. We trust it will appeal to everyone with an interest in New Zealand and anyone with a sense of humour.

That said, we expect some people to get upset; in fact we would not have written this book had there been no opportunity to get under the skin of certain fringe elements. By virtue of their very nature, most CAVE Men will outwardly abhor this book, for example. But you can bet they'll snicker awkwardly in recognising themselves in their chapter. However, as we said, it's about Good Fullas. If it was about idiots then the types who do get uptight about it would have featured.

For the record, Creative NZ did not see value in supporting us with this book — we're not sure if that was because it wasn't creative enough or wasn't New Zealand enough.

There is a saying in Spanish — 'A man should plant a tree, have a child and write a book.' We are relieved to have finally ticked the last box.

To all you Good Fullas, we salute you!

Marc and Charlie

GOOD FULLAS GLOSSARY

We know it is slightly unusual to include a glossary at the front of a book, but this is an unusual sort of a book and we thought it important that you familiarised yourselves with the Good Fullas before ploughing into the first chapter.

THE ADRENALINE JUNKY — An Adrenaline Junky (AJ) is a Fulla who needs to have the throttle on full bore at all times, regardless of what he's doing.

THE BIG FRESH — Fullas of Polynesian or Melanesian descent and by virtue of their name very large and usually very hungry. A more jovial bloke is hard to find. Big Fresh are loyal to a fault, love a laugh but demand a close eye when on the turps.

THE BOGAN — Rough as guts Fullas who surround themselves with loud cars, loud music, loud hairstyles and loud women. The following Fullas fit into the Bogan class: Wettlers, Cooters, Offcuts and Dalmogans/Bogatians.

THE BOYDOG RACER — Juvenile Fullas, disguising themselves as car enthusiasts, desperately attempting to come of age. Frequently have problems with acne, the law and most other Fullas. Not to be confused with Grommits and Wangsters (Wannabe Gangsters).

THE CARDYCRAT — Cardycrats are dull-coloured, cardigan-wearing bureaucrat Fullas, generally, but not exclusively, unravelling yards of public-sector red tape, in an attempt to tie other Fullas' hands behind their backs with it.

THE CARNY — An itinerant participant in festivals and fairs, this type of Fulla is particularly prevalent in circuses, sideshows and stalls. The Carny lives life in a very laissez-faire manner and can fix anything from a motor mower engine to a night at the dogs. The Carny has one hundred and one scams and hands that are faster than the human eye.

THE CAVE MAN — CAVE men are Citizens Against Virtually Everything. They are those types of Fullas who want to drag New Zealand back into their prehistoric ice age. The CAVEman classification includes the following Fullas: NIMBYs, NINZs, NOTEs, NOPEs and BANANAs.

THE COCKY — An agricultural or rural Fulla who lives off the land. Cockies include High and Low Country Farmers, Funters, Titpullers and Sheepshaggers. Cockies are the backbone of the Kiwi heartland.

THE FINKLE — Finkles are flamboyant, effeminate and fruity homosexual Fullas taking on the overt female role. Finkle Fullas include: Finklettes, Smurfs, Twinkies, Bears and Yestergays.

THE FUNNY WHAKA — A carefree and jovial Maori Fulla who spends most of his time chuckling, chortling, giggling and cackling. Funny Whakas can sing, dance, play any musical instrument and can cook a feast like no other.

THE GINGA — A Ginga is a redheaded Fulla who has probably been called all of the following names in his fiery lifetime: Bloodnut, Gingernut, Gonad, Coppertop, Carrotcranium, Agent Orange, Sirenhead, Fantapants, Chutneycrutch, Matchstick, Overripe, Pinky and F.O.T.

THE HENANIGAN — A mischievous Fulla who indulges in tomfoolery, roguery, rascality, waggery, diablerie and other such frolicsome baloney, usually at others' expense. The Henanigan is the life of every party.

THE HOPPER — A Fulla whose ethnicity is East or North Asian and one who enjoys studying, golf, tai chi, yum char and Japanese cars with a collection of cuddly toys in the back window. No one is sure if the name Hopper comes from hopping around the badminton court or from eating grasshoppers.

 THE KIWI BATTLER — Kiwi Battlers are Fullas who try their hardest to get ahead but are characterised and dogged by extreme misfortune. Impossible not to love and great to be around, the Battler makes even your worst day seem good by comparison.

 THE NORK — A socially inept Fulla who is single-mindedly obsessed with technological or scientific pursuit. The Nork is of similar complexion to an Emo but with a terrible dress sense. Nerds, Geeks, Dorks, Twerps and Dweebs fall into this category of Fulla.

 THE PANDABEAR — A portly and corpulent Fulla whose ethnic origins hail from or around the Asian Subcontinent, in what is modern-day India, Pakistan, Sri Lanka and Bangladesh. The name Pandabear comes from the telltale black bags sported under his eyes, which at first glance leads most to question whether he is a victim of spousal abuse or whether he works 18-hour days counting 10-cent pieces.

 THE PRANKER — A money-hungry, white-collared Fulla with large ambitions. Known for a lot of sizzle and little sausage. The following Fullas sit in the Pranker pigeonhole: Tap Dancers, Toffers, Shysters and Fronters.

 THE RUGBYHEAD — The Rugbyhead lives, breathes, sleeps, farts and sweats rugby union. A Fulla who can make or break any social event. Not to be confused with a Gym Dandy, many Rugbyheads turn into Fishheads or Couch Kumaras upon hanging up their boots.

THE SALTY SEADOG — A wiry Fulla who lives off and beside the sea and co-exists with the harshest of nature's elements. Usually a single loner, the Salty Seadog has bad taste in everything from music to clothing. He's never seen dancing in public or holding a worthwhile conversation with a Sheila.

 THE SCARFIE — A Scarfie is a carefree and irresponsible student Fulla, discovering the meaning of life (and an interest-free loan) by living it to the full — and making a fair few mistakes along the way.

 THE SKINAZI — Deluded, deranged, devout white supremacist Fulla who lives in the Land of the Wrong White Crowd. Skinazis may have originated when a racist, bald bloke from Taumarunui was duped back in the '70s by a Cocky who claimed to have found white men's bones in a paddock dating back to pre-Maori times.

 THE STORYTELLER — Storytellers are motor-mouth Fullas divided into two distinct sub-sectors: the Divide-by-Tenner, who endlessly tells tales to entertain; and the Wide-Boy, a scoundrel involved in swindles, shams, scams and scandals.

 THE THRUMPET — A working-class Fulla whose interests include the RSA, rugby league, racing, trotting, greyhounds and Brylcreem. Thrumpets are straight as a die, 'spade's a spade'-type good buggers.

 THE WAORI — A Pakeha Fulla (ironically quite often ginger or of very pale complexion) whose greatest regret is that he was born to Anglo-Saxon parents. The Waori embraces Maori culture and lifestyle and as a result always has a point to prove.

 THE WODGEWICK — The Wodgewick is a thespian and self-professed intellectual. He is a confused capitalist egalitarian bohemian conservationist and in addition to that a fervent social climber.

The Bogan

If there is a character of more colour than the common backyard Bogan living anywhere in this fine country I have yet to meet him. The Bogan is a coarse, crass and crude, and raw, rough and rude member of the New Zealand underclass. An indelible part of the national psyche, with a strong belief that blood, sweat and beers will bring him respect, and, with that, a sense of belonging. Bogandom, in many ways, is a true celebration of real Kiwi culture. And outside of New Zealand, with perhaps the exception of Australia, the Bogan is quite an exotic form of Fulla and even here in New Zealand is considered a bit of a suburban hero. With interests such as loud music, loud women and loud cars, a rather grungy aspect, the capacity to consume copious quantities of bourbon, and always sporting some form of unkempt facial hair growth, the Bogan exemplifies the uncouth, yet at the same time unsophisticated, lifestyle that many others only dream of.

The Bogan often gets a bad rap, and to call a spade a shovel, it's without a doubt justified. The Bogan does nothing quietly or by half measure. From head to toe he is a loud statement of anti-establishment and individuality — from the various style of mudflap haircut dangling over his black T-shirt, balanced by any number of exotic fringe accidents — to his black stovepipe jeans, worn on every occasion, formal or otherwise, from funeral to swimwear.

The Bogan likes life uncomplicated. He lives solely for excitement, primarily derived from women, cars, cash, piss, drugs, fights and fatty foods. A Bogan's motto is the tougher and the rougher the better. This doctrine applies to: their language and behaviour, the alcohol and nicotine content when making a purchasing decision, and often in their choice of women. Wild Turkey is a Bogan's bourbon of choice given the standard bottle is 44 per cent alcohol by volume, and if they have managed to win a bit of dough on the 'dogs' they'll go straight for eight-year-old 'Turkey' which is 51 per cent. Cigarettes will always be full strength, and hence they only smoke ciggies that come in a red packet — and by crikey do they gut drag the bastards. Have a look at the size of the ember on the end of the durry next time you see a Bogan sucking on a lung dart.

Bigger is better too, particularly with regard to hair and jewellery, but also in terms of their petrolhead endeavours: motors, mags and stereo systems. The sound system in a Bogan's set of wheels is often worth more than the vehicle itself.

As we've hinted at, and as you know doubt already know, the Bogan has some of the most offensive and outrageous hairstyles of all the Fullas. It usually consists of a mixture of both long and shaved sections of hair and his noggin very seldom sees shampoo (and never, ever conditioner). The most well known, and possibly even trademarked, haircut of the Bogan is the mullet. The mullet (short front and sides, long mane down the neck) is the style of choice among most of the subspecies of Bogan, although recently the ever increasingly popular frullet (front mullet — an inversed version) is coming to the fore.

Both the mullet and the frullet are highly practical cuts for the Bogan, as the short top and sides represent work at the front and the dags represent party at the back (for the mullet) and vice versa (for the frullet). Often a Bogan's fusty, frowzy and unkempt appearance may look like he's paid no attention to personal grooming whatsoever, but with Dalmogans (Dalmatian Bogans) and a number of Wettlers (Westie Metallers), it is quite often the opposite. The irony is, for those particular Bogans, hours are spent perfecting the bedraggled and dishevelled look.

The larger of the provincial towns are where the Bogan thrives. Kaitaia, Whangarei, Dargaville, Pukekohe, Hamilton, Gisborne, Hastings, New Plymouth, W(h)anganui, Palmerston North, Upper Hutt, Nelson, Hokitika, Timaru, Oamaru, South Dunedin and (notably) Invercargill are awash with them. Some have rural origins, but a Bogan needs the grunge of a city or town to really prosper, and Bogans seldom enjoy their own company. This is mainly because they need to be surrounded by at least three like-minded 'uncouths' to feel a sense of stability — and to talk metal and gas.

Bogans feel they need to be accompanied by only the most ferocious of pets. I'm sure if some of the larger members of the cat family were legally permitted to be domesticated animals, Bogans would own lions, tigers, panthers, pumas, cougars and leopards. But they can't, so they settle for the most intimidating dog breeds and as such West Auckland suburbs, for example, are rife with pitbulls, bull mastiffs, Dobermanns, Rottweiler crosses and other such vicious canines. Some have also been known to own snakes. Regrettably, many a Bogan has had an appendage dismembered or been tragically maimed at the hands of his own animal, usually in retaliation for general neglect or some serious mistreatment.

The Bogan is not an overly complicated or sophisticated Fulla at all. Far from it. He keeps things simple. Gladwrap and rubber bands constitute contraception. An ideal romantic dinner out is a pie and a pint (those Bogan Sheilas don't know just how lucky they are). An ideal breakfast is also a pie and a pint. Music should be four beats in a bar and either easy lyrics such as 'na na na na na na na na thunder' or dirty lyrics like 'sink the pink'. And the ultimate status symbol of the Bogan is to have his partner feature in the readers' wives section of a Gentlemen's magazine.

You can hear Bogans from a mile off. They will be yelling and swearing at their five, seven or nine children (always a minimum of five — usually in quick succession — and generally an odd number). Bogan offspring are indoctrinated into Bogandom from a very early age. They are specifically taught no moral values or any sense of sophistication. The catch-cry of many a Bogan to their progeny is KISS (Keep it simple, Shane/Sharon!).

Bogans are often divided on brands. They are either Holden or Ford, Lion Red or Double Brown, Vegemite or Marmite — there is no in between or fence sitting. A Bogan will often challenge and scrap another Bogan (including his own son, brother or father) who favours the competing brand.

Ah yes — there's a bit of Bogan in everybody, just more in some than others, as the saying goes. Well, here are a few characters with a large dose of Bogan in them.

The Offcut

An Offcut is a vicious, feral form of Bogan, often with criminal habits. He is almost invariably surrounded by liberal and loose women, but guards them incredibly closely.

Offcuts grunt and swear a lot. Grunting and swearing is their mother tongue and also their primary form of communication. An interesting fact, though, is that they very seldom hang out with other Offcuts. Like a lion, an Offie will have his own territory which he fiercely protects, patrols and owns. (Occasionally, he will also mark it with his own urine, but usually uses spray-paint.) He is, however, usually surrounded by a cast of Cooters and, running with the same analogy, the Cooters are the hyenas, who follow and clean up the scraps that the Offcut leaves in his wake.

An Offcut will smoke (and often sell) quite a lot of weed, but interestingly enough it has the opposite effect on an Offcut to what it has on the majority of the population. Instead of peace and happiness, pot promotes anger and rage in an Offcut, like picadors do a bull.

An Offie, or Wedge as they are sometimes known, will do anything necessary to protect his lifestyle. They absolutely live for the now, seldom thinking further ahead than their oft broken noses. The net result is that the Offcut's time in the public spotlight is short — the ages between 15 to 40 tops — by which time they have officially passed the mantle on to their sons by way of a huge wooden key and a bourbon-spiked yard glass at their twenty-first.

It must be said that a laugh at the expense of your closest mates is one of the true pleasures in life, and this seems to be the sole objective of the Offcut. However, Offcuts will usually have few real mates so their evil tricks will be played out on Cooters and Wettlers in their near vicinity. An Offie's favoured bag of tricks involves a tortuous array of stag-do and twenty-first party pranks to be dished out at will on any unsuspecting member of his extended group of Bogans who has, through over-excitement, rendered himself incapable of self-defence.

A couple of well-known examples, rumoured to have been carried out by an Offcut are: when some poor bastard was handcuffed naked around a tree in Hagley Park in Christchurch, and left until morning for a stag-do punishment, only to get a tap on the shoulder by some strange, sick individual who proceeded to treat him like a cellmate after whispering in his ear, 'This really is your unlucky day.' The poor bugger had no idea who was doing what as he couldn't move his swede to look because his mullet had been duct-taped to the tree trunk and therefore could give no description to the police, aside from the fact that the offender smelt of booze and Brut 33.

Or the time Reece from Henderson slipped his mate Dwayne a dose of Rohypnol (the date-rape drug), stripped him nude and tied him to a goods train bound for Wellington. Dwayne was apparently spotted by a member of the public around Taumarunui, who promptly phoned the cops. They had him on the next bus back up north with a fresh batch of op-shop clothes, and a summons to appear in court.

When we were at uni there was a guy called Fast Stu, who was not actually a Scarfie, but nonetheless flatted with a few of the Fullas. Fast Stu most certainly fell into the category of feral Offcut and was a valued member of our extended crew until he took advantage of one of the lads, who for the purposes of anonymity we will refer to as 'Giles'. (Giles has battled for the last 15 years to dump this event and I apologise in advance for making it public.) In any event, Giles had been out for the evening, doing as Scarfies do and had stumbled home on the wrong side of midnight. What he didn't know was that Fast Stu had seen a very intoxicated 'Joan the Butcher' (a well-known Dunedin street person, who it seemed spent most days ramming booze in her face and screeching obscenities to passers-by). As she went stumbling past the flat, Fast Stu had offered her a nice warm bed for the night. Joan the Butcher needed no second offer. He kept her in the lounge with a glass of whisky and shot into Giles' room and set the scene. He then put Joan to bed and awaited his prey.

When Giles arrived, the Fullas that had gathered after a few phone calls were fizzing with anticipation. Giles entered his room and shut the door and there were about eight ears jammed against it, waiting with bated breath. Giles entered and flicked the light, but Stu had removed the bulb, so he climbed into bed in the dark, only to find a warm body awaiting his arrival. Now, as a Scarfie it would be a fair assumption that this warm body was fellow Scarfess and the natural response would likely be quite enthusiastic. We can only assume that this is what panned out, as from first-hand accounts from outside the door it was alleged that there were several minutes of ruffling followed by a gut-wrenching scream.

What then followed was the sound of panicked yelps and sheer desperation as Giles ran to the door and tried to open it. Fast Stu was one step ahead, though, and had removed the door handle from the inside. Giles then tore to his windows and frantically tried to open them. Fast Stu had nailed them shut. Such was Giles' panic that he picked up his desk and threw it through the window and followed it out, only to be met by Fast Stu and the Fullas in fits of hysterics, rolling around the front lawn.

While this gag was of the utmost humour, Fast Stu had overstepped the mark and was *persona non grata* in Dunedin for quite an extended period. But the moral of the story is — beware of letting your guard down in the presence of an Offie!

Olsen, another Offcut I've known since primary school days, often brings his own sister to parties in a cat and mouse manoeuvre, just so that he can knock the block off anyone who even looks sideways at her — which most warm-blooded Fullas would, given the extremely skimpy, and quite frankly slutty, clothing she wears when accompanying Olsen. Olsen the Offcut has been studying martial arts since about the age of five. He is also extremely muscle-bound for a Bogan, but most of us suspect that is partly a result of the strange packages he's been receiving from Bulgaria for years. Nobody has ever had the guts to ask Olsen what's in the secret packages, but rumour has it that they are packed with illicit performance-enhancing drugs and some very bizarre and brutal combat weapons.

Offcuts are the most likely of the Bogan fraternity to be the 'What the fuck you looking at Fulla?' type and are known bottle and sucker punch throwers. They are also, not surprisingly, predisposed to fire starting. Good fires have, on occasion, been known to render some Offies catatonic and delusionally intoxicated, similar to a shark that has been rolled on its back.

The Cooter

A Cooter is a physically and intellectually inferior form of Bogan. The real Battler of the Bogan brotherhood. Often a lovely Fulla, but equally as often an Offcut's sidekick and fall guy — as a result of the poor old Cooter being a bit of a dipsy dullard. He has a heart of gold, yet a hollow head and lacks any direction or common sense. Knock-kneed, pigeon-toed, cross-eyed, daggy-arsed and runny-nosed, the luckless Cooter is a daft, dopey dimwit. A Cooter called Colin, who hangs with Olsen the Offcut, is so damn unlucky the poor prick will probably be reincarnated as himself.

A Cooter will set very low personal standards for himself and then consistently fail to achieve them. He has terrible delusions of adequacy but is actually viewed, even by his peers, as scummy, scabby, shabby, smutty, seedy, sordid, sloppy and slovenly and, at times, sickly. He's almost manky or mangy even — a bit like a flyblown sheep or an eye-dog with worms.

The Cooter knows better than to wear black jeans. A bit like a belt in martial arts, black jeans need to be earned. So the Cooter, recognising his inferiority, dons tight acid or stonewashed blue denim jeans with a similar, but not of course matching, denim jacket.

Cooters suffer numerous physical injuries and ailments. Most physical injuries occur from accidental circumstances such as siphoning petrol, jumping barbed-wire fences, crossing roads while being pursued, bonfires and barbecues, bike-riding accidents, car surfing mishaps and intoxicant experimentation. The ailments they suffer are usually the result of their poor blood lines, coupled with foetal alcohol syndrome, which dishes out any number of side-effects from cleft pallet and club feet, mild to extreme slowness, wandering retinas, cow eye and jigsaw mouth — where all the teeth have ignored the rules and decided to grow towards the sun.

They're loyal buggers, though. Colin the Cooter, for example, is a very faithful friend. It's just that he lacks good judgement of character — and his unwavering, devoting loyalty is mistakenly misdirected to offensive Offcuts, like Olsen. To give a typical example, Olsen the Offcut rang Colin the Cooter early one West Auckland morning, saying, 'If someone comes around to see you today tell them you walked home from the pub through Corban Reserve last night. If you don't, I'll pulverise you,' he kindly added as a warning of his seriousness. Shortly after the call, the cops were rapping on Colin's door and after he invited them in for a cup of tea, they asked him all sorts of questions about his whereabouts the night before. It was in connection to breaking and entering several houses in the vicinity. Apparently, he had been implicated in several robberies (in a clear case of mistaken identity probably a set-up by an Offcut competing for Olsen's turf).

Poor old Colin the Cooter bumbled his way through a few answers. He couldn't remember much anyway — he had filled himself so full of bourbon the night before. But he was conscious not to put his foot in it or he'd cop the full wrath of Olsen the Offcut. Well, later that month, Colin the Cooter was summonsed to appear in court as a prime suspect for the robberies. He was called to the witness stand and answered several questions so clumsily and nervously that he was almost sentencing himself for a series of crimes he didn't even commit. He was nervous, not so much about being found guilty, but more about falling foul of Olsen the Offcut.

One question he refused to budge on, however, was when he was repeatedly asked by the judge as to which route he had taken home from the pub that fateful night. 'I tell yas,' he kept repeating. 'I didn't take a root home that night!' The hearing went on for hours and not long before the judge was about to read the verdict, Colin finally burst into tears, saying, 'I've got a confession to make — I haven't taken a single root home from the boozer in nearly 10 months!'

The Wettler

Less aggressive than the Offcut, but equally as revolting, is the Wettler (a Westie Metaller). The Wettler is an awful yet relatively harmless form of Bogan. As a Metaller from the West, Wettlers tend to congregate in the western suburbs of Auckland, such as Two Tattoos, Horrendouson, Blogan Swanson, Glen and Dean's, Messy, (show us your) Titis Rangi, Glen's Eatin' and Wai-(so many)-attacks-it's-eerie. Many of them also choose to live for varying lengths of time in Paremoremo (sometimes months, sometimes years), a scenic rural locality in North Western Auckland. You will also find them in (aptly named) Hoon Hay in Christchurch, Upper Hutt (affectionately known as 'Upper Cut' which is what you will receive if you take a wrong turn and end up there) and Wainuiomata in Wellington, and Green Island and Kaitangata in Dunedin. Hamilton has a disproportionately high ratio of Wettlers to other Fullas.

The Wettler has only one pair of pants — and they are black jeans, usually uncomfortably tight-fitting ones at that. These are multi-purpose trousers performing the duties of pyjamas, togs, day wear, evening wear, formal attire, performance apparel and work pants — perfect for hiding the grease stains from working on the Commodore or Camira in the garage of their brick and tile digs. To complete the ensemble are sneakers or basketball boots (black or white), and a black T-shirt with an iron-on decal of one of the following Brutal Death Metal or Heavy Thrash Metal bands: Metallica, Megadeath, Motorhead, Iron Maiden, Anthrax, Tool or Slayer. More senior Wettlers will sport Judas Priest, Uriah Heep, Mötley Crüe, Quiet Riot, Deep Purple or Black Sabbath paraphernalia. Those with a mere modicum of taste will deck themselves out in AC/DC or Led Zeppelin gear.

Wettlers are a great addition to any party. They always have cigarettes long after others have run out (usually tucked into the rolled-up sleeve of their black tee), and after several Southern Comforts and Coke (no ice) are more than happy to liven up the party with a rendition or two of their favourite metal songs. I have never met a Wettler who couldn't play 'Wild Thing' on the guitar and most can play 'Smoke on the Water' and 'Stairway to Heaven' with aplomb. A great way to end your party, if you want your guests to head home in a hurry, is to get a Wettler to break into 'More than Words' by Extreme (the sad fact is that it's actually more than words, it's music, too — terrible music at that, and therein lies the problem). It'll send them scuttling.

Despite the prevalence of native bush in West Auckland, the area is almost void of birdlife. This is mainly due to the extreme levels of noise pollution caused as a result of V8s and metal music being thrashed, but also because the Wettler's favourite toy is the air rifle, so any deaf or very brave birds that do venture into Wettler territory are easy prey and don't last long.

I was lucky enough to attend a cracker Wettler party in Horrendouson a few years ago. It was in a reserve and basically the set-up was all number of Boganmobiles in a circle with their doors and boots open and Radio Hauraki blaring from their beat boxes. Lion Red and DB Draught were the beers of choice. And Jack Daniels and Jimmy Beam were eerily omnipresent. The majority of the crowd were grease-monkeys and without exception all were petrolheads. I could have sworn every single one of them was either called Gazza, Bazza or Dazza. The night consisted of revving engines and singing the chorus of the AC/DC and Hendrix songs that played on Hauraki.

Several fights broke out between supposed good mates and at one stage even a couple of chicks went tit for tat — and I was told in no uncertain terms that we were not to separate them and to sit back and enjoy the spectacle. The party finally died when the last car battery went flat and the last Bogan fell over in a pool of his own vomit and urine. It was entertainment at its most basic best.

The Dalmogan/Bogatian

A more refined and crafty category of Bogan is the Dalmogan, a tough yet suave Fulla of Yugoslav descent. The Dalmogan, sometimes referred to as the Bogatian, hails (or is a direct descendant of folk), more often than not, from the beautiful Dalmatian

Coast and the stunning islands located around Split in modern-day Croatia.

Dalmogans are big fans of cock rock, and a Bon Jovi or Aerosmith poster will invariably feature somewhere in their dwelling, more often than not in the dunny.

Due to being forced to go to the Yugoslav Sunday School, the Dalmogan still holds resentment towards Kiwis of British origin and annually petitions the government to have the 1898 Kauri Gum Digger Industry Act overturned. He lives on a diet of seafood and wine and pays for none of it. Between his 12 uncles and 78 first cousins they have the New Zealand wine and fishing industries sewn up.

As a side note, Dalmogans' sisters are more often than not most succulent creatures, and if they didn't insist on perming their hair and wearing flannel, and were able to spend a term in a Swiss Finishing School, they could be a good bet for New Zealand's next top model.

The CUB

CUBs are Cashed-Up Bogans, Bogans who have done well in their trade and are cash rich. CUBs pay ludicrous prices for mint condition muscle cars, and spend a small fortune just to maintain them. They buy the best house in the worst street and spend all of their disposable incomes on boys' toys. In essence this is the same stuff as standard Bogans, just better. They buy new HSV Holdens, GT Falcons or SRT Chryslers, drink Jim Beam Black Label, still wear black — although now with a high-fashion designer label stitched on at the seams, and eat at much finer dining establishments like Burger Fuel instead of Burger King.

A **Brogan,** by the way, is a Maori Bogan, usually of the Wettler or Offcut persuasion.

All categories of Bogan generally love and own six or eight-cylinder vehicles and almost exclusively those that have been assembled in Australia. Anything with less than six large cylinders is viewed with scorn and disdain. In my younger days, Wettlers invariably drove Holden Toranas or Ford Cortinas and always in offensive colours such as lime green, sunburst orange, hot pink, electric blue or flamenco red. Cooters usually had the lemon models such as the Holden Sunbird or the Ford Escort and seemed to strike endless engine trouble, exacerbated by the Cooter's inability to maintain his vehicle himself, something the rest of the Bogan population are very adept at.

These days Bogans have moved on to 80s model Commodores, Camiras, Falcons and the like. If possible it'll be the SS version and often in 'blood' red, as Bogans truly believe that red cars go faster. Most have mag wheels and a spoiler as the standard accessories and all will have a powerful stereo system with amplifiers and sub-woofers.

You see, the Bogan values his vehicle far more than his dwelling and so of course invests more time and money in it. He prefers to both eat and make love in his motorcar so needs to be wired for sound to create the appropriate ambience for these activities. And, boy, do Bogans love to go cruising around the neighbourhood. The purr of their V8s gets the stray cats in their neighbourhood aroused and the packs of vicious dogs howling in unison.

Offcuts ALWAYS have eight cylinders under the hood. With a preference for manual transmissions, they usually drive a panel-van or at the very least a station wagon. These are more often than not decorated with very intricate and ornate but horrendously heinous and distasteful panel-van art, which oft-times takes the form of mermaids (usually topless), flames, wolves, lizards, Native American dream catchers, and a psychedelic sunset scene or some such similar and sick art-form. The panel-van doubles as the Offcut's office and it is while sitting or lying on the mattress in the back that his criminal activities are planned (and occasionally carried out).

You will always find an ornamental piece draped over the rear-vision mirror of the Bogan's ride. The traditional fluffy dice is now far too mainstream (although old-schoolers will still run them) for most Bogans and has been replaced by Rottweiler or pitbull dolls, imitation nunchakus, bourbon merchandise or similar crap found in trashy park markets.

The Bogan is of the bold belief that no matter how dirty, dreggy, daggy, defiled or dishevelled he may appear, the onus to incite sex is on the female — and, besides, he looks shit-hot 'cause he's got a black T-shirt on. In his mixed-up mind, the more his breath reeks of bourbon and stale smoke, the more attractive to the fairer gender he must be and the more unsanitary, unsavoury and unsightly his behaviour and appearance, the higher his pulling power.

The Offcut will generally dress from the waist down in a similar fashion to the Wettler but will often don nothing more than a black leather waistcoat on top to show off his 'tough stickers' which are quite often self-tattooed, and always 'faaarkin' awful looking.

I recall, with little pleasure, the evening when a mate and I were outside the Golden Arches after a lengthy evening, enjoying the tail end of a fillet-o-fish, when a black Torana idled up. Clearly, it was the owner's heart and soul. It was matte black, had flared guards and had been chopped to sit mere millimetres above the wheels — and sounded like it was running a modified 454 big block. It goes without saying that we needed a closer inspection. As we drew near, a grubby little Cooter wound down the passenger's window and said from memory something along the lines of: 'What the fuck are yous looking at?' To which we quickly replied, 'Your ride, Pal! Is it just for show or can she scamper?' Well, one thing is surer than night follows day and that is that if you question a Bogan's car (even to a Cooter) it's even worse than insulting the woman who brought them into the world.

This scenario had two possible endings: a fight, or a ride. And by the end of it I would have preferred a fight. This is why:

We climbed into the back seat as the Cooter and his Offcut mate, who was at the wheel, screwed a U-turn on George Street and headed at pace for the motorway out of North Dunedin. Cruising through the city was the perfect opportunity for the proud as punch Cooter to regale us with the key statistics about his Offcut mate's pride and joy. It had a freshly rebuilt, 400+hp, 454 Chevy four-bolt big block, with a 350 transmission and a number of other things designed to make it really, really fast.

What was disconcerting was that the Offcut was drinking from a bottle of Jim Beam and, as we hit the hill leaving Dunnos, decided to bury his hoof. Well! Bugger me this thing was not all for looks. It took off like a sky-rocket. To this day I can remember the delusional look and terrestrial noises emanating from the Cooter in the passenger seat as he egged the Offie to break the 200 kph barrier — uphill. It was at this stage that my mate and I snatched the bottle of bourbon off old Coots and, resigned to the fact that it would be our last drink, started about finishing the bottle.

If ever there has been a case in my life where I believed in guardian angels, it was this, as the car skipped over the bumpy road like a go-kart, heading toward the 200 kph mark. The closer the needle got to 200, the more shrill the noise from the Cooter and the wider the eyes of the Offcut in the rear-vision mirror.

THE BOGAN

I still do not know how, but we must have cracked the 200 mark and then made our way back to the varsity campus. We were about three blocks from home when the Cooter, still riding a bourbon and adrenaline-fuelled wave, spotted the University cricket fields and alerted the Offie (who by the way had not said a single word the whole trip, deciding only to communicate through his eyes and eyebrow movements). Quick as a flash the Offcut turned his lights off and set about ripping into a five-minute burnout session of circleworks which involved leaving rubber all over the number one ground and indeed right across the cricket block and wicket. My mate and I were eventually released and headed home, a little weak at the knees and genuinely stoked to still be around to tell the tale.

Putting all the Bogans' bad reputations and notoriety aside, though, what's alarming is that it's actually a sad fact that many New Zealand Fullas are a little too embarrassed and self-conscious to release more Bogan thoughts and actions during their daily activities for fear of ridicule and contempt from co-workers, friends or family. It's even sadder when one thinks that the very people who he fears will discountenance him are also dying to unleash the Bogan from within. It wouldn't hurt for many suppressed Fullas with pent-up Bogan emotions to come out of the closet and announce their Boganity with pride, dignity and delight. It would come as an enormous collective relief for the large majority of Kiwi Fullas, with the notable exceptions being all Prankers, most Finkles, some CAVE Men and the odd Cardycrat.

If you're a Fulla, ask yourself this. On a scale of 1 to 10, how much fun is it driving a throaty yet unluxurious V8 (despite the emotional emptiness some environmental crusaders might feel), listening to loud rock music (preferably live), drinking beer and bourbon (with mates), surrounding yourself with sluts, and just generally being a lout without any sense of responsibility? Your answer will be a good gauge as to just how much Bogan you have in you.

The Pandabear

The Pandabear may be on the verge of extinction in its native Asia, but my goodness gracious me it is flourishing here in New Zealand. In fact the population is swelling and people who regarded themselves as Pandabears in the 2006 New Zealand census were well in excess of 110,000. The similarities between the Pandabear of the animal kingdom and that which inhabits New Zealand, where it is most heavily concentrated in the Balmoral and Sandringham suburbs of Auckland and on numerous corner sites nationwide, are limited to appearance and diet only (they both have a diet that is primarily herbivorous, but some have been known to eat meat).

They are poles apart when it comes to social behaviour, however, with the New Zealand variety one of the most loquacious, garrulous and talkative animals on the planet. Their behavioural differences are possibly best polarised by their breeding habits. While the animal variety has a total disinterest in copulation, the human variety's reproductive comportment resembles that of a randy rabbit. He is a prolific breeder, and fornication is usually as much a part of his daily ritual as yoga is.

Pandabears are New Zealand males of Indian descent or whose ancestors come from the surrounding areas of the Subcontinent. They are usually slightly chubby, and speak with a lilting, sing-song accent — you know, 'Oh by golly, golly gosh', sounding a bit like the Swedish chef on the *Muppet Show* but with a piping hot Hellers sausage jammed halfway down the gullet, and always putting the stress on the wrong syllable in any given word. The Pandabear has a beautiful habit of throwing random verbs and adverbs into the answering of a simple question. The standard reply to the question, 'Can I have some more poppadoms?' is 'Yes, please.' I got a taxi home from a super Sunday session the other day and asked the Panda driving, 'Did you go to the cricket one-dayer yesterday, mate?' His reply: 'Oh no, not yet.'

He is known as a Pandabear, not just because of his portly figure and swarthy colouring, but more for the big black rings which sag under his chocolate-brown eyes. The only Pandabear of European descent is the Rt. Hon. Mike Moore. The remainder have exclusively been munchers of a varying assortment of curried poultry, seafood, meats and vegetables.

Pandabears, a bit like Policemen, always feel the need to run with a moustache, generally from the age of about 15. Their favourite 'mo' is the 'Mahatma Gandhi' which in more recent times has been renamed the 'Freddie Mercury'. (A little known fact is that Freddie himself was a Parsi Pandabear, actually born Farrokh Bulsara, having grown up in Bombay.)

If you need to locate a Pandabear, they own and operate most dairies in New Zealand, occupy the driver's seats of a large proportion of our taxis, and these days sit behind the counters at most of the large retail banks. They also cook some of the most flavoursome and ferociously fiery dishes in the country. And that happens to be the very case of my mate Prashant the Pandabear, a real classic Fulla.

Prashant speaks of only two things: food and cricket.

He owns a curry stall in one of Auckland's central city Asian food-halls. Prashant looks like a large male Panda who has spent a lifetime bathing in butter chicken. I suspect he even massages it into his face every evening such is the state of his greasy and cratered dial. But my goodness, gracious me, can he cook a mean curry — and he isn't shy on the garlic or on the chilli, meaning his dishes are death for the breath and agony on the anus.

Prashant the Pandabear has three names for everyone. Those Fullas he knows are called 'Boss'. Conversely, and rather strangely, those he doesn't know are called 'My Friend'. And all females, regardless of age or familiarity, he calls 'Dear'. And he just loves to entertain. A group of Fullas I play social cricket with and I went to see him one evening for a vindaloo and a couple of Kingfishers (decidedly better than Cobra, by the way). He got wind we were coming, and knowing we were keen on cricket slapped on a movie about a small village in India under British colonial rule who challenged and beat a group of British army captains at a game of cricket, as an extra touch of audio-visual entertainment to go with dins. This was odd but certainly different. He also amused us with jokes and ditties throughout the meal.

But it was when Prashant the Panda pulled out the karaoke set that he really chased us out of the establishment quickly. Our flagrant rejection of the offer to participate must have broken his little cholesterol-clogged heart. It was a grave error on his part, and showed a complete lack of character judgement (and probably cost him another round of Kingfishers, just quietly). We have been back many times since, though, and he never fails to regale. Every single time we turn up, he treats us like long lost brothers and I swear both his butter chicken and his lamb vindaloo just keep getting better. I wouldn't want to offend him too much, though. We once saw a table-load of Bogans talking about the population growth of India and crapping on rather disparagingly about the Pandabears' disregard for contraception, and by the look on Prashant's face I wouldn't be surprised if he took things into his own hands out in the kitchen as a little bit of payback.

What many Kiwi Fullas don't really fully appreciate is that the Pandabears in New Zealand are actually divided into many distinct communities based on religion, language, caste and which IPL Twenty20 cricket team they support. You see we've got the Sikhs – the big Punjabis who wear the big turbans and grow the big beards, the Muslims from the Kashmir, Hindis from Gujarat, Jains, Tamils, Buddhists and Zoroastrians. And that's just from India. Some of the Kiwi Pandabears even arrived via Fiji, East Africa or Singapore.

What's also an unknown is one of the main reasons Pandabears make the trek to New Zealand. It's not just to play cricket or hockey or to cook us some outstanding dishes from the Tandoor. It's actually because the weddings they had to pay for back in their homeland were crippling the poor buggers financially. This is doubly tragic when the Poor old Panda is usually on the receiving end of an arranged marriage, meaning he doesn't even get to enjoy the age old game of courtship, one of every Fulla's favourite pastimes.

Pandabears fit very well into New Zealand society, particularly when out in public. One only has to look at how many have been recruited into client-facing, front-line sales or retail jobs. However, at home they follow their various customs, religions, rituals, cooking and dress, as if they were back in the middle of a New Delhi neighbourhood.

You see, unlike other Asians, Pandabears from India had it easy getting into New Zealand in the 19th century, but the Immigration Restriction Act of 1899 changed all of that. 'Aliens' were forced to fill out their immigration application in

English. (Just quietly, can you imagine the outrage if the Pommy Colonialists upon entering India were forced to fill out immigration forms in the Hindi language and script?) Smart Fullas, though, the Pandabears — most of them just stopped in at Fiji on the way through and rote-learned the application form and breezed through when they arrived at the ports of their new adopted homeland.

In fact, Fiji has been the original homeland of many a Kiwi Pandabear. Pandabears were sent to Fiji as indentured labourers in the late 19th century to work the sugar plantations. They have trickled here ever since with large spikes in numbers during the military coups in 1987 and 2000. What few Fullas appreciate is that quite a few Fijian-born Pandabears enlisted in the 28th Maori Battalion in the Second World War, having to use fake Maori *noms de guerre*, given that the Poms and Fijians got awfully nervous about how the Pandas might put their military training to use (independence in India and self-rule in Fiji) so forbade them from joining any of the armed forces.

They are not afraid to pull a swifty given the opportunity, citing the fact that if you are silly enough to fall for it, then it's your own fault. One Fulla that I know, of Indian descent, travelled back to India to visit family and hired a flash new Mercedes with some shiny new mag wheels on arrival in Mumbai to drive into the country to his family home. Along the way he drove into a pothole and the right front tyre exploded. He limped the car up the road, and as fortune had it a bloke came out of the undergrowth and offered to have the wheel repaired within two hours including getting the exact same factory alloy.

My mate was stoked as he thought there was no show on earth of finding a Mercedes mag four hours out of Mumbai, let alone in one hour. In any event, when he returned in one hour the wheel was perfect — not a ding in it and the car was ready to depart. He forked over a small fortune by Indian standards and drove up the road.

About five kilometres on, the road smoothed out into a two-lane highway and he put his foot down. Upon doing so, the car started pulling viciously to the left. So he pulled over and jumped out to check the wheels. When he checked the left front he found the good wheel had been removed and now replaced the popped wheel, and a wheel no bigger than that of a wheelbarrow wheel had been bolted on as replacement! He turned the car around and headed back to the guy who had ripped him off. When he found him the Fulla said defiantly that he didn't know what my mate was talking about and that he'd never seen him before in his life. The mate of mine cracked up telling us that one.

But we all must admit that we have a lot to thank the Pandabear for. New Zealand is in the top five countries of tea drunk per capita at over one kilo per person per year. And we source the bulk of it from the Indian region of Assam, the district of Darjeeling and Sri Lanka, previously known as Ceylon. The Pandabear has indeed been one of our most appreciated additions, assisted by his wonderful sense of humour and strong work ethic.

It's difficult to imagine a New Zealand where you were unable to catch a taxi, and on the way discuss the latest test cricket fixtures, leave the dairy on a Sunday morning feeling better than when you entered to get the papers after a quick bit of banter and a welcome smile, pop into a bank and make a quick withdrawal served by a friendly Pandabear bank teller, and then go to a curry house and eat a fiery lamb vindaloo for about $16. New Zealand just wouldn't be the same place without the popular and personable Pandabear.

The Salty Seadog

In order to find a Salty Seadog, it's best to search the areas surrounding the uncompromising waters of Stewart Island, the West Coast of the South Island, Cape Palliser, Ngawi, the Chatham Islands and other thoroughly isolated pockets along the 8000 kilometres of coastline in this maritime country as this is where the Salty Seadog inhabits when not out at sea. Some may say he's a bit of a nasty bastard, but that's generally because he only talks to those he lives with or the few that he believes, by his own standards, have earned their stripes and thus his respect. But if you need bounty from the deep blue, he's your man.

He has absolutely no time for those 'townies' who drive around in their flash cars (increasingly four-wheel-drive vehicles that never engage the second set of wheels because they are always on the road) donning their swanky clothes and swigging on cocktails, imported beers and wine. He thinks Prankers are as much use as hair on a fish, because they can't even change a tyre, or the sparkplugs on a Seagull outboard motor.

There's generally not one ounce of fat on a Salty Seadog. Days spent in the searing sun, pulling in fish, with nothing but a diet of cigarettes, tea, rum and the odd lamb chop keep him that way. He gave up on shaving his entire face long ago, resulting in the odd tuft above the five o'clock shadow. He does, though, have some excessively long eyebrows which catch your attention nearly as much as his tufty beard and the mane of sandy blond, wispy hair he has running along the tops of his ears and firing out of the end of his honk (which is actually like its own little ecosystem containing a rich vein of spiders' legs on his nose, and some flies' legs hanging out of the bottom of his nostrils).

It's tough to tell how many winters your average Salt's haggard, leathery, sun-baked face has lived through. Hard living and ultraviolet rays can add anything from five to 15 years to his appearance (not that he could give a tarakihi's tit).

Never in his life will he have worn sunglasses or sun block and the thought of putting moisturiser on his skin (which started with a burn time of only 10 minutes and can now tolerate 10 plus hours at sea a day) has never entered his mind — and frankly never, ever will.

It is interesting to note that the Salt is totally at one with nature's elements, demonstrated by the fact that he is absolutely oblivious to the harshest conditions the planet can chuck at him. This is further evidenced by him never talking about or acknowledging the weather, and by his sometimes malodorous habit of wearing the same clothes throughout summer, autumn, winter and spring (often for weeks on end without a wash, I might add).

Salty Seadogs have registered names such as Sydney, Colin, James, Stanley and the like, all of which can be abbreviated to a single syllable. That said, they are seldom known by those names because shortly after starting school, when the distinguishing characteristics which make a fine young Salt begin to rear their head, they get tagged with a handle like Sandy, Goldy or Drake (except those called Russell — shortened to Russ — they keep their name out of respect for New Zealand's first capital).

In fact, in a curiously ironic twist, this is exactly the case of a young Salt I knew called Neil, who has aged into one of the saltiest Seadogs you will ever meet. He was a chip off the old block and the son of a seriously Salty old Seadog, so his natural Salty progression was inevitable. The nickname, Sandy, was nothing to do with his prepubescent love of the sea, but more as a direct result of some rather vicious eczema, which spread from behind his already incredibly hairy ears (proof of evolution, he professed) to the backs of his knees, including stretching the full length of his appendages including his hands. As a result of this unfortunate condition, no kids really wanted to touch him, and if he got too close to the girls they would scream and scatter. (Just for the record, even though his eczema is long gone and has been superseded by some nasty sunburn, not much has changed with his luck with the ladies.)

At any rate, one day, when the taunting about his skin condition had reached boiling point, a group of girls who were in the year above Neil described his hair colour as 'rotting rust' and made the not entirely incorrect suggestion that his face looked quite similar to a butcher's block of luncheon sausage.

Well, poor Neil lost all control and unleashed a bucketload of fury on the group in a frenzy of swinging knees, feet, hands and elbows. To this day, I have never witnessed such a ruthless display of schoolyard discipline. Neil had singled out the cheekiest and largest of the girls, who was twice his size and built like a Russian road-digger, and by the time he had finished with her, her face was bright pink and swollen to the point of rupture, not from any direct blows or the manner one might expect of an obese person after such exertion. No, Neil had dished out a 10-second facial, rubbing his little salt-hardened mitts all over her chubby, lily-white cheeks, chin and forehead.

The girl was kept from school for four days while her skin was bathed and tended to by her equally pudgy and pallid mother. We suspect she must have spent that time sympathetically eating herself back to health because she returned even larger. But it has to be said that, after that, she and her mates kept their pie holes shut when we were around — a pleasant change from their previous taunts and jeers. From that week on Neil was called Sandy out of pure respect, and just quietly I think he was pretty stoked with the nickname too.

It should, however, be noted that Sandy has never again entered a physical altercation with a woman since that day, and never will. However, the rumours in seaside pubs around the country are that when he does manage a 'land-catch', he can be slightly overzealous and enthusiastic, in the manner one might expect from a bloke who goes from drought to drought.

These days Sandy the Salty Seadog sports a reddy-grey moustache and is distinguishable by two poo-brown stripes under the nostrils from years of exhaling rum-flavoured Port Royal tobacco. He has one front tooth missing which he lost as a teenager when he fell off the Whitianga wharf while fishing for kahawai and face-planted the edge of a dinghy on the way down. His other front tooth has the wiggles and is on its last legs — hardly surprising given it hasn't seen a toothbrush since the day Sandy left primary school.

Like every true Salty Seadog, Sandy smokes like a chimney, and steadfast to Salty traditions, rolls his own smokes. He has the uncanny knack of being able to do this with just his left hand and without looking, despite his hand having only four fingers. He lost one while undertaking some maintenance down in the bilge room of *Smelly Hooker*, a charter fishing boat out of Ngawi (rumour has it the finger is still lying around down there somewhere). He throws off at anyone who smokes tailor-mades, but you will be sure to find him bludging from anyone that pulls out a pack, at any chance he gets.

Sandy the Salty Seadog's working life has always been connected to the ocean. As a matter of fact, if he spends too much time onshore he gets 'landsick' through a lack of motion. Shortly after leaving school, at the age of 15, Sandy the Salt had his sights set on qualifying as an able-bodied seaman. He went along to the ports to find out how he could get on an international cargo ship as soon as possible. He was told to head up to the Maritime Club and speak with a Fulla by the name of Bobby who was the Boatswain, which he promptly did.

Bobby had a quick chat to Sandy and soon realised he had the potential to be a fine Salty Seadog indeed. Bobby put it like this: 'You'll make an excellent seafarer, you will — you've got no fucking brains.' Sandy was ecstatic. After a huge night on the rum with Bobby and the boys at the Maritime, he was off the very next day. Sandy started as a Scavenger, cleaning the carbon waste from an oil tanker, and spent weeks on end at sea.

Occasionally, they'd pull in at some port in South East Asia or somewhere similar and indulge in some sordid sprees. A few years of that was enough for Sandy, though. His best mate on board jumped ship in Jakarta and married a prostitute he fell in love with at first sight, and Sandy couldn't have stood another serving of Colonial Goose (a cheap mutton-flap stew which was the staple diet on board the liner). So he decided to jump ship and go work on the wharves instead.

The Wharfies were always giving the Seafarers stick, so he thought he'd like to join in with them instead of being on the receiving end of their taunts. But work on the wharves was tough, and Sandy the Salty Seadog decided to opt for an easier income. He arranged for one of his Wharfy mates to run over his foot for him with a forklift, and with a crushed big toe off he went and signed up for permanent impairment through ACC, and to the best of my knowledge he still receives a decent weekly payout for loss of earnings, a decade or so later. Coupled with some under-the-table freelance commercial fishing it's not a bad little cashflow he's got coming in, particularly for a Salt with no financial responsibilities and some pretty bloody low overheads.

Salty Seadogs are of the opinion 'if you can't fix it, don't own it', which is why most of them actually own very little. In fact, the vast majority of their amenities have been borrowed or salvaged — in the case of Sandy, the boat he picked up from a bach in Waikanae in 1987 when a wealthy stockbroker went tits up, a 1952 Seagull fibreglass, which he uses as a recreational vessel, or the 1972 XA Falcon, which a local Cocky had sitting in his hay-shed until Sandy offered to take it off his hands — he undertakes all maintenance himself. That's not to say he's a great mechanic or handyman, though. Sandy's Falcon, for example, hasn't been what I would describe as roadworthy for years and runs like a vibrator on wheels.

A Salty Seadog's adrenaline glands will have long since exhausted their supply of adrenaline. After countless hairy experiences during his seafaring days, a Salt knows no fear and feels no pain. It is remarkable that, given the time they spend on the water, very few have actually ever learnt to swim. In fact, if a Seadog were to fall overboard, he would paddle straight for the bottom, rather than flopping and flapping around in the vain hope of being rescued. As far as any true Salt is concerned, a meeting with Old Davie Jones himself is the only true way to sign off. He never wears a life-jacket either. You know why? Because he's in charge.

An interesting characteristic of the Salty Seadog is that they very seldom eat fish, living by the motto you can't sell what you've already eaten. To be fair, most Salts just prefer the taste of fatty lamb chops and fried eggs which, given the opportunity, they will knock off for breakfast, lunch or dinner. Not that they ever eat breakfast, lunch and dinner. Far from it, eating is no more than a necessity for the Seadog, not something to get excited about.

As a result, your average Seadog is not a big man. Tom Jacks (a bloke we met down on the West Coast), for example, is about 5' 9" and weighs about 70 kilos, wringing wet. By Jesus he can arm-wrestle, though. Never seen him beaten. (Never under any circumstances take a Salt on in an arm wrestle, no matter how much weight they are giving away.) Most opponents are just plain intimidated when they see his forearms or cop a feel of his calloused hands. Or they are mesmerised by his forearm tattoo ('if a tattoo is good enough for Popeye . . .') — that of an anchor (meaning he has fished the Atlantic waters), a snake (meaning he has fished the Pacific) and a naked woman (apparently meaning he has crossed the Tropic of Cancer — but I have a sneaking suspicion that he just wants to have pornographic material handy at all times).

Tom Jacks is single and has very few qualities that draw women towards him. He is broke, ugly, unclean and not the slightest bit romantic. Having said that, though, he did manage to pull a fair few land catches in different ports during his commercial seafaring days. This is normally comprised of a game of attrition whereby all of the attractive 'top-shelf' sorts had long since left with their friends or other Fullas and Tom was left with the remaining talent (although that is definitely not the right word to describe the women that let Tom have his way with them). Tom reckons he has had the odd purple patch; however, these all occurred overseas and as such cannot be verified. To call a spade a shovel, I'd put money on the fact these alleged purple patches coincided with times when his bank balance took a hammering.

Part of his difficulty in connecting with the fairer sex is that he lives by the philosophy of 'it's what you don't say'. Sandy the Seadog is perfectly capable of having a good catch up with his mate Gritty and only saying about a hundred words, usually involving ordering rum, asking how the rum tastes, to which Gritty replies with the rhetorical question, 'What do you think?', borrowing a lighter, and ending up by saying, 'Good to catch up with ya, Mate.'

Salty Seadogs do enjoy observing other Fullas, with less salt running through their veins, battle with the very environment, atmosphere or conditions that the Seadog thrives in. I can well remember when a Good Fulla I knew from my Scarfie days and I randomly decided, while having a cup of tea in his flat one day, to do a roadie to Bluff at the start of the Oyster season to get among our finest delicacy. We left that very same morning, swung past Nightcaps for lunch (just so we could say we had been there), and had an afternoon in Bluff sucking back some slippery ones, when we came up with the smart idea that we should continue on to Stewart Island.

So we jumped on a ferry and cruised over to Halfmoon Bay, and within an hour and a half we were sipping on a few sherbets at the South Seas Hotel with some beaut Salties. We booked a room there, and a silly night ensued. Just as the publican was shutting up shop and serving last drinks (well after his licence allowed him to, I might add), one of the Salts asked if we'd like to head out fishing with them the following day. We readily agreed and he said he'd give us a knock on our door next morning.

Well, I swear, no sooner had I entered into blissful sleep than there was a rap on the door and a gruff and gravelly voice said, 'Wakey, wakey, hands off snaky. We're off.'

THE SALTY SEADOG

It was four o'clock in the bloody morning. By just after half past four we were heading out of the bay and as we rounded the point we hit a four-metre swell and a bloody choppy open sea. It was about then the boys cracked open a big bottle of Speight's each and were back on the sauce. We had no option but to join them.

We spent about three or four hours fishing for blue cod and drinking beer. My mate and I blew our necks several times as a result of some severe seasickness. But the highlight was when one of the Salty Old Seadogs gave himself a firm uppercut in the nose then hung his head over the side and bled profusely into the water. When we asked what the hell he had done that for we were told to just keep an eye on the water. He was trying to attract a six-metre white pointer that had been seen off Stewart Island having the odd seal for breakfast the weeks previous and it had gained a reputation for trying to intimidate fishing vessels like the one we were on. Luckily, no Great White turned up but a few makos got a hint of the Salty Seadog's nose-bleed and started sniffing around the boat.

We were only at sea for about four hours but it seemed like an eternity. It was a massive relief to enter the port again, and we were straight back into the pub where they pan-fried a couple of the blue cod, which we had landed, for lunch. We had completely emptied the contents of our stomachs so it was nice to take in some healthy solids, although we did then settle into a decent session with the ragged bunch of Salts until well into the evening. It goes without saying we didn't accept the offer to head out again the next morning with the Fullas.

It's not surprising that it's when on land that the Salty Seadog is at greatest risk of mishap. For most Salts there is no need to waste money on a car with a warrant and there is certainly no bloody use wearing a seatbelt. This belief, coupled with the need to ply themselves with a few sherbets prior to hitting town to calm the nerves and to save on paying marked up prices for pub booze, means that sadly the Salt, on occasions, does not make it as far as the local pub.

One upside, however, is that if a terminal accident occurs, they can usually be thrown straight in the casket as they are undoubtedly in their best attire. On the 99 per cent of times they do make the pub (Tom reckons he can't remember the last time he drove sober) they will usually have their own handle hanging pride of place above the bar. Undoubtedly, it will be an old school pint that actually measures 600 ml! Not the 480 ml pints they give you these days. The Salt takes pride in the fact he gets 120 ml over every other mug for the same price.

After sufficient booze, the Salty Seadog may very occasionally hit the dance floor, although the better explanation might be that the dance floor hits him. Given the Salt will never dance unless a full five sheets to the gale, whenever a Dr Hook song like 'Silvia's Mother' comes on the juke-box, the haggard Seadog will be reduced to a whirling dervish, spinning around and around until he vomits or ploughs head first into a hard wooden object like a floor, bar stool, leaner, wall or fist. Take this as a first-hand warning that if you see a Salty Seadog dancing it's time to pour yourself a final drink and to take a grandstand view somewhere out of harm's way.

When we went down to visit Tom Jacks, we got to his shed full of everything a Salt needs, from a cooking hob to a transistor, a whitebait net to a teapot with crochet cosy, a bed to a long drop only to find him repairing a hole in the front wall where he had parked his car the night before! I reckon he must have been travelling at about 20–30 kph as you could have shoved a miniature pony and a dwarf through the hole! His repair job, like most things he does, was practical but by no means permanent. A tarp was hammered over it, in the same way he fixed the back window of his car, which was apparently taken out by a stone (I'd love to know who threw it).

The Salty Seadog is no mug but he can be parted from his money by most half-decent con men, pool sharks and dart throwers. One such cock Tom was telling us about was the Fulla who convinced Tom to shout him drinks for the night in return for a water bed. It hurts to tell the story as he should have known better. The guy was apparently a salesman from up north who had been passing through the Coast and had called on a bad debt for which he had been offered a water bed as payment. Reluctantly, he had accepted and had headed to the pub to find a sucker prepared to trade anything for a water bed that was at some address just out of Hokitika.

According to Tom, the moment this prick found out he was a man of the sea he started on him about the water bed replicating the rocking of the ocean and being a real novelty with the ladies, and so on and so forth. Whatever he said he got Tom to agree to shouting him a skinful in return for the address of the bed. This Fulla certainly made the most of it too, ordering for a local lass who was buying his big city bullshit and leaving Tom 230 bucks out of pocket and with a Post-it stamp with an address on it.

The next day, Tom went to borrow a mate's trailer only to find the back axle had broken, so he shelled out another $25 to hire a trailer from a gassy and headed to the address and arrived there just after lunch. He knocked on the door and was greeted after an extended time by a scruffy scrubber in her early twenties (with two young kids around her ankles) who knew nothing about a water bed, but woke her flatmate (a dreadlocked no-hoper) who got Tom's dander up without saying anything.

'Ah, the water bed,' he finally managed. 'The only one I know of is on the back lawn.' Tom Jacks was well pissed as he trudged around the back of the house looking for a water bed (not even knowing what one looked like).

As he drew around the corner, he could see nothing that resembled a bed at all, so he banged on the back door and waited for the dope-smoking drop-out to answer. Eventually, he did and told him it was behind the creeper on the far fence. He wasn't lying either. As Tom rounded the fence he saw it — a piece of foam the size of a single bed lying in a kids' paddling pool like a sponge, full to overflowing with dirty, green water. So much for a bloody water bed! He was so annoyed at himself at being conned he didn't say a word to the home owners. He just quietly slipped back into his car and drove over their letterbox as he left.

Predictably enough, Salty Seadogs have zero time for the America's Cup. 'Fancy nonsense with no bloody risk,' according to most, unlike the Sydney to Hobart and solo navigation of the globe. Tom reckons he has travelled the equivalent of four to five times around the globe during his 30 years at sea, and given he exclusively fishes the deep zone 20-odd kilometres off the coast, I wouldn't doubt him.

Salty Seadogs aren't renowned for their wit. It's more their demeanour and habits that Fullas find quite funny. But Tom Jacks for one can tell a great joke. Quite literally — he only has one. But it's a goodie and, as you would expect, it involves booze and has a nautical theme, in that the lead character of the joke is an octopus. From memory, it goes something like this:

A Fulla walks into a pub with a pet octopus, orders a beer and jumps up onto the bar and loudly exclaims, 'I will give a thousand dollars to anyone here who can bring me an instrument my octopus can't play. The entry fee is a beer for me and another for the invertebrate.'

As you would imagine this causes quite a stir and it's not long until a member of the band offers the octopus his six string. The octopus takes a minute to tune it then bangs out a fine piece of classical guitar. Gob-smacked, the band member buys a round. Then a little Thrumpet steps up and pulls a harmonica from his top pocket. The octopus takes a sip of his beer to wet his whistle and then cranks into a bit of blues. Again the crowd is in awe.

Same thing happens with another band member and his saxophone and a Fulla with a hand drum, before the hotel manager suggests the crowd shoot into the dining room where there is a grand piano. Same result. The octopus tinkles the ivories to an awesome overture and he and his owner get yet another pint each.

By this stage the octopus is three sheets to the wind and is getting a bit obnoxious and loud. So a Scottish bloke steps up and throws a set of bagpipes down on the bar. The octopus goes quiet and starts fumbling with the pipes. One minute passes. Two minutes pass. The owner is getting worried and the crowd is drawing in. Finally, after five minutes, a member of the crowd calls out, 'Come on, Buddy. Are you going to play it?' To which the Octopus replies, 'Play it? If I can work out how to get the pyjamas off it, I am going to fuck it!'

Tom reckons it doesn't matter how many times you hear it, it's always funny. I'm not so sure. But I laughed the first time around for sure.

Salty Seadogs are quintessentially Kiwi, ingenious yet simple, carefree yet sincere. Abel Tasman, Captain Cook and Maui will be proudly looking on at this latest batch of Salty Fullas! Long may they prosper!

The Salty Seabag

Another version of the Salt is the Salty Seabags, a veteran surfer. One called Peter the Seabag was drawn to salt water from an early age. By his early teens, surfing had taken over his life, and he spent his school days staring out of the window wondering if there were waves to be had after school. Sometimes he'd sneak a quick surf with his mates before school, during a storm, and being at the self-conscious age that he was, would wear undies under his wetsuit so his mates wouldn't see the size of his shrivelled, chilly willy. Many a day was spent wearing wet, salty undies that got itchier by the hour — not to mention the tell-all wet patch on the shorts as a result, on arrival at school.

By Peter's late teens, the weekend surf trips were of epic proportions. The Salty

Seabags would pool their hard-earned apprenticeship coins to fill the tank with gas and buy a scone to accompany the customary joint on the way to the waves. Post surf, one wet towel would be shared between four, with the unlucky last guaranteed of having three bums already rubbed through it.

Peter got to the wild twenties and thirties with the ultimate experience being surf trips to Indonesia with the boys — surfing all day over sharp coral reefs with mandatory sunset beers the order of every day. The Salty Seabags had freedom and energy to party all night, and the once-awkward teenagers learned the value of slippery tongues and if you're away from home how the lovely girls were unable to check if you were really a chopper pilot working on the rigs or a pro surfer here on a promo film shoot. These days the Salty Seabags have traded in beers and doobs for tea and dunkers post surf, but still spin some great yarns — if their missus gives them a leave pass for a half-day surf mission.

The Big Fresh

The Big Fresh hails from the stunning tropical islands of the South Pacific — islands full of trees laden with fruit of high sugar and calorie content such as the mango and the coconut. These islands are scattered around the Pacific Ocean, and just how the Big Fresh and their families managed to arrive there remains one of the great navigational seafaring marvels of history. Big Fresh (plural also Big Fresh) here in New Zealand have traded in their fine white sandy beaches of the Pacific for the Otara Creek, the Tamaki Estuary and the Mangere Inlet. Actually, one perturbing irony of the Big Fresh's love of the water is that very few can actually swim more than two lengths of an Olympic pool. That said, they are second only to Maori when it comes to dropping a bomb or pulling off a staple dive from a bridge or a cliff.

Big Fresh have numerous local heroes and icons, primarily from sporting or musical backgrounds. However, all of these high achievers pale into insignificance by comparison to one old Palangi (white Fulla), Colonel Sanders. Every Big Fresh, without exception, has a deep emotional and physical addiction to the Colonel's secret recipe of herbs and spices. The Colonel's outlets attract Big Fresh with the appeal and awe of the Pied Piper, which coincidentally is why you will never see a KFC outlet in the Pacific Islands. While such a venture would be a gold mine, it would cripple the economy and would require the security of Fort Knox.

Anyone who has flown to Apia, Suva or Nuku'alofa will have seen and smelt the kilos of KFC being crammed into the overhead lockers of the plane as the Big Fresh takes back the ultimate present to his relatives. In fact, back in the Islands many Big Fresh are led to believe that KFC stands for Kai For Cousins.

During the 1990s astute businessmen were so astounded by the consumptive abilities of the Big Fresh that one of the main Auckland food distribution and retail companies named a supermarket chain after them, based on a traditional food market-style layout of fresh foods complemented by the No-Frills range of products. They widened the aisles to future proof their investment and cunningly increased the size of the trolleys by 25 per cent so that they gave the impression of being empty. Big Fresh Supermarkets even sponsored some Big Fresh sports tournaments, Pacifica events, markets and musical extravaganzas to reach and appeal to their target market.

Taro is an essential part of the Big Fresh diet. It's a bit like your average spud, but with more starch, fibre, vitamins and minerals. Pop into most veggie shops in South Auckland and pick some up for yourself. You'll find no shortage of fellow shoppers who are keen to teach you their favourite way to prepare it, if you just ask them. The yam is another staple. Not the piddly little orange and red designer veggies that we know as yams, which are not yams at all, but ocas — Big Fresh yams are the big stodgy, starchy ones.

Big Fresh of Fijian lineage have an affinity with the moustache, and the majority are partial to what is known in most parts of the world as the 'Burt Reynolds', a thick, broad moustache bordering on, but not quite, the walrus variety. In fact, in many quarters of New Zealand it's most appropriately called the 'Bernie Fraser' out of respect for one of New Zealand's great Fijians. Most Fijian Fullas can grow a mature 'Bernie' in just over 72 hours. Gold teeth are a sign of wealth and as such often replace perfectly healthy teeth to beautify a grin. The size of your wife and numbers of children can also be seen as an indication of your living standards as a larger wife needs more fuel to sustain her, as too does a large family.

Big Fresh often have a fondness for Christian names with both significance and literal meaning. Internal Affairs have refused to register an astounding array of unique names proffered by Big Fresh. Fish and Chips (twins), Masport, Mower, Yeah Detroit, Stallion, Twisty Poi, Gas Axe, Keenan Got Lucky, Post Office, Otara Busstop and Sex Fruit all tragically fell short of realisation.

However, a few crackers slipped through the cracks! Apparently, there are Petrolinas, Gasolinas, Cinemas, Golden Jubilees, a USNavy, a Tomcat and even a Chocolate running around the playgrounds of South Auckland. Predictably enough, there are a disproportional number of Colonels hot footing it around North Island playgrounds.

A Big Fresh I played league with was a real Good Fulla by the name of Deputy.

He called his first son Boss, which raised a few eyebrows among our teammates when he told us at practice one night, as he invited us to Boss' Methodist christening (and of course the enormous post-service feast, including several pigs on the spit).

Without mucking around he had a second son about 11 months later. We had had a few bets at the clubrooms the week his missus was due with Director and Chief as odds on favourites with the bookies. But our club captain got lucky when he took a punt on Manager, which was the eventual winner and name of Deputy's second born. No doubt Deputy has several more sons that now sit around the executive table. The mind boggles as to what he might have called any daughters he may have had.

I also played for Otago with a top bloke who named his son Carisbrook Gordon after both the ground and the coach.

New Zealand has had a strong connection to the Samoan family of Big Fresh ever since ousting the Jerries from what was then known as German Samoa, during the First World War, even if there was a cock up or two during New Zealand's administration of Samoa — such as when we sent a ship called SS *Talune* up there with a crook crew who unleashed a nasty flu epidemic through the islands. But it's predominantly been a great relationship. In fact, not long after Samoa regained independence in 1962, Auckland became known as the de facto capital of Polynesia, with Manukau City the most populous Polynesian city in the world. This is only set to continue. In fact, Big Fresh are prolific breeders by comparison to the average Kiwi, having twice the number of children in half the amount of time, leading to the prediction that in the next 20 years the majority of Kiwi kids could well be Polynesian.

The dawn raids unkindly put the Big Fresh in the headlines during the 1970s. Quite why they conducted the raids at dawn was beyond most, as the Big Fresh is just as likely to be sleeping in the middle of the day. At any rate, this atrocity resulted in wide-scale stampedes as terrified Polynesians were chased through neighbourhoods from Ponsonby to Mangere with Officer Plod in hot pursuit.

If it were not for a strong Christian belief and equal moral fortitude, the dawn raids might have turned nasty. Had the Big Fresh been anything other than a gentle pacifist at heart, the taser would have been called for long before 2008. It was not that Big Fresh were intentionally flouting the law. It was a simple case of the average Big Fresh being on the lower side of average when it came to organising paper work. It's for this reason that the issuing of Maori passports by Hapu Tino Rangatiratanga Atawhai Whangai in 2009 was pure commercial genius. For the small price of $500, the tedious hours of filling out forms to appease the Cardycrats at Immigration New Zealand was averted. While morally bereft, and legally daft, the scam was a cracker until it was exposed.

It's not just feasting and procreating that's important to the Big Fresh. The sense of family too is paramount. The Samoan and the Tongan cultures have the *Fa'asamoa* and the *anga faka-Tonga* respectively. These are ways of life which teach the importance of respect, family and elders. Charlie and I were catching a taxi home one evening and struck up a conversation with a friendly Big Fresh who was driving the taxi. I had just found out that I was a father to be and Charlie and I were talking about the delights and challenges of raising children. Salesi, the Big Fresh (coincidentally Salesi is Tongan for Charlie), said, 'Wait until you haf your fourf an fiff child — dat's when the real work starts.'

Turns out that Salesi had five children of his own and what's more was the primary caregiver for another four of his nephews and nieces. He and his wife were directly responsible for nine children. Not only that, but his sister, his sister's husband and their three children all lived in the same house. He reckoned most nights his wife cooked about six kilos of lamb flaps, opened five big tins of mackerel or corned beef, boiled four kilos of taro, roasted three kilos of yams, fried two dozen eggs, toasted a loaf of bread and peeled and sliced seven pineapples for pudding. But every one of the 16 people living under the roof contributed in kind and there were very seldom any disagreements except over which channel was shown on the tele in the evenings: TV1, TV2 or TV3. Quite remarkable, really.

Salesi did add, however, that he warns all under his roof that some serious 'boy justice' will be administered should anyone bring shame or disrepute to the wider family.

It makes you kind of wonder who has it right, the nuclear (Mum, Dad and two kids) Palangi family who set out on their own chasing the dream of the better house, car, school, etc., or the Big Fresh family content on spending as much time with their extended clan as possible, perhaps at the expense of the bells and whistles. I would bet that the thing most of us regret on our death bed is not spending more time with our family as opposed to not living in a larger house.

Big Fresh like nothing more than a good kava session. This is the opportunity to sit around sharing the special root drink with mates, and awaiting your lips, mouth, throat, neck, head, arms, shoulders, chest and abdomen to go to sleep, usually, but not always, in that order. It would be fair to state that the taste is an acquired one, which for want of a better description is not dissimilar to drinking directly from a muddy puddle. The effects of this intoxicant can deliver the full spectrum of emotions from absolute peace and calm to euphoric excitement. One clear side-effect, if you can consider it that, is that it makes the Big Fresh very amorous.

At the opposite end of the spectrum is the white man's fire-water or top-shelf spirits! Fire-water was first shared in significant volume as the Anglo-Saxons descended on the islands. Rum in particular has been a hit with the Big Fresh, especially when combined with Coca-Cola (this delightful mix is known as Samoan Champagne). Consumed in significant volume, this is a recipe for disaster as the Big Fresh is genetically predisposed to effects from the fire-water that will often border on antisocial (to be fair that could often be said of anyone who is full of rum).

However, the sheer scale of devastation a motivated Big Fresh can cause makes this a very risky business indeed. Demolitions, fires, assaults, letterbox removals, food theft, crossed eyes, colour blindness, car conversion and trespassing are all to be expected if the white man's fire-water is plied too liberally to a Big Fresh.

One Fulla we attended Otago University with, who we will refer to only as Tongy for the purposes of this story, gave us a first-hand example of the risks associated with excess consumption of hard plonk. Not that his logic was flawed at all, more that boyish enthusiasm got the better of him. He had invited a mate called Stu over in the middle of a winter's day to have a few whiskies (evidently, his tropical blood was needing some warming, given the strain of days and days of negative temperatures). Without dragging out the finer detail, Stu turned up in his pride and joy, a lime green Vauxhall Viva, and made his way into the flat where Tongy welcomed him with a poor attempt at a Scottish welcome and a glass of Wilsons Whisky of Dunedin.

It was not long before they had finished the whole bottle and started to make a sizable dent in the cooking sherry (cunningly bought to convince the female flatmates of the boys' intentions to assist with culinary delights). A few hours into this absurdity, Stu stumbled into the restroom and was woken from his day-slumber by the piercing screech of the neighbour venting her spleen at someone for some serious breach of the law. By the time Stu stumbled to the front door, all that was left of the fracas was a dishevelled Tongy being strongly berated as he stood beside her flattened *brown* Vauxhall Viva!

It seems Tongy thought it would be a hell of a laugh to jump up and down on Stu's car until the roof was resting on the seats (of little significance was that this took only about seven jumps). Plied with a skinful of whisky and sherry, Tongy had made the honest mistake of thinking *brown* was *lime green*. Fortunately, Stu managed to unwind the damage by giving the lucky lady the keys to his pride and joy, an unexpected windfall for the lass whose brown Viva was in considerably poorer condition. In fact, Stu later tracked down a steel cutter and turned it into a positive by lopping the roof off and converting it into a convertible! (Really handy in a Dunedin winter.)

Clothing for comfort, cooling and ease are the preference of the Big Fresh. Known to break into a sweat in a New Zealand winter given the work rate of his pump, the Big Fresh will usually step out in Jandals, a lava-lava and a T-shirt or short-sleeved shirt. The Jandal, trademarked over 50 years ago, was a revolutionary design which has been embraced by the entire South Pacific and in particular by the Big Fresh. Buoyant, lightweight, cheap, cool (both literally and in look), and available in any array of bright colour combinations, this footwear was rated third behind corned beef and religion as the most loved things among the Polynesian community.

By direct contrast to the Chinese, who were renowned for placing women's feet in wooden shoes that prohibited the natural growth of the foot (known as 'binding') for about a thousand years until the 1940s, the Big Fresh often spends north of 95 per cent of his time 'unleashing', wearing Jandals or in bare feet, resulting in the Big Fresh having the widest feet on the planet — on occasion as wide as they are long — or square.

A good mate of mine called Tavita (David) has been known during summer to go barefoot water skiing around Orakei Basin in Auckland and is to my knowledge the only man alive to attempt a barefoot ski-jump (see advice above re: white man's fire-water).

It was in no way the prettiest sight, but it was one of the funniest things I have ever seen. Firstly, because of the fact that he could get on the plane at half the speed of any other barefoot skier given the size of his steaks and, secondly, that he was mad enough to have a crack at the ramp at full noise. To cut a long story short, he hit the ramp at about 50 kph, or I should say it hit him at 50 kph, and after his feet stuck to the surface of the ramp, he slammed forward onto his shoulder and bonce, smashing into the ramp like a crash-test dummy. To his credit he didn't let go of the rope and was torn off the ramp and flung 20-odd metres into the water head first. We had our hearts in our mouths until we saw him grinning and waving to us. Clearly, Tavita is built to withstand much greater impacts than most.

I saw Tavita recently at a friend's wedding, sitting in the corner looking a bit sheepish, and went over to him and asked, 'What's wrong, mate?' He said that the loafers he had shoe-horned his feet into were killing him so he had to sit down. I left the wedding well past curfew and waved goodbye to Tavita. He was still sitting in the same chair, feeling quite sorry for himself. Not even several generous servings of wedding cake had cheered him up.

The Big Fresh is an expert in diffusion. If you are ever in trouble and need to enter a negotiation of any kind where there is the likelihood of it turning for the worse, ensure you do so with a Big Fresh at your side. There is no such thing as an uncoordinated Polynesian and this, coupled with a childhood of ducking Jandals and a general fearlessness, makes them more than talented in the art of self-defence.

One situation in a bar in Queenstown where a good mate (a Storyteller called Waffle, all of about 55 kilograms and five foot nothing at a stretch) had somehow brassed off a group of Bogans who were spoiling for an altercation. Little did they know that Waffle had a trump card. Once his good mate Lavalu the Big Fresh became involved, it resulted in a mauling, the likes of which are best seen on Discovery Channel. It is quite amazing the sound that a Bogan makes when he has seen the other five of his mates mauled and is sprinting for the hills.

Big Fresh are almost always religious, spending Sundays at church with friends and family socialising and singing hymns. It is a curious trait of the Big Fresh that their voices increase towards a higher pitch in direct correlation to their size. It is quite extraordinary to see a 150-kilogram Fulla singing with the voice of a choir girl. This is particularly prevalent in Fiji.

I knew a clever Fulla called Palusi (Bruce) who lopped off his little digit in the meatworks back in the day of the bulk ACC payments and received a cheque for $7000. He was so stoked with this scam that he wanted to have another crack. However, the finger had really hurt, not just at the time but for a couple of weeks after, so he studied the ACC guidelines and hit them up for $3500 for a loss of potency in the scratcher as the direct result of an old back injury. He had his girlfriend of the time support his application with a signed affidavit, claiming that he had lost his mojo in bed and supported it with doctors' letters and specialists' reports. The problem was that he told so many people that a vicious Chinese whisper developed and no woman would touch him. But still, I think he got another hefty lump sum after that too, so that should've helped him in the pulling stakes.

Sadly, very few Big Fresh venture to the South Island, put off primarily by the cold southern winters. It's a real shame as those who do venture south have many similar qualities to the warm, open Southerners and are greeted with open arms. One such chap, who had made the trip south to Dunedin, would always turn up to watch University rugby matches. From memory his name was Sa. Well, to call a spade a spade, his grasp of the Queen's English left a bit to be desired. But that did not stop him offering a few bits of great advice to the players. One had to listen very intently to understand what great insight was being shared, but occasionally he would pull out an absolute cracker. He once came up to me and said, 'You know, Harris (he could not say Ellis), you eat the rabbit, you run fast!' Well, how on God's earth do you reply to that?

The Big Fresh is undoubtedly the strongest human on the planet. Numerous tests on bone density and muscle mass have concluded that they are without peer when it comes to physical gifts. This has both upsides and downsides. The upsides relate to the shorter contact-based sports which is why a decent percentage of the All Blacks and Kiwi league players are of Polynesian or Melanesian lineage and a large number of American Footballers too. On the downside, there are very few Polynesian marathon runners or cricketers as lugging the excessive bulk around during endurance sports takes a special kind of dedication. What's more, you don't have the chance to pop in a few head highs or grass cutters during a marathon.

As a nation, we as Kiwi Fullas like to think of ourselves as great sailors, and of course the Big Fresh are some of the greatest navigators in human history.

Polynesian navigation was far more sophisticated than any other, even if it only relied on the sailor's senses and traditions passed down through the generations. In fact, Samoa was originally named the Navigator Islands by a Frog who went by the name of Louis de Bougainville, such was his impression of their superb seafaring skills.

The long and short of all this is that the Big Fresh is a Fulla you will undoubtedly come across and whose company is a wholly rewarding experience. While predominantly located in Auckland (more specifically the southern suburbs), you will also come across them in Wellington and in small number dispersed around the North Island. As yet, they are few and far between in the South Island (aside from a limited number in Christchurch) but should global warming actually occur, outside the imagination of a few scientists on the gravy train, then we should expect to see them down south for the short period between a pleasant temperature and our inevitable global incineration.

Big Fresh are an integral and valuable part of New Zealand society, contributing to our cultural, sporting and economic endeavours. Their big, fresh, smiling faces are a treasured part of the Kiwi landscape!

The Pranker

The Pranker is a prize wanker. A real prick. Quite often he can be quite a nice prick, and nine times out of 10 he's a bloody generous prick, but nonetheless there's never a shadow of doubt that he's a fully qualified, gold-plated, prime spanker. And, to be frank, he wouldn't want to be classified by the masses any other way. In addition to being wankers and spankers, Prankers are often bankers. But regardless of their profession they are always surrounded by, or in hot pursuit of, cash, which they refer to as Rutherfords, or Crayfish. They will stop at nothing until they are millionaires, preferably many times over. Interestingly, they refer to millions as 'bricks', often referring to the deals they have pulled off in this way, or to their cars and houses as being worth a 'quarter brick' or 'five plus bricks' respectively.

The Pranker should not be mistaken for, or confused with, the Prankster, who is a bodacious, ballsy and brazen Fulla of the Henanigan variety, renowned for his practical jokes, pranks and general horsing around. The Pranker's sole modus operandi and raison d'être (to use Pranker terminology) is to make as much money, or certainly give that impression, while doing the least amount of work for it. He is pretentious, ostentatious, overambitious, spurious and vainglorious. He is also pompous, specious, captious, meretricious, surreptitious and supposititious, and totally prankericious but frequently quite likeable in a funny sort of a way. He is economically energetic and does his best to surround himself with what are deemed by society as high-status items (but what many other Fullas see as frivolous wastes of money; for example, why buy a Porsche Cayenne when you can buy a Toyota Hilux for a quarter of the price and actually use it off the road?).

The Pranker spends a lot of time testiculating, which is an interesting Pranker term for waving your hands around in the air a lot and talking absolute bollocks.

He also thinks of himself as one of the world's great boulevardiers, even if deep down he knows he is ridiculed by all of his fellow countrymen, with the exception of those like-minded Prankers living in their lily-white world, the white ghetto that is the Eastern Auckland suburbs. Between about 9.30 am and midday Prankers can be seen socialising at spots such as: The Chancery in Auckland, Oriental Bay and an assortment of flavour of the month cafés on the Quay in Wellington, and Sumner and Fendalton in Christchurch. They'll be dressed to the nines and exuding wealth, and crapping on about deals, interest rates and the value of the dollar or the current price for gold bullion. For them, bugger else really matters.

It's of interest to note that Prankers seldom live south of Christchurch as they battle for an audience with straight-shooting Kiwi blokes who inhabit such areas. That said, Queenstown is being infiltrated by these Prats who have gravitated to the adventure capital so they can buy the toys and prattle on to the mates up north about their winter home, referred to as 'snow and tell'. The Queenie locals know just the buggers we are alluding to and humour their existence by having two price lists for everything: one for Locals (20 years plus as a resident) and one for Prankers.

A wise (and green-eyed) Fulla once said, 'At the end of the day Prankers are so poor the only thing they have is their money.' If humans were birds these Fullas would undoubtedly be magpies — attracted to anything that glistens and shines. Clearly, they are not shy of jewellery and will exclusively wear gold over silver or platinum. The reason for their attraction to gold is simple — it contrasts best against their fake tans.

A Pranker will never be separated from his pair of designer label sunglasses. For him, these are purely a fashion accessory and will seldom, if ever, be used with the actual intention of shielding the sun's rays from the eyes. They're there for show and show only. When cloudy or after dark they are worn on the head, and, even if a Pranker has longer hair, a direct line of sight to the brand and logo will never be obscured from view.

For this reason, the Pranker primarily buys women's glasses that could just about pass as unisex, like Gucci and Prada. These brands have huge logos in gold which match the range of medallions and chokers that the Pranker is draped in, as well as the clasps on his man-bag — although this is more typical of the Nouveau

Riche Pranker as opposed to the Old Money Pranker who uses his dough with more sophistication and finesse.

Most Prankers will drive around in a Remuera tractor which, by the way, will never have seen mud. His vehicle will only ever be black with matching black leather, and they will be exclusively European: Range Rovers, Q7s, X5s, XC90s, Cayennes, M Class Mercedes, Touaregs and the like, and usually with a very Pranky personalised plate. Most of them will have the turbo version — fat use when you can't go over 99 kph on New Zealand roads (and, of course, they never go off-road to be able to get up to a decent speed there either). Their excuse for owning such a large and powerful all-terrain vehicle is that it is a complete necessity for the annual ski trip to the mountain, but in reality they just crave the height and perceived prestige of such an urban assault vehicle.

The Pranker's property will always be north-facing and with views of the sea, because according to many a Pranker 'they are not making any more coastline'. It will undoubtedly be equipped with an infinity pool and jacuzzi. Young upwardly mobile Prankers will pay through the nose for run-down, pokey and impractical villas in former working-class areas, then spend a small fortune on them and turn them into well-decorated, pokey and impractical villas in former working-class areas. These ridiculously overpriced properties will have virtually no section, no parking and be claustrophobically jammed into a narrow street — but will of course be within walking distance of a trim soy latte.

Prankers seem to be cursed by this horrible habit of throwing bad business buzzwords and buzz phrases into their conversations, willy-nilly. A couple of years back I had to sit through a painful presentation from a Pranker from Parnell. After we'd heard a buzzword soup about the value proposition of his business and its brand values and identity, strategic intent, comparative advantage, core competencies, value-added solutions and bleeding-edge technology he concluded like this: 'So, I will shrink-wrap the information I have just relayed, and I ask that you cascade it down through your business units, and revert with feedback after you have brain-dumped outside of the box, so we can hit the ground running when the rubber hits the road and get some runs on the board.' Or words to that effect — I actually didn't have the 'bandwidth' to 'digest' his 'elevator pitch' in its entirety. None of us actually had a bloody clue what he or his company did, but it certainly sounded flash. I did get a little concerned, though, when he approached me after the meeting and said, 'Mate, I'd like to touch base with you so we can take advantage of some low-hanging fruit.' I had a feeling he was referring to making contact with my genitalia and then sexually harassing some Finkles with saggy scrotum sacks.

He continued, 'Let's aim for a mindshare and put our heads together, so we can connect the dots, get our ducks in a row and sing from the same song sheet to ensure we can get closure.' If feeling me up wasn't enough, he now wanted to get a condominium in Taupo used for group meditation, frot, play board-games, go duck shooting and serenade me so he could go all the way! When he said something about the 'upshot' being that he just wanted to give me a 'heads up', I left the venue immediately, my hands trembling feverishly and my palms extremely sweaty.

A Pranker will undoubtedly never have been in a blue despite his attitude and verbosity. The one thing he rates more highly than all else is his looks and he will run for the hills at the thought of a straight left on the bugle. He may not be a handsome bloke but he will have tapped out every iota of natural talent he has and then added to it in the form of cosmetic surgery.

From a 'punch and grow' hair transplant, dyed hair, fake tan, botox, chin implants, designer teeth (way too white to be natural) and collagen, the Pranker will stop at nothing to appear younger, fitter and healthier than is, in fact, reality. That said, this peacocking behaviour does attract the female equivalent who will have undergone more elective surgery than the late Michael Jackson and Cher combined.

Both the Pranker and his prospective mate will have selective amnesia and will have destroyed all photographic proof of what they looked like prior to meeting each other. This can all come horribly unstuck when they breed and the resulting child is a true reflection of the pre-cosmetic genetics. This will sadly mean a life of limited social contact for the child until they have run a full cycle on the treadmill of enhancement. They then blossom at their coming-out parties at around 16 years of age with a look that only money can buy.

There are various other close relatives of the Pranker species, which fit into the broader Pranker family category.

THE PRANKER

The **Tap Dancer** is a rather fascinating form of Pranker. The Tap Dancer sports a full head of hair (quite frequently a punch-and-grow transplant), unusually tanned skin (particularly for an Anglo-Saxon in winter), a white shirt (to emphasise the tan) with a heavily starched collar, a pressed suit, a power tie, black polished shoes, and is a real Fronter. More often than not he is a high-flying Auckland businessman, but Tap Dancers can be found strutting their stuff up and down the country. Having said that, I have never spotted one south of Christchurch or north of Whangarei. And my word can they talk the talk. But in reality they deliver Sweet Fanny Adams and are responsible for bringing New Zealand's productivity per capita crashing down around its ankles.

A lower profile and usually younger version of the Pranker is a **Toffer**, a tosser with a lisp. Toffers graduate into fully blown Prankers, often of the Tap Dancing variety. **Shysters** are a cross between a Pranker and a Wideboy (see Storytellers for Wideboy description), the wheeler dealer, 'pull a fast one'-type Pranker.

But thank heavens that the offensive and rather sycophantic metrosexual **SNAG** (a Sensitive New Age Guy), who began to spring up in the 1980s and flourished in the 90s, has disappeared from the scene of late. He was held up on a pedestal by the ladies as an example of the perfect Fulla and made life unbearable for the average Fulla by setting some unacheivably high standards of hygiene, charm, romanticism and general contributions around the home, particularly in the laundry and the kitchen.

The SNAG smelt like a whore's handbag such was the pot-pourri of aftershaves and colognes he doused himself in, knew how to make beds and iron clothes (properly), could bake and bake well, enjoyed romantic movies and books and loved reviewing them, knew the scientific names for most flowers, took notice and commented on women's hair, jewellery and clothing, pretended not to be interested in racing, beer or cricket, wore high-neck, pastel-coloured skivvies, ate salads and drank cups of chamomile tea, cried at weddings, and even went as far as to have a vasectomy.

The SNAG was destined for extinction because he was simply unable to keep up the unattainable pace he had set, and he found that the bar was being subtly and unrealistically raised by the very women he had tried so hard to please and appease in the first place. You see, the SNAG never cottoned on to the well-known and universally played game of fluffery and false advertising that goes on early in any relationship. As all Fullas and Sheilas realise, there is a three to six-month entry period where your partner is lying to your face in a flagrant attempt to pervert your thinking. Still, it goes without saying that the snuffing out of the SNAG came as a huge relief to the rest of the Kiwi Fullas.

A Pranker's primary form of leisure activity is golf. If he could, a Pranker would spend every minute that he is not making money playing golf. And most Prankers are bloody good at it. It's just that they have appalling golf etiquette. Prankers will talk during other players' tee shots, cast shadows over the hole, walk through a fellow player's putting line, and pepper slower players in the group ahead and yell abuse at them for not keeping a quick pace (Prankers will always use carts — regardless of the conditions).

Conversely, they will never let a quick twosome play through them if they are dawdling along themselves. A Pranker will never repair divots or rake the sand bunkers. They are far too busy being angry with themselves for not hitting a clean shot or for picking out a hazard. A very good mate of ours, Frankie the Pranker, is so renowned for having such a foul temper on the course that very few people are actually willing to play with him. In fact, more often than not he can't find a single soul keen to share a round with him, so he has to pull two balls out and play with himself.

In addition to golf and property, a Pranker's interests will include horses, shooting and international travel. On the travel front, he will only ever travel on 'lie-flat seat' planes, decrying the cheapness of all those airlines who do not offer such service. However, international travel has an unnerving effect on the Pranker as it cements his relative insignificance by comparison to the real wealth of Europe (his favourite travel destination). As he just thrives on being a relatively fat fish in a small pond, he loves arriving home and takes great pride in regaling all and sundry about how much he enjoyed the Amalfi Coast, Dubrovnik and Prague despite the fact that they have become overrun with tourists since his last trip 18 months ago.

A Pranker will bore you batty prattling on about wine, although as a handy side note, if you show sufficient interest he will buy you some to assist in your education.

The Pranker has a walk-in wardrobe, often referred to as a 'wank-in wardrobe', as they spend a ridiculous amount of time staring at themselves in the full-length 270-degree mirrors as they preen and prance and peacock and dress. In terms of clothing, his work attire will consist of: a pair of distressed denim jeans, leather lace-up shoes, possibly Loakes or an Italian brand, a belt two shades off the shoes, a crisp shirt with English collars and double cuffs for his gold cufflinks that draw out the gold of his IWC or Rolex, a navy blazer with pocket handkerchief and the mandatory jewellery in the form of a chain, worn both around the neck and the wrist, are all essentials.

When going casual, he will wear light-coloured loafers with knee-length chinos and Ralph Lauren polos tucked in and, again, the belt two shades off, with a designer jersey draped over the shoulders regardless of the season or the weather conditions.

On all occasions, his hair will be well groomed and with a wet look and quiff of hair that would have taken a most painstaking 20 minutes to get sitting flat but to him it was 20 of the best minutes in his favourite place — the 'his' side of the 'his/hers' bathroom.

The bathroom is the most important part of the house for the Pranker as it houses every conceivable concoction for his most valued asset — his face. Starting from the throat up he will have (in no particular order): the latest Gillette five-blade razor with vibrating handle, the matching shaving gel, cut cream that can be applied to any shaving nick to stop bleeding, aftershave lotion to add post-shave and pre-moisturiser, tweezers to pluck any errant hairs on his face, ears and eyebrows, eye-drops (the same brand that the Hollywood superstars use for the crystal-white eyes), electric toothbrushes, specialised dental teeth whitener, lash curlers, brow combs, and an ungodly assortment of hair shampoos, conditioners, gels, mousses, sprays and waxes. Of course, he will never, ever run short of a touch of women's make-up to hide any blemish that might pop up at an inopportune time (pimples love parties, remember!).

If single, most of the above will obviously be under lock and key so as to ensure that the high number of slim duskies wearing a path to the bedroom don't discover just how deluded the Pranker is. At least, not until he has had time to work out how much of a gold digger she is, anyway.

The net result is that the Pranker battles to find the right girl, which in itself can have some serious challenges. Having been quite verbose in his opposition to dating Cougars, Bobcats (small androgynous blokey-looking chicks) or Rattlers (in their forties with withered skin from too much time doing everything they shouldn't, with a venom that can kill a man if they are scorned — which they incidentally like doing as the knowledge that they are a fall-back option has left them bitter) he refuses to swallow that bitter pill. So the Pranker will invariably meet a woman through other contacts of a similar social standing (in Auckland, the Parnell tennis club is a good start) and a marriage of convenience will occur. Convenient for him, as he can do as he pleases, and for her, as she can buy whatever she wishes. Shallow as it may sound, this is the best type of relationship for the Pranker, on every level.

If the Pranker has children he wants to name them differently to ensure they stand out from the crowd. Popular choices for girls include Brooklyn and Chelsea (after suburbs of their favourite cities), Harmony, Faith, Summer or Isla (and similar such un-proper nouns), Savannah or Maya (after exotic holidays) or the name of the latest gossip magazine queen. And for Fullas the name is often that of their old man followed by 'the second'. Other names that have been used are celebrity surnames such as Carter, Spencer, Cooper, Haden, Jackson, Harrison, Hunter, Dylan, Miller, Ryan and Riley.

Pranklets (a Pranker's progeny) are not at all interested in traditional sports. Any sport where the barriers to entry are small, you will find few Pranklets. Given that all you need to play rugby are some boots, you won't find many there. All you need for cricket is a bat, so not many there either. Individual sports such as skiing, sailing and go-karting where both the fixed and marginal costs are high are where you find Prankers' posterity.

There is one exception, however. Pranklets contribute to the dire rise in soccer player numbers among our young. Some shocking statistics show that there are now more soccer players at primary school level in New Zealand than rugby and league players combined. Pranklets are largely to blame for this sad situation. What's worse, when out in public, these poxy Pranklets wear wanky round-ball jerseys from such far-flung places as Madrid, Manchester or Milan, instead of the blue and white hoops of Auckland, a Blues franchise jersey or the mighty

Warriors black number. Sadly for these kids, this is highly encouraged by their Pranker fathers.

The Pranklet is likely to suffer an array of minor physical conditions only correctable by expensive consultation and tidy ups from New Zealand's elite cosmetic surgeons. Given the Pranklets' predisposition to settle down with only blue bloods from the right pedigree they often suffer, as do the European royals, with undershot chins, buck teeth, hog nose, sloping shoulders and ginger hair. That said, the early detection of such conditions will see the Pranklets having teeth wired the moment the milk teeth fall out or in severe circumstances the extreme measure of the steel frisbee or glockenspiel hammer may be called for, where the child can be shipped to the dental beautician in the 'am' and have a new set of chompers in by the 'pm'.

Chin implants, hair dye and fake tan are all employed to ensure the Pranklet reaches his or her 'full potential' and does not embarrass the folks. Dressed from head to toe in designer clothes, they are never allowed to feel warm bitumen on bare feet as they stroll to the local shops for an ice cream (shoes are a necessity on all levels). Pranklets are direct reflections of their parents and, in much the same way as a handbag dog, they must be in show condition 24 hours a day and seven days a week.

Pranklets grow a penchant for the more desirable foods and beverages and are oft seen asking for delicacies that any normal young palate should not have a taste for. Crayfish, scallops, oysters (only Bluff), scampi, eye fillet or wagyu beef and lamb cutlets, buffalo mozzarella with vine-ripened tomato and basil, capers, balsamic vinegar, and pâté de foie gras are favourites of the Pranklet who has never, and will never, attend a birthday party at McDonald's or a party with all you can eat at Denny's.

A special treat is a thin-based pizza from an authentic up-market Italian restaurant or an icy pole made with fresh crushed juice.

Heaven forbid a Pranklet suffers from a weight condition! Years of Mum fingering her own tonsils to ensure she retains her wedding weight means that the Pranklet, despite a relatively indolent lifestyle, will never exceed his designer weight. It is not unusual to see a Pranklet being walked by his nanny to keep him trim. There is an exception, however, for uber-rich male offspring who can be afforded a few additional pounds as they are guaranteed a bevy of women to choose from in later life as they use their weighty wallets to solicit young money-hungry blue bloods with the desire to better their parents.

Where most Kiwi kids have to buy their own car once they've saved enough money, or may be given a cheap Jap lawnmower-sized shopping basket if they have generous parents, Pranklets will be given European sports cars as their first car. This ridiculous situation results in the oxymoron of a Maserati with a 'learner' plate dangling from the back window.

Prankers will never use an au pair as a child minder, with live-in nannies the only applicable option. Travel will be yearly with the European summer as the ideal time to discover Italy, Croatia and other Mediterranean destinations. The Prankers will travel First Class and leave the nanny and the Pranklets in Business to ruin the trip for those unfortunate enough to be in the same compartment.

Funnily enough, I was once in business with a Pranker who, at a Christmas party, loudly proclaimed to all in earshot, in a gross assumption that anyone was interested, that he had 'never been wrong!'. A quite preposterous assertion at the best of times. Had we known him any less we would have put it down to the three glasses of champagne (champagne makes Prankers sing like canaries) he had had over dinner. But after further investigation it was clear that he was deadly serious. Goes to show just how delusional a Pranker can get if no one tells him to get his hand off it. Recent rumour has it his wife has since shot the gap so he can't have been doing everything brilliantly.

It must be said, though, that Prankers, for all their drawbacks, are among the most generous people you will find. A Pranker will constantly have people around for dinner, and my word can a Pranker cook a mean barbecue (on his stainless steel six-burner with double-skinned hood for maximum heat retention and push-button electric ignition, gas wok and rotisserie of course). Large cuts of lamb or beef are prepared and nobody is allowed to even prod it as it cooks on the barbie (usually for 17 minutes on full heat, before it's turned and left to roast with the hood down on low flame for a further 12 minutes, our mate Frankie the Pranker reckons).

Prankers often suffer from tall poppy syndrome and are victims of the great Kiwi clobbering machine. But it must be recognised that Prankers are high net worth individuals (if not already, they have the ambition and hankering to be so) and if on the surface they appear to be nothing more than a mercenary menace, their financial and aspirational contribution to New Zealand cannot be underestimated. New Zealand actually needs to keep our Prankers right here. They are some of the best employers and customers any Fulla could have or wish for. Embrace the Pranker!

The Ginga

A Ginga or Gonad is a Fulla whose hair (including facial, bodily and pubic) is bright red or bright orange and whose skin looks like luncheon sausage.

Constant adversity from their first memories of disappointed parents, relatives and friends looking and pointing at their ginger swedes with supportive and condoling comments, to schoolyard ridicule and limited interaction with the fairer sex, the Ginga is the master of entertaining himself. It is this industrious, never-say-die spirit that makes the Ginga a valued member of every set of mates from North Cape (where there is a very high incidence of the rare Whaka Blond or Pink Maori) to Bluff. A Ginga is one of life's gifts and a joy to be around.

According to a recent DNA study out of a Scottish University, there is irrefutable evidence that Gingas are directly descended from the Neanderthals. This little-known fact should surprise nobody. Sadly, a recessive gene means that we may only have a few more generations to enjoy them.

In many ways, mocking Gingas is the last form of tolerated racism, discrimination and prejudice, so it is fortunate that the Ginga has a good sense of humour. That sense of humour is a vital part of being a FOT (Fuckin' Orange Thing), given the genetic propensity for poor health. They are fiery, and as such can suffer stress-related blood pressure issues, such as blackout in extreme rages and in later life massive heart attacks brought on by puerile incidents such as slow traffic lights or the Wallabies scoring a try against the All Blacks.

Their translucent skin means that the sunny summer months can be nigh on intolerable, coupled with the fact that bees, wasps, mosquitoes and sandflies find the Ginga's luncheon skin ripe to bite or prick. Not that they tend to enjoy winter much either as they suffer horribly from snow blindness. That said, years of schoolyard beatings and taunting make them both resilient and handy with their dukes and excellent rumblers, brawlers and scrappers when it comes to a good old stoush or a decent donnybrook.

The Celtic variety, with the bright red bulbous nose, is something of a rarity and can explode at the drop of a hat. Little doubt, due to the arduous circumstances endured by his forefathers and the need to fight like savages against the marauding English.

Despite the fact that Judas was a renowned Red, Gingas are remarkably trustworthy and stand-up blokes. They will always have a good read on fairness, having suffered horribly for no good reason at school, where a litany of names and knees and elbows would have been thrown at them.

Despite what you may have heard there is no such hair colour as strawberry blond. Think about it . . . is there anything redder than a strawberry? This misappropriation has simply been offered by the 'PC' brigade and the odd hapless Morringe in defence of the indefensible. If your hair colour is not primarily black or brown then you are a Ginga. Albinos or 'Milkies' are simply the magnified form of a bloodnut suffering intensified symptoms and sporting an uncanny resemblance to a pink-eyed newt. In a cruel twist, the 'Milky' seldom has any of the desirable Ginga traits.

One Milky I went to university with called 'Beno' was a hell of a Good Fulla. He played footy as a loose forward, and when the weather was overcast he was a great roving number seven. But when the sun was out, he spent the whole game burrowing into rucks in the desire to escape the fire from above and moved into a tight forward role. He was never more at home than at the local pub, the Gardie's Sports Tavern, and would weave his way home with a smile from ear to ear, avoiding bright street lights and oncoming cars, which at high beam could paralyse him like a possum.

He had a marvellous sense of humour, and rumour had it he got a few pranks too many over his flatmates who, as a result, decided to up the ante by putting a sunlamp on him as he slept off a night on the plonk. If one is to believe the Chinese whispers circulating years later, the ruse was apparently foiled by a female flatmate who returned home to the faint smell of pork sausages cooking and after searching the kitchen, woke poor Beno with a bucket of cold water which almost sizzled on contact with his overripe helmet.

Given the Gingas' intense dislike of the sun, coupled with Neanderthalic and more recently Celtic ancestry, it comes as little surprise that they love nothing more than a good old knees up in the local pub. This allows them the ability to cast aside their inhibitions and really let their Ginga hair down in a safe environment — well, safe for them at least. A little known fact is that Gingas are on average 15–20 per cent larger than the average Fulla. In New Zealand, the average weight is 78 kg and growing at a ready pace! The Gingas' average weight is well over 90 kg; this can make them very hard to control when they decide to let their hair down.

One of my closest friends, who happens to run a similar shade to a test cricket ball, and is a lot larger than the average Ginga even, has a habit of really living life to the full. His run of overexcited behaviour started at the tender age of eight, when after watching *Edward Scissorhands* and drinking too much Fanta, he attempted to emulate his new big-screen hero and in the process lopped off his best mate's index finger with the garden shears. As if that was not bad enough, in a state of panic, he grabbed the amputated digit and hurled it deep into dense bush to hide the evidence. An extensive search by 20 neighbours and relatives came up empty and his relationship with the amputee was in tatters and has never been the same since.

Since then he has moved on to some of the most brazen acts of passion known to our group of pretty liberal mates, including starting a riot in Sydney at a league club karaoke night, by responding to the heckling of the crowd to his Neil Diamond rendition by dropping his tweeds and depositing the mesh head of the microphone firmly between his ginger cheeks. In his mind, if they did not have the decency to give him a crack, then he would give them a crack of his own. It would take a desperately brave patron to continue singing after that.

This same chap has been a constant source of entertainment to all and sundry and has had to go by a number of noms de plume to ensure his errant behaviour is not attributed to one single individual. A lot of his over-exuberant behaviour in the summer months is passed off as a side-effect of sunstroke. Pinkies are obviously not cut out for temperatures above 14 degrees Celsius. Temperatures in excess of this safety zone can melt the Ginga's on-board thermostat and fry the motherboard, resulting in deranged behaviours ranging from 3 to 10 on the antisocial scale.

As a word of warning, trying to regulate the thermostat with cold lager is bloody foolhardy at best. Some of the behaviour we have personally witnessed from the FOT mentioned above includes:

- Biting two eye holes in a garlic naan at an Indian restaurant, peeling it over his face, removing his clothing and running around the restaurant offering direct advice to diners, calling himself 'Naanman'.
- Trying to drive a jet ski, parked on the beach, at full throttle to catch a ferry he had just missed, only to be tackled off the ride by the owner as it dug itself into the beach it had been dragged up onto.
- And a number of others not fit to record.

Not surprisingly, Gingas have a pain threshold many times superior to Fullas of other hair pigmentation. One extraordinary example of this was a dear Ginga friend of ours whose foot was lopped off by a boat propeller out at sea. Once we got him into the boat, on seeing his nub, the girls on board lost the plot, as too did most of the Fullas. The only one who kept it cool was the victim, who ever so calmly asked for a cigarette!

There are several websites developed by and for gregarious Gingas, providing a sense of unity and pride among the brotherhood of Bloodnuts. Ginga.co.nz, for example, is sponsored by Lion Red, Fanta, Gingernuts, Red Bull and Frank's Gingerbeer and provides all sorts of Ginga trivia. What is really needed, though, is an online Ginga dating website. The benefits of this would be twofold: (1) Gingas often battle when it comes to attracting the fairer sex — and a website may facilitate courtship and alleviate this issue ever so slightly. And (2) Gingas are in serious danger of extinction.

The first point is obvious. The second point, however, needs further attention. Believe it or not Gingas are on the endangered species list. You see the Ginga gene — which is a mutation of the Melanocortin 1 Receptor, a mutation which causes great hormonal imbalances and random fluctuations in mood and also causes red pigmentation of the follicular cells — is recessive. This means that Gingas need to mate with Gingarettes or at the very least fair Blondes to create Gingalets. Only this way will the Ginga not suffer the same fate as the dinosaur or the dodo. And all this time you probably thought that Ginganess was caused by high blood pressure causing blood vessels in the scalp to burst and as a result staining the hair follicles, I bet.

The Ginga gene is unique to Gingas. For this very reason, those Fullas that have an accident with peroxide, or even worse — intentionally bleach their hair ginger, are not the same on the inside. They may look Ginga, but they don't, or can't, act it. They can't just flare up like a pack of haemorrhoids at the drop of a hat, like a true Ginga. They lack the red-hot fire and passion that comes from within a genuine Ginga. They lack the total unpredictability and irrationality of a bona-fide, unadulterated, authentic Ginga.

A true Ginga's nose is always smaller than the average Fulla's. (Or occasionally temporarily larger as a result of stepping in to defend what's right and just.) This is from years and years of peeling after being burned by the harsh New Zealand summer sun. As a kid, young Gareth the Ginga from Greytown spent the months of December to March with a scabbed-topped snoz, and to this day those layers of peeled skin have never quite regenerated fully. Gareth doesn't mind though coz he reckons a smaller nose is better in scraps. 'No one's ever broken my nose,' Gareth once told me. This is not an insignificant feat considering his head's had more hits than the Beatles.

The Maori even have a special name for a Ginga. It is Urukehu. Now my Te Reo has never been that flash, but if I'm not mistaken (and I may well be) Urukehu is loosely translated as '*an unpredictable and frequently irrational Fulla with a heart like a Lion and a head the colour of the inside of a Kumara*'. The Urukehu were regarded as some of the most fearsome and fearless warriors of all time, and were instilling panic and fear throughout New Zealand at the same time that their Viking and Celtic copper-headed counterparts were also terrorising Europe.

You only need to ask any club footy player who they most respect on the field. Without exception it'll be the Ginga. It's funny that you can mark some hard as nails Offcuts or some massive Big Freshes or even some very fleet-footed Funters, but invariably it's the crafty Ginga in the team (and there always seems to be one in every team — or more than one if you're playing a Catholic team) that instils the most anguish, anxiety, apprehension, angst and affliction.

I'm not sure if it is their unpredictability or their propensity to bleed profusely (from the face more often than not) without flinching that creates the unease, but marking a Ginga is a harbinger for a game which starts with pang and ends with pain. I played a couple of seasons with a Ginga, whose name escapes me, we just always called him Ginga (normally followed by nads, pubes or ring) who, despite being one of the smallest hookers in the competition, was undoubtedly the most effective. On countless occasions he'd come flying out of the middle of a maul with the ball in hand, just as the referee was about to blow the whistle, and charge off down the park, elbows and knees flailing. This vigorous thrashing about of his appendages made him very awkward and tough to tackle. He'd throw his body around with reckless abandon, bouncing into and out of tackles, hitting rucks like a runaway train and scavenging the ball like a hungry farmdog.

I'm sure he would have had a stellar rugby career had it not been catastrophically cut short. In a desperate attempt to stop an opposition try he ran head first at full tit into a goalpost. It was a pre-season game and there were no pads on the posts. Poor old Ginga ended up with a gash from his red-hairline to the bridge of his nose, and was quite obviously suffering from a serious case of concussion.

In a cruel twist, it wasn't the vicious head injury that halted his career. No, what happened next was truly remarkable. The ref blew his whistle, called on the St John's boys, and walked over to pick up the ball until Ginga was helped from the field. But Ginga stood up with a glazed look, rubbed the blood and mud out of his eyes, glanced around and spied the ref holding the ball. Well! In his confusion, he mistook him for an opposition player, and charged at him, unleashing a textbook ball and all tackle that nearly cut the referee in half. He then leapt to his feet, and, as the tackler, he assumed he had rights to the ball, ripped it off the ref and sprinted down the park scoring a try under the posts at the other end with a death-defying dive. The ref suffered some whiplash and post-traumatic stress, but this was nothing compared to poor old Ginga who was banned from the game for life by the NZRFU judiciary.

It is a bizarre fact that despite Gingas' natural ability to stand out from the crowd, they all consistently find the need to be a little eccentric. When it comes to cars, they tend to drive vehicles with personality: the Citroen DS (or Frog), the Austin 1100 (Land Crab), the Triumph Stag (the Snag), and other generally unreliable and troublesome automobiles.

Given that very few colours go well with red, and that Gingas are all extroverts, when dressing they will throw all number of offensive colour, material and pattern combinations together and pull it off. The most obvious worldwide example of which is Ronald McDonald, who not surprisingly is sitting at 10th equal on the all-time list of significant FOTs.

If looking for birthday or Christmas gifts, a sure hit is either a bow tie or a cravat (for those over 45). They may pretend not to like them, but underneath they will be tickled that they have an excuse to unleash their exhibitionism in a social situation.

Another random cautionary note, that it would be remiss to exclude, is a general warning about combining a Ginga of any age with fireworks. This is a recipe for disaster, along similar lines to handing a social retard a rifle (we have all seen what happens in the southern states of America). As discussed, they have an extraordinary pain threshold, and thus minor (or for that matter major) burns do not affect Pinkies when fuelled by adrenaline. They are drawn to any firework that explodes or that can be aimed and shot. With little or no encouragement, they will start holding and lighting fireworks and within minutes will be aiming them at people.

I first witnessed this phenomenon in the early 80s when a few families combined their stash and held a neighbourhood Guy Fawkes party for the kids. A mate of mine called Adam, who was as red as the bonfire we stood around, would have been about six at the time and even at that tender age was known as being clumsy and at risk. The old routine was to fill milk bottles full of sand and stick the sky-rockets into them to control take-off. This was prior to the ludicrous rules controlling rocket size and the big rockets would shoot the best part of one kilometre up with four or five explosions on the ascent and one huge eruption at maximum altitude.

Well, Wellington is a windy city and it was no surprise that when one of the milk bottles blew over with the fuse a split second from detonation, the rocket picked Adam as its target. It was a free-for-all! Everyone was diving for cover in an attempt to save themselves except Adam's folks who bravely stood in front of the little carrot-top to shield him from being skewed and flown off the property. The rocket had a mind of its own and shot in the total opposite direction at about 200 kph.

The problem was that it hit a log for the bonfire that redirected it 90 degrees and it then took another fortuitous change in direction off the kitchen wall, before heading directly towards Adam's back, having circumvented his parents' protective cover. It hit him at maximum velocity just prior to its first explosion and pinned him face first against a wooden trellis with a creeper growing on it.

There were five problems at this stage: firstly, that Adam's old man had, about one week earlier, doused the creeper with Round Up so it was dry and extremely flammable. Secondly, the rocket was just hitting full speed. Thirdly, Adam was incapable of moving against the rocket's propulsion. Fourthly, everything was happening fast — very fast. And, finally, some silly bugger decided to try to throw a stick at the rocket that by now was hanging out of Adam's back in the way a perfectly shot arrow hangs out of the target.

Well, the stick missed the rocket and hit Adam square on the ear, which in a strange way possibly averted a disastrous demise, and his attention from the rocket, and surely saved him from more serious damage (but which ended the relationship between the families).

Adam fell to the ground and the rocket slid off his back straight up and into the dead creeper, letting out its second explosion on cue and igniting the entire creeper, which was tied to the trellis with a woman's stocking. Everything was happening in slow motion by now and by the time Adam's old man reached him the rocket let out its third explosion, a royal display of blue and white phosphorus that drove his old man out of reach and burnt through the stocking tie, collapsing the entire flaming bush on the poor, prone Adam.

At this stage the rocket broke free and shot skyward, letting go its penultimate plume as it rose above the neighbourhood. Suffice to say that pandemonium and chaos reigned as one of the parents opened the garden hose on to the trellis bonfire with the crumpled Adam beneath it. Just as Adam was being dragged from the ash the rocket let out its last climactic explosion and fell back to earth.

I hate to sound sick, but if I were to expire and had the opportunity to relive 10 experiences, this would be one of them! Poor Adam was bloody lucky to have been wearing a woollen, hand-knitted jersey and beanie because while both of them were poked he was only slightly charred. The worst injury was the split ear where he had been sconed by the errant stick. Believe it or not, the story had one more glorious chapter, for the rocket still had not made it back to terra firma.

Weighing about half a pound (empty) and plummeting back from about a thousand feet, this damn thing landed perfectly on top of Adam's old man's bald, Ginga head, dropping him like a Tua left hook! I mean, what are the odds? Slim but a lot higher than you might expect if you are celebrating Guy Fawkes with a family of Gingas — so let this be a warning. It would be wise to wear ski goggles and flame-retardant clothing if you wish to celebrate in complete safety.

There are very few Ginga cricketers for obvious reasons. Those rare buggers who do make it are so bloody angry they have to stand in the sun for days on end that they are invariably aggressive fast bowlers, such as the Aussie pair of Craig McDermott and Rodney Hogg. There is even speculation that the fastest bowler of all time, Jeff Thomson, was a Ginga. Apparently, even more use to their team than their quick deliveries was that they were also brilliant sledgers.

Gynaecologists and obstetricians are now able to check for certain birth defects by pulling a hair and testing for the additional chromosome — for those terrified about bringing a child into a world of ridicule this offers the ability to kill two birds with one stone.

PROOF OF THE CALIBRE OF **REDHEADS** THROUGHOUT THE AGES COMES IN THE TOP 10 GINGAS OF ALL TIME:		
1 Adam	**6**	Prince Harry (could end up top 3)
2 Eric the Viking	**7**	Johnny Rotten
3 Napoleon	**8**	Custer
4 Churchill	**9**	Ron Howard
5 Richard the Lionheart	**10=**	For those in the Taranaki, Paul Tito (who is the perfect example of a Pink Maori) and Ronald McDonald

While these days you can still see Gingas the full length and breadth of New Zealand, let's hope the Ginga doesn't die out. It'd be a calamity for us all if we didn't have his colourful character and his colourful head in our classrooms, sports teams and workplaces. God save the Ginga — they are custodians of all that is right and true!

In fact, you Sheilas reading this, if you have hair of any shade of blonde it would be a great service to future generations if you thought favourably about a relationship with a Ginga. You will find your partner, loyal to the nth degree, with a fine sense of humour and of what's right, great tenacity, a glass is half full outlook, very sociable, an extrovert showman, hopelessly romantic, creative and complete with the desire to please . . . what more could you ask for?

THE CARDYCRAT

We all know Cardycrats. They're the Cardigan-wearing bureaucrat Fullas who spend hours trying to put up official roadblocks and barriers to everything you want to do, causing nothing but a serious brain-ache to all. They have appalling dress sense (and often atrocious body odour too), dressing in dull coloured (usually grey or brown) cardigans in summer, autumn, winter and spring, weekdays, weekends, and even around their own home, with matching coloured slacks, shoes and socks — and always an earthy-coloured tie to look important. In summer they may even break out knee-length walker shorts with long socks, resembling a hiker who is donning formal neckwear so he can have a passport photo taken on his way to the bush. Their demeanour is so dull and their bearing so boring, the Cardycrat would even give an aspirin a headache.

I once heard Roger Douglas say that under the recent Labour Government the number of public-sector bureaucrats had ballooned 40 per cent in nine years. 'That would be no real problem to me as a taxpayer,' he said, 'if they just sat around all day drinking tea. It would act as a sort of welfare benefit to quasi-unemployable people. But the problem is they actually do do a few things and those few things inhibit the average person like you and me by creating unnecessary red tape and headache, and preventing any form of progress.'

Everybody has had at least one encounter with a Cardycrat in their time. If they were to realistically describe their profession it would be 'Papershuffler', but generally they are involved in local government, councils and public sector roles. They take sick enjoyment in turning down applications, holding people up and generally dicking people around over trivial matters. The private sector too (usually the large corporate fraternity) has strategically hired Cardycrats when they want to frustrate clients or customers. They unleash them on anybody who is: trying to get a refund, make a complaint, discuss an erroneous bill, or attempting to speak with someone of importance in the organisation.

Wellington has a disproportionate number of Cardycrats (apparently, over 40 per cent of the core public service posts are there), but they are scattered throughout the beautiful New Zealand countryside, slowing down administrative processes, regulating an already over-regulated state, and frustrating the be-Jesus out of unprofitable corporate customers.

A mate of mine told me the other day of his adventures in attempting to get some childcare subsidy support for his kids' education from the relevant government agency. He rang them, and after eight or so options to push one, two or three he finally got to speak to someone who said, 'Ah yes, you need to bring in documents A, B, C and D for childcare support.'

So this Fulla went along to his local service centre office and after standing in a queue for half an hour or so he finally got to speak with an expressionless Cardycrat. He produced documents A, B, C and D, and was promptly asked where documents E and F were. My mate said he was only told to bring A, B, C and D and that he wasn't even sure what an F was. The Cardycrat rolled his eyes and said, 'You can get an F from over there.'

He wandered over to the desk and a frightfully polite Cardycrat told him, 'Oh no, sir, to get an F you need to go over there, but they're on a tea break, so you'll have to come back after eleven o'clock.' So my mate wandered over to the desk when it opened back up — about half past eleven. The Cardycrat there was very grumpy indeed about having to work so soon after his tea break. When asked how one can get an F document for childcare subsidy support he snapped back, 'But what the hell do you want an F document for? You only need an A, B, C and D!'

At any rate, after all the kerfuffle, it turns out that this Fulla and his wife earn a smidgeon over fifty grand a year each, so some smug Cardycrat took great delight in advising him he was far too 'rich' for any sort of support.

When they're not busy disrupting hard-working citizens' days, or sipping on their tea, delivered by Doris and her tea-trolley, they have a habit of simply going AWOL. I remember reading in the late David Lange's autobiography, *My Life*, that one warm January's morning, not long after he became Prime Minister, he decided, as Minister of Education too, to pop over to the Ministry of Education. He arrived to find the building resembling an abandoned Central Otago gold mining ghost town. He wandered around scribbling a few notes and strategically leaving them on a few of the desks in the building. It was some hours later that a bunch of senior departmental Cardycrats from the Ministry paid him a visit at the Beehive with their tails between their legs, explaining sheepishly that as the Ministry of Education, there was little to do during the school holidays, and that it was customary to take a daily long lunch during the months of January, May, August and December.

In general Cardycrats are just vexatious, annoying, irritating and nettlesome, but occasionally they can become so overwhelmed with their own power that there is a point where they can metamorphose into something quite viciously evil. A prime example of this is the case of the bunch of Cardycrats at OSH going hell for leather after some poor Cocky because a beekeeper was tragically killed when a bridge that was built by the Army collapsed on Crown land leading to the Cocky's farm.

Cardycrats at the IRD have even been known to push some Fullas over the edge by placing so much heat on them just chasing up a bit of overdue GST or income tax. Like rust corroding a beautiful old car, they just never stop in their pursuit to be viciously officious.

As an example of how powerful they have become, the staff at a small company in Wellington that I have a few shares in were informed that someone in the wider New Zealand workforce had attempted to sit down on their chair, misjudged the mount and landed square on their tail-bone. This had caused some minor bruising and discomfort and this Fulla had had to have time off work courtesy of ACC. As a result, Cardycrats, via the company human resources department, insisted that everyone in the organisation undergo some training and practice on how to sit safely on a chair. You can imagine just how ridiculous the staff felt going through this comical and worthless exercise.

But Charlie tells of a similar story where a mate of his attended a workshop in his local community and was ticked off by a pedantic and puffed-up Cardycrat for calling it a 'brainstorming' session. The reason? It might be disrespectful to those who may have become mentally incapacitated as a result of a lightning strike. With his tongue planted firmly in his cheek, Charlie's mate then proposed that this particular session be called 'thought-showers' only to be told in no uncertain terms that this name could cause trauma and gross offence to those that might be thinking about relatives in drought-stricken areas. It was agreed that it should be referred to as a 'multi-party meeting' — nothing more. Although Charlie's mate couldn't help but throw one last suggestion on the table, directed at the Cardycrat facilitating the show, before deciding his time was better spent elsewhere. That suggestion? 'A mass debate.'

But, as I mentioned, don't think for a second that they are just the domain of the civil service and SOEs. They are commonly found in private industry too, to repel unprofitable customers or to create a layer between Joe Bloggs the consumer and senior management. Airlines, banks, telcos and utility companies are full of the buggers, causing pain and delay for the average Fulla to the point of exasperation and resignation.

It is easy to think they are among the most bothersome, officious and self-righteous wastes of space that God gave breath to. And for the 35 hours (maximum) of the week that they 'work' they quite probably are. However, it should be known that these boring bastards actually selflessly contribute to society in unseen ways that most Fullas are totally unaware of.

First of all, they are so ruthlessly by-the-book that New Zealand is classified as the least corrupt country in the world, according to the United Nations' corruption index. The Cardycrat's form of payment, fulfilment and gratitude is the pure enjoyment he gets from rigidly sticking to the rules, even if it makes absolutely perfect sense to bend them ever so slightly occasionally. Therefore bribery is of absolutely no interest to them — in other words, they are totally incorruptible.

Secondly, what they get up to in their spare time will surprise you. It certainly won't interest you because it's as boring as bat-shit, but it will surprise you. Cardycrats perform all sorts of chores for which they get no monetary remuneration. For example, a Fulla the old man went to school with, Clifton the Cardycrat, a Customs Officer at Wellington Airport, volunteers every spare minute he has to helping his local community. He umpires youth cricket all weekend (and of course takes great delight in shaking his head and uttering the words 'not out' when there is a huge appeal for a close run out, LBW or caught behind) and even manages to find time to mow the lawns at the local church.

His greatest ever moment was umpiring the 1979 secondary schools cricket final. That particular morning he had already mown the field and rolled the pitch, and then for about six hours he was a match official in front of a bumper crowd of 400. He was king for a day. Unfortunately, some members of the losing team took exception to one of his umpiring calls and engraved a large image of a dufus on the roof of his car which took some of the gloss off what had been a most memorable day in the sun for old Cliff.

Cliff the Cardycrat could well be mistaken for yet another moustached moron making life difficult for others but he more than makes up for it with his selfless community services. He is a Rotary member, delivers meals on wheels to the elderly or indisposed, is a volunteer fireman, and was even a lifeguard at the local public pool for many years until the administration received so many complaints about his vigorous over-use of the whistle that they had to ask him to retire and look for something else to do with his Sundays.

The most outrageous thing Cliff has ever done, when I asked him at his Plimmerton home recently, was fart in a fridge at a party when he was studying his BA at Victoria (where he majored in the enthralling subject of Latin Literature). But Cliff the Cardycrat's biggest claim to fame was when he appeared as an extra in Roger Donaldson's 1977 movie *Sleeping Dogs*. There isn't a person Clifton meets who doesn't hear the whole story, especially the part where he asked Sam Neill if he could borrow his lighter to light a ciggie (off the set, of course).

Many of his workmates believe he has a secret ambition to be a revolutionary, just like the main character, Smith, and that he is still hopeful that New Zealand may some day slip into civil chaos so he can live his dream.

The excellent news for Wellingtonians is that, with such a severe concentration of Cardycrats in the town, those who have real estate interests are laughing all the way to the bank. The central business district has full occupancy and in fact, given that other countries send an assortment of seconded foreign Cardycrats into the city as well, there is a shortage of office space and rental properties in the central city, forcing property prices through the permanent Wellington cloud cover.

The Finkle

The Finkle is an effeminate and fruity homosexual Fulla with a weak wrist and a strong lisp. For years Finkles had to live a secret life hiding their Finkility for fear of ridicule, marginalisation and the more than occasional hiding at the hand of a redneck. However, one of the few positives to come from the political correctness movement is that Finkles, and other minorities of persuasion, have been able to show their freedom of expression, openly and proudly.

While more often than not clearly male, a Finkle will adopt the traits of a woman. He is submissive, but verbose and as camp as a row of pink tents (obviously not the Native American version). Finkles can either be Tops, Bottoms or Versatiles. This does not require further explanation, I hope. They will often wear a goatee, and there are various reasons for this that I'd rather not detail, but probably the most commonly accepted is that it hides the stretch marks.

A Finkle will talk loudly as to his sexual prowess and will have a peculiar passion to lure male members of heterosexual persuasion over to the dark side in much the same way as Big Ears tried to deflower poor young Noddy under the tree stump in the dark, dark woods. A Finkle will, when telling a story, often talk of himself in the third person and refer to himself as 'she' as in 'she loves it'. Quite what 'it' can be applied to varies.

Finkles love music and will jump around the place like a teenage girl after two glasses of wine, should the right pop song come on. Finkle anthems by prominent 'Gaycons' (gay icons) are 'Like a Virgin' by Madonna and 'I Am What I Am' by Gloria Gaynor. Immaculate dress sense is another defining characteristic of the Finkle. Major top-end European brands (or rip-offs) being first choice. Prada, Gucci, Louis Vuitton are 'to die for . . . mmmmm . . . yummmmmmmmmmy'.

A Finkle will have no ugly friends as appearance is of the utmost importance. He would rather die than be seen with plain Janes or (even worse) a plain James. He will be at the cutting edge of fashion, and eats only the best when in public but will have a fridge at home consisting of no more than bottles of wine (predominantly fruity German varietals like Riesling and Gewürztraminer), cheese, tomato chutney, chocolates and a couple of microwave meals. He'll have his hair cut every two to three weeks, just like a 14-year-old Pranker, and will have lots of friends in the hair game. Despite having the equivalent of a 'number 4' buzz cut, they can spend upwards of 30 minutes getting it correctly shaped and, if they cannot, will simply throw a sickie and stay at home depressed until they can remedy the problem by having a local queen swing by home with the scissors. In fact, many Finkles take up hairdressing as a profession and specialise in *Manscaping*, the act of grooming, shaving or trimming hair on the male body.

Finkles' sexuality affords them the presumption to redecorate their friends' apartments, arrange flowers, arrange their wardrobes and, occasionally, even cut their friends' hair (qualified or not). Finkles find it hilarious that often 'Breeders' (heterosexuals) are sometimes stupid enough to let them loose on their lid with a pair of scissors.

One mate of ours, who we will call Shamus, spent six days in bed ordering pizza and refusing to take visitors or answer the phone after a dreadful bout of misfortune with Veet depilatory cream (for hair removal). He had just applied (quite liberally) a tube to his nether regions — in preparation for a big weekend ahead where he was due to hook up with a Muscle Mary (a buff Gym Dandy Finkle) whom he had met casually on a girls' 'shopping' weekend in Sydney — when a close friend phoned him. Oblivious to the fact that Veet has a maximum 'on skin' time of eight minutes for coarse hair, Shamus kept yapping away until he smelt a strong burning odour, upon which he screamed like a choir girl and ran for the shower where he turned it on full pressure, as cold as possible, and proceeded to do a hand-stand in the shower box in order to get maximum direct spray on his crutch region.

The last call duration on his cell phone was 19 minutes. He had melted his bread box and spent six days waiting for the snake to 'shed its skin' so to speak. What was worse, according to Shamus, was that the Muscle Mary from Sydney thought he was a 'silly bitch' for not turning up and, despite Shamus' protestations, didn't want a bar of him from then on. Shamus is able to tell this story for at least 40 minutes and, as if anyone in the group wants to hear, often describes his post-skinned nether regions as 'brand new' and the process as actually being 'so incredibly worth it'.

Finkles can have a very cutting bitchy streak and love nothing more than to laugh at others' expense. One of their favourite pastimes is people watching and they adore tearing innocent folk to bits, about their look, style, mannerisms or redeeming features. This is why they used to love the HERO parade so much as they have hundreds of friends, usually Bears, the butch masculine half of a relationship, who would sport tight shirts, bulging muscles and full facial beards or handlebar mos with matching thick body hair. Heaven forbid they ever got too close to a naked flame or contract a case of crabs.

Finkles will usually drive two-door sports cars that, frankly, no man should ever be seen in, such as: Porsche Boxters, Mazda MX5s, Mercedes C Series, Mini Ragtops and similar such cars which were designed with wealthy Prankers' teenage daughters in mind. One theory is that they are too weak in the wrist to operate a larger vehicle. Another is that these cars are impractical for 'Breeders' and therefore overtly advertises a Finkle's Finkleness. As they love to be seen, they never have tinted windows and will often buy the convertible option. Canary yellow or bright pink are the colours of choice.

Finkles love bitches. They will own Chihuahuas, Miniature Poodles, Bichon Frises and other similarly ridiculous and neurotic types of canines. And they take great pride in dressing them to the nines with all sorts of silly paraphernalia. His pooch is a fashion accessory and most of these breeds are small enough to be carried in the Finkle's man-bag as he minces his way through shopping centres and cafés during the weekend.

The bitch-slap is the Finkle's (rather effective) form of defence. It's an open hand stinger to the cheek, where the technique is all in the snap of the wrist. The bitch-slap, when used mildly, can also be a type of friendly, affectionate, caressing gesture and when used between fellow Finkles often replaces the standard handshake greeting that other Fullas employ on seeing one another. It can also be a very provocative, flirtatious gesture — particularly when thrown into thin air and accompanied with the comment, 'Oh stop it!'

Every Finkle has a Fag Hag. More essential than their mobile phone, and more fashionable than their Gucci glasses, their Fag Hag is their mentor, support network and second opinion all wrapped up in one slightly overweight, often loud and inappropriate but completely smitten package. Fag Hags, also known as Fruit-flies, are Sheilas who help Finkles get in touch with their feminine side. Then there's the Fag Stag, a very unusual type of Fulla, indeed. The Fag Stag is heterosexual who enjoys hanging out with Finkles. Sociologists and psychologists have not yet found the reason for this, but one can only assume it is to increase their chances with the ladies, by slimming the odds of competition.

A good friend of my wife's, Freddy the Finkle, drives a pink Audi TT (always with his white leather driving gloves), has a Maxi Priest CD permanently playing and a Flock of Seagulls CD in reserve in the glove-box. He smokes Fleur cigarettes which he refers to as 'fags' with a wink, giggle and a swish of the wrist. ('You know, Sweetheart, they are the long skinny type with gold-wrapped filters — oh I do like the long skinny ones but I like the short stubby ones too.') He works in a design agency but wants to leave because his ex-lover, Bryce, is now the Creative Director, and therefore his boss. His BFFN (best friend for now) and he might go into business in competition to 'shunt that slutpipe pillowbiter Bryce in the ass'. Besides, Bryce has developed some tragic rack rot and is looking as rough as guts, according to Freddie.

He's quite a bombastic Fulla is Freddy the Finkle. He once told me in passing, 'You know, Sweetheart, I'm not gay.' I raised my eyebrows, rather perplexed and perturbed until he continued: 'I once fucked a guy who reckoned he was, though.' And if hung over, Freddie calls himself and his partner the Sisters Grimm.

Freddy the Finkle tends to drink only double-shot decaffeinated organic trim soy lattes to break the fast and has a pet hate for small-town New Zealand where he can't get hold of the aforementioned beverage to flop around in his limp wrists. And he only ever pees sitting down. That way the last elusive drop (you know the one you get no matter how carefully you shake post urination) doesn't show up when he wears his best beige slacks.

Even though in general Finkles couldn't give a flying Frenchman's arsehole about rugby, a mate told me about a Finkle who owned a florist shop on Parnell Rise in Auckland and when asked by the local publican, who was doing the rounds of the stores up the strip, if he wanted to enter the sweepstake for the Bledisloe Cup game that Saturday, the Finkle replied, 'Oh sure, Darl.' The publican then went to lengths to explain that the person who picked the closest aggregate score for the game won a $100 beer voucher redeemable at his pub. The Finkle decided to take a punt and said, 'I reckon the French will win 2–1.' It goes without saying he didn't win the sweepstake that day.

Freddy the Finkle is a mighty fine chef, indeed. If you ever get the opportunity to be invited to a Finkle's house for dinner — snap it up. If you are a little apprehensive about being confined to a Finkle's abode, just find out which restaurants in your home town have a Finkle operating the oven and you won't be disappointed. Freddy the Finkle, for example, is the proud owner of an autographed copy of Hudson and Halls' gourmet recipe book which he follows without any deviation whatsoever. He has his own signature specialities too, though, such as his much-loved meatballs which he makes by grinding nuts, mince and ginger then hand rolling the meatballs, and he serves them with hot buttered, honey-roasted carrots. He makes a mean starter too — a spicy Thai soup called Cream of Sum Yung Gai. For pudding he pulls out a selection of Perky Nanas and Pixie Caramels, and it is usually about then I decide it's safer to blow him an air-kiss goodbye and leave for the night.

Freddy is one of the country's greatest entertainers, throwing the best parties almost every weekend. He's also an excellent dancer and he just loves holding balls, which fellow Finkles from all over the globe are invited to come to. One of the most legendary parties to ever have been held on these shores was Freddie's 'Coming Out' ball where he confirmed his Finkility to the nation in scintillating style.

An interesting characteristic of Freddy the Finkle is that he has the most amazing, intuitive ability to distinguish other Finkles from heterosexuals. He can do this at just a single glance (or apparently by noting the aroma of a Fulla's musk). It's like a sixth sense or intuition based on the observation of physical movements, traits, trinkets and what have you. He nails it every time too. He calls this his Gaydar.

Just a word of warning: you should always exercise caution when buying a second-hand computer or laptop from a Finkle as there will always be three keys on the board that are worn down:

C : ENTER

You'll find Finkles in the strangest places and doing the queerest things. A very fruity little Finkle from Featherston, commonly known in the area as the Fish, recently bought a lifestyle block near Colonial Knob, just north of Wellington. He believes there is a market for organic carrots, parsnips and other kinds of 'root' vegetables, and that the cool climate of the Porirua region is ideal. I asked him what market research had identified the organic carrot opportunity, and he sheepishly said it was his own private investigation. Naturally, I didn't probe any further. Nonetheless he has planted several acres in taproots and strictly uses no herbicides, fungicides or pesticides.

I was lucky enough to get invited to his 10-acre farm for brunch one cold but sunny Sunday. He has a gorgeous little cottage at the front of the property which he daintily, yet rather inappropriately, refers to as his weekend getaway Frottage. You can't miss it from the road; it's got an enormous Rainbow Flag out the front.

As I pulled in, the Fish was sitting on the front porch and he leapt up and waved so vigorously, flopping his hand around, I feared it was going to fling off. I congratulated him on the lovely maroon towelling tracksuit he was wearing. 'Thank you, Breakfast,' he lisped back. (Finkles always have odd terms of endearment and an apparent genetic disposition to lisp.) 'Does it make me look gay?' he continued. It most certainly did.

Not long after I had arrived he said, 'Let's go out the back for brunch. You can come and sit on my big deck.' A little uncomfortable with the suggestion, I asked him to refer to it as his veranda in future. We had a lovely, big breakfast with stunning views of the Knob. Over brunch the Fish began to tell me all about the Finkle Fullas in his life. And there are many, I must say. He has recently been seeing a Smurf. A **Smurf** is a young, smart, opinionated Finkle with a swishy long fringe and plenty of attitude. Smurfs are almost solely responsible for keeping high-street fashion stores in business and are regulars on the cocktail circuit. In the words of the Fish, they are scrumpable screws, but too high maintenance to get emotionally attached to.

He prefers **Twinkies** — frivolous, flighty, flaky, fatuous and fickle Finkles who are young and cute and shallow and come with no strings attached and no excess baggage. Why are they called Twinkies, you ask? Because they are yummy and full of cream, but have no nutritional value. Bet you wished you hadn't asked, right?

But then he really opened his heart up and spoke about his true love. His first real boyfriend. His soulmate for nearly 10 years — Moe. Moe had left the Fish and run off with a woman and has chosen a heterosexual life for himself ever since, turning his back on his Finkle roots (not a wise move, frankly). 'A typical **Yestergay**!' laments the Fish. 'But he'll be back. He's a **Sneaky Butcher** (likes to deliver his meat to the back door.)' The Fish is now trying to convert a happily married man who he believes is eyeing the back of the closet door, just itching to come bursting out.

A **Finklette** is an extreme version of the Finkle and is a very entertaining yet, at the same time, extremely dangerous 'man'. Beware! You can get scorched skin and seriously singed eyebrows from standing too close to a Finklette — they are such absolute Flamers.

When all is said and done, though, Finkles' artistic, creative and innovative contribution to New Zealand must not be underestimated. They are the spine of New Zealand's creative industries. And if most Fullas could take off their homophobic glasses for just a while they'd find just how gregarious, energetic and classically funny most Finkles are too!

the Kiwi Battler

The Kiwi Battler is just one of those really unlucky bastards. A Fulla who perseveres through his commitments despite untold adversity. Kiwi Battlers never quite manage a fair suck of the saveloy. Even when trying to do a good deed, things always go tits up. But Battlers roll with the punches, bounce back, then get knocked straight back down again.

By sheer dint of the name, the Kiwi Battler is a bloke who has given life 110 per cent and received only about 60 per cent back. A real 'salt of the earth' type with whom most Kiwi Fullas can relate, and for whom most have genuine empathy. That said, the Battler doesn't want your bloody sympathy, thank you very much.

The usual story for the Battler is one that starts in childhood with a run of bad luck that everyone around him thinks will dry up at some stage. The most usual form of misfortune for the pre-pubescent Battler is a long run of physical injuries. Broken bones from bull-rush and jungle gyms, missing teeth from slips and slingshots, bluebottle stings, errant dart piercings, boiling water scalds, dog bites, wasp attacks, poisonings from drinking from stagnant streams and eating brightly coloured, delectable looking berries, fireworks mishaps from blowing on duds, cars rolling over feet, nits, worms, savage sunburn, grass burns, gravel burns and multiple butterfly stitches are all a major part of growing up for the Kiwi Battler.

One Fulla I know lost his front teeth and knocked himself clean out during an innocent lolly scramble. As he darted around desperately trying to gather lollies he made the fatal error of reaching for the same lolly as a South Korean Hopper kid who had a head like a mule and was clearly being groomed for sumo. His front teeth gave way on impact and his poor little button nose was flattened and in the aftermath looked like a trodden-on cherry tomato. It was like the poor little sod spent his entire youth walking under ladders, or lived in a house where the windows always opened just at head height. That said, however, the little bugger would never stop trying. An attitude that in anyone else you would admire, but in a Battler only serves to ensure his life remains a thick stream of raw deals.

The standard rule of thumb is: the older you get, the bigger your mistakes — and this rule certainly applies to the teenage Battler. At a time where relationships, vehicles, studies and extra-curricular activity fill your day, the Battler could spend 90 per cent of his time pushing the proverbial uphill or squirting it into the teeth of a gusting gale.

A guy I went to school with, called Derren (he even had bad luck with names), endured the most absurd run of ill fortune I've had the thrill of being privy to. It started on the very first day of term when he started in standard two, which as we all know can be a bit nerve-racking. In an admirable attempt at manliness, Derren decided to break into the caretaker's shed and start the five-tonne cricket roller. In a stroke of luck he managed to turn the engine over. The problem was it was actually poor luck and as he was gloating to those in attendance, the roller gently ran his big toe flat before continuing at an unassuming pace straight over the work bench and tool cupboard and conking out against the door, prying it open. Poor old Derren was caught by the caretaker as he hobbled off into the bushes in tears with a toe that resembled a dropped mince pie.

Derren's run of luck with girls was consistent if nothing else. From his first kiss to his first home run, things were appalling. With a face like a bulldog swallowing a wasp, he started behind the eight ball even before his rotten luck set in. The first girl he planted a smooch on was a girl called Natasha, who was a stunning little number and who had Derren convinced that his luck might change. They had spent the year in the same class and had been paired up to walk hand in hand from school to the library. Lord only knows what happened on those supervised walks, but the net result was that Derren found himself behind the bus stop swapping saliva with his first true love.

Well! Word got back to her brothers (Natasha was of Italian descent) and the next day at school we found Derren hanging by his undies from a coat hanger in the changing room. He had been there for about 90 minutes and, as well as a black eye, had been given a black-and-white ultimatum.

Not too long after we left school, I heard Derren had become a father — of triplets no less. Rumour, according to a notorious Storyteller, had it that he had used precaution but his younger brother, who he had been feuding with ever since

Derren shot his front tooth out trying to William Tell an apple off his head with a slug gun, had gone through Derren's drawers and had stuck a pin into all his joeys. I saw Derren many years later and he confided in me that he could never work out why people called it 'getting lucky'.

Another one of my first mates at school was a diligent and dedicated Battler by the name of Bevan. We're still good mates today. But my first memory of him was as brutal as it was indelible. You see, there was a nasty Offcut called Eugene at my primary school who lost his prize beanie one morning at playtime while playing bull-rush. Later, at lunch time, Bevan the Battler was cleaning up the play-fields (as punishment for talking during a spelling test — even though poor old Bevan just happened to be in between two other kids chatting, the teacher had singled him out for detention) when he came across a black beanie at the base of the rugby posts out on the far field. Thinking he'd take it back to Mrs McGarvey, who was the teacher in charge of the lost and found pound, he stuck it in the pocket of his snug-fitting stubbies.

After lunch had finished Bevan wandered back into class, when lo and behold, Eugene caught sight of the beanie peeping out of Bevan's pocket. Eugene the Offcut threw an unmerciful beating on poor old Bevan the Battler which had the girls crying and even the toughest of the Fullas wincing. Of course, the teacher came in to catch the tail end of the donnybrook and to see Bevan bashed, bent, bruised, bleeding and blubbering on the floor. Out of pure fear, Bevan refused to tell the teacher exactly who had left him in such a state, so he was punished with another lunchtime detention for insubordination and the withholding of incriminating evidence. This was just one of many early episodes of adversity that have plagued Bevan throughout his luckless life.

Battlers tend to understate absolutely everything. Poor old Bevan the Battler got crushed in a game of paper, scissors, rock and as a result was sent out to pull up the cray-pots one freezing mid-winter's day when we were down at a mate of mine's place on the Wairarapa coast for a long weekend. After about an hour, when we realised he hadn't come back we got a tad worried. It was getting dark and a nasty storm was brewing out over the ocean.

We soon realised that poor Bevan the Battler had taken the dinghy out without any oars and the outboard had run out of petrol and he was being swept towards

Chile. In a panic, we ran to the neighbours' digs and jumped in their boat to go out and pick him up. When we got to him, there he was: soaking wet, teeth chattering, lips blue and obviously suffering from hypothermia. 'Yeah, thanks for coming out to pick me up, Fullas,' he managed to squeeze out between shivers and lip quivers as we approached the dinghy. 'It was starting to get a bit nippy out here,' he said as nonchalantly as possible for a Fulla resembling a lemonade ice-block.

Battlers also feel the need to apologise profusely and repeatedly. I asked Bev the Battler the other day if I could borrow his bottle opener to open my stubby at a barbecue we were at. 'Oh shit mate, sorry mate, here you go mate, sorry mate,' he said as he handed me the bottle opener he had in his hand. Inadvertently, I slipped the opener into my pocket after opening my beer, and a sheepish Bev later approached me saying, 'Sorry to be a nuisance, mate, but I couldn't have my opener back by any chance could I, mate? Sorry mate.' When I pulled it out of my pocket, explaining myself, he said, 'Thanks mate. Sorry mate.'

Lotto was designed for the Kiwi Battler in everyone, and in most cases serves as a reminder that optimism at great odds is nothing short of a waste of time. It would, however, be a great idea (but cruel to the extreme) to run the great Lotto scam on a Battler. The scam, for the uninitiated, involves recording the Lotto results from the week prior and buying a ticket for a Battler, with the same winning numbers, and replaying the show at the exact same time the following week to the unsuspecting victim. It would be hard to imagine what was going on between the Battler's ears when they thought that their luck had finally changed.

The Kiwi Battler never wins a bloody thing. Bevan the Battler, for example, buys a Big Wednesday ticket every week — goodness only knows why. Having said that, though, I did witness him win a bottle of champagne in a raffle at an opposing team's rugby club once. He was so proud that he put it pride of place on the leaner we were standing around sharing a few yarns. Then he got so excited telling a story, waving his arms about furiously, that he knocked the bottle to the floor and it semi-shattered, semi-exploded, making a hell of a racket and such a mess the club captain threw him out, no questions asked, for supposedly being too pissed.

In actual fact, the poor prick had drawn the short straw and been chosen as the designated driver, so he had only had two light beers. Unbeknown to us, he made it worse by trying to get back in, once he had realised that his car keys had been used to open a big bot of Lion Red and were sitting on the leaner. This time the bloke, who had caught sight of him coming back into the club, threw him out using a bit of brute force and apparently managed to break his nose for him, in a display of savage boy justice, according to those who witnessed it. Of course, with his bloodied face, no taxi would pick Bev the Battler up, no matter how hard he tried.

After about an hour of hailing cabs in vain, nature called so he whipped out his whizzer and took a pee up against a tree on the roadside. As luck would have it a patrol car happened to drive past and catch him in the act and he was fined $280 for his troubles. Good old Bevan wasn't too upset when I spoke with him the next day, however — it was just a typical night out for the unfortunate Fulla.

The Battler's run of luck is no more obvious than with vehicles. If he is not crashing them or falling off or out of them, then they are seizing, rusting, blowing up, burning, being ticketed, towed or stolen. I met a guy when I first moved to Auckland who came around to my house to do a bit of painting. I got a call halfway through the job to say he couldn't work for a few days as his work van had been stolen. That was just the start of it! To cut a long story short, he had pulled into a mate's driveway for a beer after work and left the keys in the car and some Fulla had helped himself to the work van. The story really starts to go downhill from here.

The poor bugger had all his paint and gear in the car, which, while being driven at break-neck speed, had flown across the van and burst open. The resulting fumes had overwhelmed the occupant who had crashed the car into a barrier and vomited all through the vehicle, then taken off like a robber's dog. Of course, the insurance company would not pay as he had left the keys in the car. The paint that spilled through the van was worth as much as the van itself, and was a special blend that needed to be batched, but the supplier was out of a certain ingredient which meant he needed to wait for the next batch to be made which was 10 days off. I had a contract for finishing the work by a certain time, which this delay made impossible. And not only that, when he did get the paint the rain set in for two weeks and he couldn't work. So the job, which was two days off being finished and invoiced, took another month! You could only laugh. . . . I don't think this particular Battler could at the time, though.

I must admit to not having witnessed this first hand, but I once heard of a blighted Battler from Hamilton who, while playing lock in a game of rugger at Ngaruawahia, fell awkwardly from a great height after being lifted in the line-out, and dislocated his hip upon crashing to the ground. The match stopped for a couple of minutes, as this Fulla was quite clearly in serious discomfort. A young junior doctor was on the bench for the opposing side and quickly diagnosed the problem. He suggested that the longer a hip remains out of the socket, the more prone it is to dislocate again in future and promptly offered to pop it back in, right there on the spot — to which the Battler readily, but reluctantly, agreed. The junior doctor got himself into position and, using his own full body weight and the leverage of the long leg of the Battler, with an almighty shove managed to manipulate the hip ball back into the pelvic socket.

Well! The Battler let out a blood-curdling scream and yelped like a stuck piglet, writhing in absolute agony. The junior doctor was at a loss as to the Battler's reaction, and while realising it was a painful procedure, told the crowd that had gathered around to rubberneck that normally the dislocation tends to be far more painful than the relocation. All the while the Battler continued to bawl like a baby as he lay in the foetal position in agony.

It turns out that what had actually happened was that in the same motion that had caused the dislocation, one of the Battler's testicles had retracted up the inguinal canal and popped through a hernia in his abdomen. When the well-intentioned junior doctor had corrected the dislocation, the Battler's stray nut, which had actually ended up in the hip socket, had been crushed and was jammed in there behind the ball of the femur.

No doubt you can imagine the intense pain and acute agony that that would produce. And a ball without blood is like a brain without oxygen. They both die within minutes. So the luckless Battler had to be rushed to Waikato Hospital, have his hip re-dislocated, the nut massaged back into place and its cord untangled, then have his hip re-relocated, and apparently needed several months of tender loving care before he got over the trauma of his tragically trapped testis — which on being discharged from the hospital was the size, shape and colour of a large, ripe avocado pear (according to the rumours floating around the nursing wards).

I also heard another tragic tale the other day — this time right from the horse's mouth. A most unfortunate Battler with a history of bad breaks called Brian had been asked by his boss to do a presentation on his company's product range at a seminar in central Auckland. He had practised it for days and was pretty confident he was going to nail it. But he was terribly nervous and it showed in the build-up on the day. He had a long morning, having to sit through some other very professional presentations and his nerves began to play havoc with his bodily functions.

About 10 minutes before he was due up the butterflies began fluttering in his tummy and he decided to head to the dunny. He snuck out into a stairwell and could only find the 'Ladies'. He tried to get back out of the stairwell to look for the 'Gents' and that's when his problems began. He hadn't realised that he needed a swipe-card to get back into the conference area. The panic brought on the movement at pace so he had to whip into the can and by his own admission laid a most malodorous deposit. He then realised there was no dunny-paper — remember this was the 'Ladies' and the enormity of their loo paper consumption has always been a mystery — so he had to improvise when tidying himself up. He managed to do this, apparently — although he wouldn't admit to how. But he was still stuck in the stairwell and was now due up to speak.

One of the conference organisers decided to go and look for him, and she sent a bloke to look in the 'Gents' while she popped out to the 'Ladies'. She entered the heavily polluted ablutions block, squinted, covered her nose and mouth and saw Brian splashing his face with water in an attempt to calm himself down. With a face as red as a tree-tomato he had to wander out into the conference to a snickering and sneering audience and as you can imagine he bumbled, mumbled, fumbled and stumbled his way through the presentation all the while looking like a beaten-up beetroot.

Then there was the evening where I was trying to get a good night's sleep prior to a big game of league, when my flatmate Scott, who was a true blue Battler, came home at some ungodly hour and started making a hell of a racket. This was not unusual. In fact, he had made quite a habit of interrupting my pre-match evening's rest with all sorts of odd behaviours — from falling asleep with the gas turned on because he wanted to cook some grub (which earned him the nickname Adolf) to falling asleep on the throne with the drone of the extractor fan just enough of an irritant that I had to go and wake him up and show him where his bedroom was.

(Without doubt, this Fulla had a tight relationship with the bottle.)

On this particular evening it sounded like he was attempting to re-enact the philharmonic orchestra, using cutlery and crockery. This continued for the best part of an hour while he cooked up anything that he could get his mitts on. I finally nodded off, only to be woken by two other mates saying, 'Geez mate, you'd better get up. Scott has shat all over your carpet.' Well, suffice to say I was about ready to explode when I hit the corridor to see all the white carpet in the house had muddy footprints all over it. The boys took me into Scott's room, where he was unconscious, and showed me the shoes caked in dirt and filth sitting perfectly at the base of his bed.

My Tegel timer popped and I dragged Scott from his slumber and gave him a prehistoric barrage of dead arms, dead legs and kidney punches. All the while he kept on denying any responsibility despite the incriminating evidence. This without doubt added to the punishment, as my position was: 'If you're caught red-handed then just apologise.'

It was not until a few days later that the true story emerged. The two Fullas who had woken me up to dob Scott in had realised, en route to my house, that they were short of the taxi fare and so had jumped out at the lights and done a runner over a few parks and a couple of back lawns. By the time they burst through the door at my place and raced up the stairs to hide out, they had destroyed the carpet, which they only later realised on seeing the mess. They hatched their ruse as a great way to pass the buck and lumped Scott right in it by putting *their* dirty shoes by Scott's bed.

Poor old Scott the Battler. We all felt pretty average about that one. But he didn't mind. Far worse things have happened to him and he even has a chuckle about it now when we remind him.

There's another similar type of Fulla to the Battler called a **Muddler**. A Muddler is a Kiwi Battler without the competitive edge — the most unlucky, unfortunate, inauspicious and afflicted of all the Fullas. Unlike the Battler, he doesn't even need to go looking for bad luck; it chases him like a gundog after a shot duck. If it weren't for bad luck, he wouldn't have any luck at all. Everything he touches turns to custard. Any project he's involved with goes pear-shaped.

One Muddler I know called Ralph would be the funniest Fulla I know. You just have to love him. His run of misfortune is so spectacular, and his attitude towards it so casual, that he appears not at all affected by anything that the cruel, unkind world can throw at him.

Once, when living on the bones of his posterior, he had made the foolish move to head to Australia in search of fortune and, in desperate need of gainful employment, he decided to set to sea as a deck hand on a deep-sea trawler. In his eagerness to impress, he headed to the wharves 30 minutes before call time, which was just as well as he got there to find the whole crew sitting around having a few beers and a few rollies.

Soon after he arrived, one of the crew offered him a smoke which he accepted. A few puffs into it he worked out it was one of those special ones, so special in fact that the crew had been saving it for the entire three weeks they had been at sea. Yep, you've probably guessed it. In his eagerness to impress his crewmates he had actually met the old crew who had just hit land ready to celebrate after their 'tour of duty'. About 10 minutes later, the new crew with whom he would set to sea arrived — all well rested and ready to head out despite the stern weather warnings.

His new mates farewelled him and set off into town, leaving him with a bunch of new people, all of whom had been at sea together for years and none of whom had just been through the celebratory session that had left Ralph feeling like Sonny Bolstad (the New Zealand wood-chopping legend) was applying the long arm chop to the back of his head with a 15-pounder at world record pace. To make matters worse, the oldest of his crew, a gnarled old Salty Seadog of north of 60, was convinced that Ralph had been brought in by the skipper to replace him. This Fulla took a grave disliking to poor Ralphy from the moment he met him and kept the remaining crew pretty cold on him too. And when he found out poor old Ralph was a Kiwi to boot, the guy had to be restrained.

Anyway, the special cigarette was really hitting home as the boat pulled out of Sydney Harbour straight into the teeth of a massive southerly low. This, coupled with the burning eyes of the old Fulla, turned Ralph into a paranoid fool who, by the time he straightened out, was so far behind the eight ball that he gave up any hope of getting chummy with anyone. They gave him the worst jobs, including climbing along the stabilising arms (that had been in the water since only a few hours after they had left port, to counter huge swells rolling the boat) to ensure they were secure, baiting the hooks and being lookout on the 2 am to 6 am shift.

They never offered him a cuppa. They gave him the last helping of the tucker and then made him do the dishes. The toilet paper always seemed to run out when he needed it. His bed had no pillow. And he was the guy who missed out on the wet weather gear.

After 12 nights at sea, the captain decided it was time to return to port. Not, however, because the tanks were overflowing but instead because the storm had totally poked the fishing grounds. Ralphy the Muddler was ecstatic when he finally saw land. He reckoned he even got a bit misty-eyed. When they berthed, the crew all got handed their cheque envelopes — including Ralphy — and they hit the road. Ralphy was pretty stoked to hit terra firma and he raced to the closest pub to open his cheque and enjoy a cleansing ale. A cleansing ale (or at a long stretch two) was literally all he could enjoy, though, as when he opened the envelope to reveal the cheque, he saw a grand total of $16.35. As bad as I feel telling this, Ralphy started blubbing into his beer and spent the remaining money on a long-distance phone call to his folks, begging them to wire him some loot. He'd truly hit rock bottom and was starting to dig.

He came right again (though temporarily) in fine Kiwi Battler form. In fact, another great yarn about Ralph the Muddler happened a few years later after what Ralph would call his 'purple patch'. Ralph had managed to hold down a job for a couple of years and given he was single had saved about 40 grand. That was when he heard about futures trading. Given his history, the logical decision would have been to forget about his future, but like all good Muddlers, despite some major shoes to the nuts throughout his battled and muddled life, Ralph remained eternally positive.

Rather than invest just a small amount, after a few conversations with a broker, he decided to place it all on black. In effect, futures trading involves betting on the movement of the stock market — in this case the NASDAQ and Dow Jones in the US. If the market moved up a point Ralphy would earn dollars. If it fell he would lose. In a relatively short period of time, he had somehow got himself into a very strong position. His broker assured him the plan was bulletproof.

Such was his confidence he invested his gross savings including tax liabilities, and by the time 2001 came, Ralph the Muddler had turned 40 grand into 160 grand on paper, and was convinced his luck had changed for good. He started looking at real estate as his next big investment and had earmarked a decent lakefront plot in Wanaka that cost 280 grand. He was going to need a mortgage — but what the heck. He signed on the dotted line and was the proud owner of some prime South Island real estate (worth well into the millions these days).

A few short days later came the 9/11 terrorist attacks in New York. Ralphy phoned his broker to ask, 'How much did that hurt us?' The answer was that he had lost the lot, including the tax he owed. He was on the bones of his arse again and needing a serious change of fortune. Later that day he received an email from his broker summarising his position and including a bill for the brokerage fees. The only bit of luck he had was the real estate agent allowing him out of the purchase if he paid his fee. So, in the space of 24 hours, Ralphy had gone from $160K in the black to about $40K in the red. Still, what doesn't kill you makes you stronger according to Ralphy. You've got to love his attitude, if not his execution.

But Battlers and Muddlers are beaut blokes. Real good Fullas. They are the most earnest, persevering and determined of all the Fullas. They never give up. Ever. In fact, old Bev the Battler keeps on smoking even though he knows the dangers and the damage he's doing to himself — and he doesn't even really enjoy it anyway. When he's asked why he won't give up he replies resolutely, 'Because no one likes a quitter, do they?'

Kiwi Battlers are here to remind us all just how lucky we are and to show us just how much spirit some people have. They are absolute champions at enjoying the little things others might call mundane and they appreciate every little bit of good fortune which many others take for granted.

Long live the Battler!

THE FUNNY WHAKA

The Funny Whaka is a Maori Fulla with a sunny disposition, a side-splitting sense of humour, a humdinger smile and a great giggle. He's a gummy grinner, an eternal optimist, a witty lipshooter and downright dag. The epitome was the universally admired and much-loved New Zealand legend, Billy T James. But the original Funny Whaka, and first to sing a song about one, was Sir Howard Morrison, who sadly passed away while we were writing this chapter.

These are the Fullas from whom the Maori gained their reputation and, despite the media's preoccupation with portraying their Maori antithesis, these guys are fit and well throughout the country.

Grabbing any musical instrument from spoons to the requisite guitar, these Fullas have a beat and manner that is unique the world over. It seems their single focus is to make whatever environment they enter better than it was prior to their arrival. That's *not* to say they are showy but that *is* to say they are often the last to pull stumps. If there is festivity, food, music and a few beers, these Fullas will be there and if they aren't then find one or a handful.

One Funny Whaka called Whetunui, from Whangarei, who I used to spend a bit of time with, was the master of putting on a knees-up — and I mean master. He made every occasion look informal and unrehearsed, but seldom would you ever be in need of anything. If it were the Bluff oyster season you would only need to think to yourself, 'Gee a few Bluffies would be nice' and there would be six dozen still unshucked that appeared from who knows where. What's more, he would always let you have the first shot at them.

He had hangis with wild pork, mutton, chickens and even eel with all the requisite veggies too. He would always have a boil-up going at 3 am if you needed a meal on your way home. If the boil-up was not on, it would be muttonbird in ice cream containers stored in lard with punnets of kina. He would always have the music at the ready and a voice that sounds like only Maori voices can, with that distinct melodic warble that often led us in song (Bob Marley, more often than not, from memory).

His cars all had bench seats so that he could fit six of the Fullas in and his girlfriend always seemed stoked when we woke her at any hour with a carload of blokes intent on eating and singing and keeping hydrated. He had crayfish, paua, scallops and fresh fish in such a quantity that I was sure he was always planning for a tangi or a birth, which, to be fair, given his number of friends, he probably was. And if the music died down, he had an artillery of jokes and stories which seemed like they had been passed down throughout the generations and had stood the test of time because they were all side-splittingly funny.

He got most excited when he played tricks on the Fullas, and he had every conceivable routine imaginable in his artillery. It was like a rite of passage. If Whetu played a prank on you then you were one of his mates, and the more elaborate the prank the more he liked you. I remember one Fulla called Waffle, a legendary Storyteller, who Whetu was just getting to know and who we knew would be not too far from the receiving end. Sure enough, he was welcomed to the group with a real cracker.

Waffle had been putting in hours of spadework on a lovely young girl he had fancied for a fairly long period of time. The challenge with Waffle was to ascertain whether his claims were reliable. Most of us kind of gave up listening, but Whetu was uncharacteristically interested in how well Waffle was getting on. Quite remarkably, Whetu managed to crack Waffle's verbal code and work out the exact night that Waffle was going to invite his new infatuation home for coffee (code for trying his luck). He had also, through feigning interest, worked out that his particular love interest was Jewish and a bit of a clean freak. Thus the embryo of a plan was hatched.

On the night in question, Waffle had single-handedly spent the day cleaning the flat, even picking flowers and placing them strategically — including a few petals leading upstairs to his place of slumber. He had meticulously tidied his room, changing the sheets, burning incense — all the usual prep — in readiness. Later, once he had wined and dined his lovely and had convinced her to accompany him home for a coffee, when the taxi arrived home to his beautiful, clean flat, Waffle suggested to his delight that she stay the night. She had readily agreed and

Waffle told her to follow the petals as he went and brushed his teeth and splashed some water over his face and under his pits. Just as he was doing so he heard a blood-curdling screech, followed by a huge commotion upstairs and was met by his sweety literally falling down the stairs just as he came sprinting up them.

Old Whetunui the Funny Whaka had pulled off an all-time beauty. He had somehow managed to get his hands on a kunekune pig, and waited outside for Waffle to leave the flat before shutting it in his room with a bucket filled with baked beans and a large chocolate cake as fuel. The pig had never been happier and had eaten the offerings, two pairs of undies and a couple of books.

So by the time his (Jewish) princess entered the room, having followed the petals like Gretel, she walked straight into a bomb site which smelt like a tip and had dozens of offerings of the pig's own as decoration. To make matters worse, Whetu had left a lamp on in the corner of the room which the lovely moved towards only to be met by a snuffling, oinking swine halfway there.

After months of shovel work, Waffle had his nirvana destroyed by Whetu. Luckily, Waffle saw the funny side of it. Little surprise they are still best mates to this day. And even smaller wonder Waffle never spoke to the dusty in question again.

There's a Funny Whaka I know called Hemi, who drives a bus for the Auckland Regional Authority or whatever the hell it calls itself these days. He treats his passengers to some marvellous percussion while driving. Tapping his toes, slapping his thighs, clanging his ring against the steering wheel and even adding the hiss of the air brakes for a special touch, in all perfect rhythm. A rare talent, indeed. And my word does he have a superb singing voice to go along with it. When he's not singing, he's whistling — and beautifully in tune too. It's fascinating to note that nobody whatsoever on his run ever wears an iPod because they are too busy listening to his captivating and busy beat.

Hemi the Funny Whaka gets some interesting reactions from your average inanimate and unexcited Joes who hop on his bus. He often makes a joke about the main news item of the day. When someone in Masterton won $36 million in the Big Wednesday lottery he asked everyone if they had any rich nieces in Masterton they could introduce him to as they got on the bus. The week before the general election, he asked passengers not to vote for his uncle Winston, as Winston was going to be too busy painting Hemi's house for the next few months to get involved in politics. When the Silver Ferns had a win against the Australian Diamonds he said, 'My daughter's netball team had a win over the weekend in Melbourne, folks.'

People are often initially unsure how to react, but even the most dull and dry Fulla says something to him as they get off his bus, in recognition of Hemi's radiating and contagious happiness.

Hemi is so happy that nothing fazes him, not even heavy traffic or mad drivers. I was talking to him once while travelling through Newmarket, even though there was a sign plastered above the dashboard which said 'PLEASE DO NOT CONVERSE WITH DRIVER WHILE BUS IS IN MOTION', when a mad Pranker pulled across right in front of him. Hemi the Funny Whaka had to slam on the anchors and swerve to the right to avoid the Pranker's Porsche. Several scared passengers let out a scream and a couple were shaken in the aftermath. Hemi just said loudly, 'Sorry folks, hope everybody's all right!' with a chuckle and continued to chat away with me and giggle. Any other warm-blooded alpha male would have let out a barrage of abuse the Pranker's way. But not Hemi. He just stayed as cool as a cucumber and continued on unperturbed.

More often than not the Funny Whaka is a devout man of faith. It's his pious belief that Jesus is ubiquitous and permanently at his side and on his side that keeps him everlastingly happy. And he has no need whatsoever for cannabis (although it does help a story and you sound better singing), but most evenings he will enjoy a nice cold can o' piss.

The Funny Whaka chooses jobs based primarily on two simple rules — the job needs to have a social team spirit and have a ready availability of perks.

The team environment is paramount as the Funny Whaka is the most social man on the planet and needs to be yakking, laughing and taking the Mickey. The availability of perks is another key and is the primary reason the Funny Whaka is often employed in the food industry. Meatworks, fisheries, pubs and restaurants are ideal vocations allowing both the requisite social interaction and fantastic perks which can assist his great love of entertaining.

Barter is a widely used form of trade among the Funny Whaka, with roadworks vehicles, for example, often loading a little too much bitumen for a job which can then be dropped on a mate's driveway for a side of hogget or mutton. Some Funny Whakas even strategically seek employment to ensure their group of mates has all the bases covered. To do this you need one mate who either works for the breweries or owns a pub, one mate who works in the meatworks and one either on boats or in a fish-processing plant, one mate who works for Tip Top (bread, ice cream) or a bakery, one mate who is part of a building gang (preferably with sparky/plumbing know-how) one on the roads and one with a job at Placemakers.

If I have left anything out I'll be surprised. It is not unusual to walk into the pub with six crayfish and to stumble out with a couple of lamb legs, a muttonbird, a loaf of bread and a fair glow on. It's just a matter of who you know! I can't help but think that New Zealand would be better if this were the norm for all the Fullas.

The Funny Whaka has mates all over New Zealand — and they all seem to operate under the old code of 'when in my neck of the woods, I look after you and vice versa'. This will mean that if you are anywhere from North Cape to Bluff, the Funny Whaka will have a Cuzzie in town who will ensure, in no particular order, that you are fed (with anything the land or sea can provide), entertained, housed and chaperoned and sometimes accompanied.

It is like getting the Rolls-Royce treatment in all that is Kiwi by the best tour guide in the land in every port. It's little wonder the Funny Whaka is happy. He has nailed all that is important. He can holiday anywhere with the best of all the sensory delights guaranteed and is always assured of plenty of friends coming to visit him in return. It seems the more your guests enjoy themselves the better the host feels — something some Unhappy Honkies could learn from.

That said, the Funny Whaka often has a shorter life expectancy. This is a small sacrifice for the life he leads; rich food and plenty of it, late nights entertaining and being entertained, plenty of social lubricant, the pressure to have the freezer and fridge stocked all the time for a drop-in guest, and a manual job with long hours, ensure that this character is here for a good time, not necessarily a long time. However, I would argue that these Fullas cram in a damn sight more of the good times than the average Fulla on the treadmill of life.

The Funny Whaka is not a good traveller, preferring to stay at home savouring the well-earned delights that being a good sort brings. I mean, what is the upside of travelling if all your mates are at home and you have to go through the 'front door' every time you want something — it's just too damn hard. And don't get the Funny Whaka started about Aussies. He has little time for those buggers, despite the fact that he has lost a few mates who have hopped across the ditch. In fact, I guarantee that the majority of Funny Whakas' favourite trans-Tasman sporting moment was when Kevin Tamati unleashed an unmerciful beating on that bearded Ginga called Greg Dowling in the Kiwi League test vs. Australia at Lang Park back in 1985.

Food is something which the Funny Whaka has on a string. You name it — he knows where it is and how to get it, from eel to wood pigeon, mountain oysters to venison, puha to paua it is a phone call away or, at the very least, a short drive. There is no type of food that the Funny Whaka cannot have delivered from anywhere in New Zealand within 24 hours.

The hangi is the ultimate environment. It takes hours of preparation and involves a fair swag of people from digging the hole to sourcing the kai and wood. It's the perfect social setting and is what slow cooking (a relatively modern trend) is all about. This is the environment where the Funny Whaka is on his 'A' game, ensuring everyone is laughing and enjoying themselves. He will have brought his own hangi stones (about which there will be a few stories) and will undoubtedly have the guitar and an array of jokes at the ready. I am not sure what it is but all of the jokes include a Maori and some an Aussie and an Irishman.

Here are a few of Whetunui the Funny Whaka's favourites:

- He told us a tale about a Funny Whaka mate of his called Hika, who hailed from Hastings. He was an All Black fanatic and had dreamed of seeing them play at Twickenham ever since he was a chipper young whipper-snapper. He'd been saving for years and finally one November bought some airline tickets and some tickets to a test and jumped on a 747 to Heathrow. Having never been to Europe before he decided to take a couple of weeks and have a good old butcher's hook around. He caught the chunnel to Paris and had a café au lait and a croissant on the Champs Élysées, caught a train from there and paid his respects at Flanders Fields. He caught an overnight train up to Edinburgh and enjoyed some haggis and a few scotches and just chuckled when the Scottish Fullas spoke 'coz he didn't understand a word they said.

  However, when he got back to London he began to feel a dull ache in his cods, which progressively got worse until he decided he'd better go and see a quack. So he found a medical practitioner in Belgravia and popped in for an appointment. 'I've not got good news, I'm afraid, old boy,' said the toffee-nosed physician as he delivered the diagnosis, 'I'm going to have to remove your testicles immediately.' 'Oh, bugger that!' said Hika. 'I'm going for a second opinion.' So he found a cockney doctor in Hackney, who had a look over his knackersack and said, 'Sorry, me old china plate, I'm gonna 'ave to remove ya testicles straight away.' Once again, Hika the Funny Whaka refused to believe this and decided on a third opinion. He tracked down a Kiwi doctor in Earls Court this time, and after a quick check over his ballbag, the Kiwi doctor said, 'Look, it's not great news unfortunately, Hika. I'm going to have to cut your balls off.'

'Oh, thank God for that,' Hika replied, 'those bloody Pommy doctors wanted to take my test tickets off me!'

- The Pope was on an official visit to New Zealand and took his entourage to the beach to watch some fishermen do their stuff. He looked out to sea to see a helpless Fulla wearing a green and gold Wallaby rugby jersey, struggling frantically to free himself from the jaws of a five-metre great white shark. As the Pope watched horrified, a waka cruised up alongside with two other Fullas wearing All Black jerseys. One of them, Tane, quickly threw a harpoon into the shark's side. The other Fulla, Tipene, reached out and pulled the mauled, bleeding and semi-conscious Aussie from the water. Then, using long clubs, Tane and Tipene killed the white pointer and hauled it into the boat.

  Immediately the Pope summoned them to the beach. 'I give you my blessing for your brave actions,' he told them. 'I had heard that there was some bitter and ugly rivalry between New Zealand and Australia, but now I have seen with my own eyes that this is not true.'

  As the Pope drove off, Tane asked Tipene, 'Who was that, Bro?'

  'That was the Pope, Cuz,' Tipene replied. 'He's in direct contact with God, Bro, and has access to all of God's wisdom.'

'Well,' Tane said, 'he may have access to God's wisdom, but he doesn't know bugger all about shark fishing. . . . Is the bait holding up okay, or do we need to get another Aussie?'

- There were three Fullas in jail: a Funny Whaka, an Aussie and an Irishman. They were all trying to break out of prison. The Aussie Fulla went first — he jumped over the fence and the prison guard said, 'Who's there?' So the Aussie Fulla said, 'Meow.' The guard said, 'Oh, it's a damned cat.' Then the Funny Whaka had a crack and he jumped over the fence. Again the guard said, 'Who's there?' And the Funny Whaka said 'Meow,' and the guard said, 'Oh, it's that damn cat again.' So the Irishman followed third and he jumped over the fence and the guard said, 'OK, who's there?' And the Irishman said, 'The pussy cat.'

- After having dug to a depth of 10 metres in 2008, Irish scientists found traces of copper wire dating back one hundred years and came to the conclusion that their ancestors already had a telephone network more than a hundred years ago. Not to be outdone by the Irish, in 2009, Australian scientists dug to a depth of 15 metres, and shortly after, headlines in the *Sydney Morning Herald* read: 'Australian archaeologists have found traces of 150-year-old copper wire and have concluded that their ancestors already had an advanced high-tech communications network 50 years earlier than the Europeans.' In 2010, Maori TV reported the following: 'After digging as deep as 30 metres in his back yard in Te Kuiti, Tangaroa Te Pura, a King Country kaumatua, reported that he found absolutely nothing. Tangaroa has therefore concluded that 300 years ago Maori had already gone wireless.'

- Two Aussie Fullas are sitting down for a break in their new store. The store isn't ready to be opened yet, but the shelving is all in place. One Fulla says to the other, 'I bet any minute now some Dork of a tourist is going to walk by, put his face against the window and ask us what we're selling.' No sooner are the words out of his mouth when, sure enough, a curious bloke walks to the window, has a butcher's hook and in a Kiwi accent asks, 'What are you selling here, Bro?' One of the Fullas replies . . . 'We're selling arseholes here, Mate.' Without missing a beat, the Kiwi Fulla (a Funny Whaka) replies, 'Geepers, you must have had a bloody good day, I can see you've only got two left!'

- There was an Englishman, an Irishman and Funny Whaka and they all wanted to join the army but they had to first pass a test. The Englishman went in and the Sergeant asked, 'What would happen if one of your eyes got stabbed out?' The Pommy Fulla said, 'I'll be half blind then.' The Sergeant continues, 'What would happen if both your eyes got stabbed out?' The Englishman said, 'I'll be full blind.' 'You pass. Next,' said the Sergeant. So the Irishman came in and the Sergeant asked the same questions and the Irishman gave the same answers so he passed as well.

  The Funny Whaka had been listening at the door for the answers. The Sergeant had caught on to this so he thought he'd change the questions. 'What would you do if one of your ears got cut off?' The Funny Whaka said, 'I'd go half blind.' Then the Sergeant said, 'What would you do if both your ears got cut off?' and the Funny Whaka goes, 'I'd go fully blind.' So the Sergeant asks, 'Why's that?' And the Funny Whaka replies, 'Cause I'll have no ears to hang my glasses on.'

So, in conclusion, as you can see, they're the original Good Fulla, the Funny Whaka. If you find yourself hit by a case of the 'blues' and in need of a pick up and some good cheer, then locate your nearest (and hilariousest) Funny Whaka and have a cuppa with him. It'll be the best remedy in the country, and in our experience, possibly the world.

THE THRUMPET

The Thrumpet is a marvellous man. A true working-class hero (which is something to be). Unassuming, unassertive, unpretentious, unostentatious and unobtrusive. Yet at the same time he's clannish and cliquish, contumacious but conservative, obstinate, obdurate and opinionated. He's also a touch dry. Attempting to initiate a conversation with a Thrumpet is about as tough as chewing up four dry Weet-Bix in your mouth and trying to whistle.

If I can be so bold as to make several suggestions, if you do wish to try, they would be: ask him for tips at the trots or gallops (this could also be considered fiscally prudent advice if you rush off to the TAB), ask him about the state of rugby league in this country, try to get his opinion on civil unions of same-sex couples, his thoughts on Winston Peters (Thrumpets are divided on Winny but deep down most have the utmost respect for the man) or similar such topics. Be warned, though, once you do get a Thrumpet started, he is bloody hard to shut up.

The best place to run across one, outside the race-track, would undoubtedly be the RSAs, Cosmopolitan Clubs or Working Men's Clubs around the country. Charlie and I discovered this as university students around the same time that we discovered it cost $30 to become a paid-up financial member of the RSA which, depending on your thirst, could often be more than paid back in your first evening in the place, as jugs were subsidised to $2.50. It is for this reason, and indeed out of a great respect for *God's Own*, that the Thrumpet spends his money at such places as the RSA, rural fire stations and footy clubs.

A warning for the uninitiated: if you find yourself in the RSA around 9 pm, be prepared to sing 'Old Lang Syne' and play the dancing game — where if you don't have a partner when the music stops, you're out. On the upside, if you get a good one, like we had in Dunedin and where we made the acquaintance of many a fine Thrumpet, you might find small-bore rifle shooting (I think Thrumpets still like to keep the senses in check just in case the Huns or the Nips attack).

Actually it's funny that they might still refer to the Germans and Japanese as Jerries or Nips in today's politically correct world, but each to their own, I say. In fact, I was brought to tears by one remark as I left the RSA one night with a fair dinkum Thrumpet also among the last to leave. As we got out into the freezing Dunedin winter he let out a shiver and said, 'Gee, she's a bit bloody Pearl Harbor out here!' which naturally solicited an innocent enquiry as to what he meant. The very nonchalant reply muttered under his breath was: 'There's a nasty nip in the air.' After a few sherbets that parting comment had us rolling in the frost with laughter.

The Thrumpet drinks nothing but draught beer when in public, and preferably by the jug via a bulbed seven-ounce glass. (Be prepared to pay the Thrumpet for his time with beer until such time as you have earned his respect at which stage you can settle into a round with him). For his consumption at home he buys pub-pets, the two-litre plastic flagons. He rues the fact that the chubby, a 550 ml bottle released by DB in the 90s, didn't catch on. It felt so comfortable in his mitts, and was able to be drunk before the dregs got too warm, unlike a 750 ml big bot.

The meal he asks his wife to prepare him on his birthday is tripe followed by trifle, and of course he washes this down with a pub-pet of draught and finishes with a strong cup of Choysa tea. He's big on eating offal and reckons that the younger generation don't know what they are bloody missing out on. It's fine with him if they dodge offal, though, 'cause he reckons he can get a few black puddings, some kidney, heart and brains as cheap as chips from his local butcher and moreover it's heaps better for you than the lean meat. Although the only way to really appreciate the flavour is to cook it in pork lard or beef dripping.

The Thrumpet wears earthy-coloured suits (although those with just a dash of extrovert in them might opt for light blue), generally well pressed, and his ensemble will almost always be topped off with a lemon-squeezer or cheese-cutter hat which he wears at all times outdoors, except when talking to a lady.

When he takes his hat off on entering an establishment, such as the RSA, in a flurry he whips a broad-toothed comb out of his pocket and swooshes his heavily waxed hair into form. The Thrumpet is not a fan of facial hair other than some compulsory mutton-chop sideburns, which also receive a healthy dressing of Brylcreem.

In fact, when it was rumoured that Brylcreem's parent company was thinking of ceasing the manufacture of the product, an old Thrumpet I know from my days at the Warriors, often referred to as the 'Ox-Tongue' given the appearance of his Brylcreemed swishy fringe, stockpiled 200 red pots of original Brylcreem in his garden shed. When the rumour proved false, he dumped the product to mates at the Cossie Club in return for a pint a pot. He would walk in with a brick of a dozen Brylcreem pots and stagger out with three of them stuffed into his top pocket and jeans and with his eyes going all over the show like a cicada in an empty jam jar.

The Thrumpet donates his suits to the Salvation Army when he feels they reach their use-by date, which is generally after a decade of heavy use. He is generally a generation behind fashion trends anyway so his suits are often real classics. He'd be devastated to know that the biggest market for his second-hand suits is the Scarfie, who buys them and wears them to bad-taste and rude-suit parties around the country. Like seagulls at the tip, Wodgewicks also hover around the Sally Army op shops, swooping on anything retro or cool that Thrumpets may have discarded.

The 'Ox-Tongue' was most upset when reading the *Alexandra Park Annual Report* to see that there are now more brands of wine on offer than beer at the trots. He blames the fact that there are now so many women members. And he can't fathom why those women members are allowed into the Members' bar. 'They can go anywhere else on the bloody course but they get their knickers in a knot if the Fullas have a quiet place just for themselves,' snorts The Ox-Tongue.

Being a true John OATS (Jack Of All Trades), the Thrumpet will have a garden shed that any Fulla would be envious of. To the Thrumpet, his garden shed is his shrine. Being a king of Do-It-Yourself handiwork, nine times out of 10 the Thrumpet will have built his own backyard shed from scratch. He'll often use it as a retreat when he wants to escape the nagging of his wife, or just sit there and listen to the wind, the rain, the birds, the motorway or whatever background noise there may be. Sometimes he'll sneak a little snooze in there (or even sleep the night on the fold-out camp stretcher), and occasionally he'll drill a bottle of scotch and smoke a cigar in there and just reflect on his Thrumpetness.

Depending on how extroverted the Thrumpet is, the garden shed will often be situated on the prime part of his section. It'll normally be a backyard shed, but in the case of a loud and proud Thrumpet it could well be a frontyard shed. It'll have his tools, usually meticulously placed and hung in orderly fashion for easy access (and for showing off), and house a few old racing trophies, some league club paraphernalia, and a couple of old number plates and hubcaps that he's collected. The more cheeky of the Thrumpets will have a few nudey magazine centrefolds or a smutty calendar from the dirty Bogan down the road's mechanic shop nailed to the wall.

The Thrumpet we've got to know best while researching this superb stereotype, Theodore, gives his frontyard shed a generous dousing of creosote every summer and even recently built a small deck with a corrugated iron and four by two awning on the north-facing side where he enjoys a pub-pet or two in the late afternoon sun. In the old days he hung a sackful of sand in there and used his shed as a training gym to practise his boxing — he entered a few amateur bouts in the 60s and didn't have too bad a record, actually. These days it's used as an office (of course it has electricity hooked up), for all number of home handyman activities, and for rest and relaxation, particularly when he's offside with his missus. In fact Theodore frequently refers to it as the 'dogbox'.

His backyard shed is also where he practises darts — for hours on end it should be noted. Thrumpets are unbeatable when chucking a steel-tipped dart into a bristle board. Charlie and I decided to pop into the Onehunga Workingmen's Club one Saturday afternoon to study the Thrumpet and his traits further and that's actually where we met Theodore for the first time. He was sitting in the corner wearing a tweed jacket with leather elbow patches and a beautifully immaculate, felt pork-pie hat. He was sitting alone and a bit aloof when we asked if we could join him and shout him a jug.

We explained that we were writing a book on Good Fullas and doing a bit of research so he suggested we should talk over a game of darts. Reckoned he hadn't played for ages. But he thought we should have a little wager on the game — perhaps 20 bucks — just to keep it interesting. Impassive and reserved was our first impression of Theodore. And Charlie and I exchanged a quick wink when we saw the shake he had in his arm as he raised his seven ounce to his lips. 'You're on,' said Charlie foolishly overconfidently. The game we opted for was 501, and the bluff was over as soon as Theodore lined up his first biff. The constant tremble of his hand miraculously disappeared as he prepared to toss and he became as steady as she goes. The triple 20 he threw first up was inevitable. So too was losing our 20 slides.

Theodore taught us that most Thrumpets love to gamble. They'll bet on anything. In fact, it's the pokie machines that keep the RSA and Cossie clubs afloat. They are shrewd but conservative gamblers. My first brush with a proper Thrumpet came at university when taking the first Tuesday of November off for the Melbourne Cup. I went into the pub to place the mandatory bet and was, as fortune had it, standing opposite your stereotypical Thrumpet. He had the race-book, with notes scribbled all over it, hanging out of his back pocket, a pen behind his ear and appeared to be as pissed as a parrot.

I slipped out of my line and pushed in right behind him as he was placing his bet. When he moved on through, I just said to the lady behind the till, 'Give me exactly what he had . . .' Well, without a word of a lie, we struck the trifecta — 1200 bucks — which, as a student, was like winning Lotto. From that day forth, I have had an even greater respect for the Thrumpet, and if you are that particular Thrumpet who was drinking in the Captain Cook on Melbourne Cup day in 1991, and reading this, then I owe you a few seven ounces when our paths next cross.

Anyway, back to our afternoon with Theodore. So impressed were we with the facilities at the club — about 1000 square metres built for pure entertainment and social intercourse — that we enquired about applying to become members. The President there gave us a royal tour and told us about the proud history of the club. He mentioned that there are 250 affiliated clubs around the country and you can pop into any of them for some fine tucker and a tipple — handy when you're on road trips. 'There's one rule,' he said, 'and that rule is that there is no swearing allowed. Some of the older bastards get fucked off if they hear too much foul bloody language.' He continued, oblivious to the irony — perhaps.

He saw us neck a couple of $4 pints quite quickly and he also reminded us: 'Here at the club we serve cheap piss, we don't serve pissed people.' And it was true. While there were quite a few Fullas in there with a happy glow on, the majority of which were Thrumpets, although there was a decent representation of Funny Whakas and Big Fresh as well, there was a very positive atmosphere throughout the joint. We settled in for the afternoon, enjoyed a plate of steak and chips (that you could hardly jump over) for $8, and realised (for those who mind their pennies) that the best-value beer was actually a quart bottle, which came in at well under a cent a millilitre.

One of the Thrumpets brought over an empty crate and as we finished our beers we just put the bottles in there until it was full. The best feature was these mobile 50-inch telly screens on wheels, which you could just wheel over to where you were and plug in. We soon realised that this was a necessity at about 7.30 pm, because in our group there were a couple of Thrumpets who were following the trots and flicking between that and the gallops, a couple of Funny Whakas who wanted to watch the Warriors and a couple of Big Fresh who wanted to watch the Super 14 — so we were boxed in by three screens!

After that, the Fullas suggested we head down the road to the Onehunga RSA where they were meeting some old Vietnam and Korea vets — and that's exactly what we did. Although upon leaving the club, there was a lot of confusion as to whose gumboots were whose.

Theodore the Thrumpet can easily be spotted buying his meat at the Mad Butcher. He reckons he knows Peter Leitch from when he was deputy assistant to the Manager of the Carlaw Park Trust in the early 80s. However, I happened to be at a function with both of them just recently, when Theodore got Peter in a corner and chewed his ear off. Peter was polite and talkative but later professed he'd never heard of Theodore. I didn't have the heart to pass that on, but I have a sneaking suspicion that if I had, Theodore might have started buying his meat at the Aussie Butcher from that day forth.

Your average Thrumpet will only ever own two cars in his life. Not long after leaving school and while doing an apprenticeship, the Thrumpet will buy a cheap old car to get to and from work. It'll be what you'd expect from an old dunga, but he'll methodically maintain it and systematically service it and keep it in perfect working order. Normally, about 10 years later, when he has gone out on his own and doing a roaring trade, he'll buy a new vehicle, usually a large, mid-range sedan in gold or brown. He will have become so fond of his previous bomb that he'll keep it, and then painstakingly restore it to original mint condition over the following years. Meanwhile he'll treat his new car like a newborn baby and own it until he can drive no longer. It's usually when a Thrumpet is retired to a rest-home that you'll see an ad in the paper that reads:

Genuine unmolested example of thirty-year-old iconic vehicle, original paint and upholstery, excellent running order, mint condition, one old man owner. (Be careful, many Wideboys will try to advertise like this to fob off an old dunga, so be sure it is an authentic ex-Thrumpet vehicle.)

And:

Genuine classic, restored lovingly from the ground up, will only sell to a good home.

Both cars will have a leather strap hanging from the rear underside of the car. The Thrumpet swears this stops carsickness.

As you no doubt know, the Thrumpet is unmistakeable — a classic Fulla. And he has some close relatives:

- A **Frumpet** is a slightly fruity Thrumpet. Frumpets are very uncommon. As rare as rocking horse shit, in fact. I have never seen one. Neither has Charlie. We believe them to be nothing other than urban myth, as they are a contradiction in terms.
- A **Grumpet** is a grumpy Thrumpet. Also rare.
- A **Plumpet** is an overweight Thrumpet, and a **Slumpet** is one with a slouch.
- **Crumpet** is not a Thrumpet. You know this.
- But a **Thrumpette** is a Thrumpet's wife.

Sadly, the average Thrumpet is a dying breed. The youngest are now in their late fifties, and there is nothing to suggest that any younger generations are looking to follow suit. They are relics of a simpler, honest life, of the real New Zealand and as such should be embraced. In fact, it should be mandatory to enjoy a few ales with one. You will learn a thing or two and will likely leave with a happy glow and a few good tips to race off to the TAB with. Please, help save the Thrumpet!

On that note, let's finish this chapter with a minute's silence and reflect on the mighty Thrumpet.

THE BOYDOG RACER

Boydog Racers are the love birds of the new generation — preening, puffing and squawking in an attempt to attract the attention of the fairer sex with 'look at me' style acts. This is a glaringly obvious example of the mating season behaviour of the animal kingdom with juvenile adolescent Fullas 'drifting', 'cruising' or 'drag racing', all in the attempt to entice the fairer gender.

Their cars themselves are designed to be subliminally phallic, with big shiny bonnets, sleek lines and a dangling set of mufflers.

Boydog Racers are named as such after their behaviour which is reminiscent of dogs on heat, sniffing each other's arseholes as they drive up and down inches from each other's exhausts, all the while staring at one another. Coincidentally, the net result is exactly the same as dogs on heat, as their desire is to enter a brief physical encounter with females attracted to their attention seeking.

Extraordinarily, this attracts the female yoof in hordes, who, like magpies, are attracted to all things shiny and loud. Clearly, attempting to curb this antisocial behaviour is an ambulance at the bottom of the cliff. The focus must be attempting to interpret why attractive young women are drawn to this nonsensical behaviour attributed to pubescent car enthusiasts, and what can be done to snap them to their senses. It's an interesting fact that the Boydog Racer attracts young ladies of a calibre directly proportional to the car they drive. This is the fundamental reason we have Boydogs hitting the headlines most weekends for acts of bravado. The simple time-proven fact is that young men think with certain parts of their anatomy.

Put it this way: if you were a yoof of particularly average looks but you knew that if you had a nicer car than your attractive mate you would get his girl, you would be working three jobs!

Again women have a lot to answer for here . . . any twit can interpret the boys' behaviour, but it would take a genius to understand the motivation of the young dusties.

Without fail, Boydogs roll around in crappy Jappas that have been lowered, cosmetically modified with body kits and one-off paint jobs and stuffed full of after-market performance accessories in quite a preposterous manner. You can easily spot them burning away from traffic lights, needlessly revving their engines, and driving around listening to bad, heavy, bassy, techno music which you can feel as well as hear from about a kilometre away.

They usually run with tinted windows, but if they do have them down, you'll see them wearing a baseball cap backwards or a beanie, and baggy clothing with the mandatory bling in the form of either shiny necklaces, rings, watches or a combination. Standard vehicle modifications include: large, loud and (aptly named) big bore exhaust systems (which serve only to make more noise rather than actually increase performance), aftermarket mags, lowered suspension, silly-looking spoilers and bonnet scoops to house the thousands spent on tweaking every last drop of brake horsepower out of the motor. There are usually a couple of stupid stickers.

Believe it or not, there are numerous small Japanese four-cylinder cars packing north of 500 bhp under the bonnet with 0–100 kph speeds of under four seconds! They will leave a Porsche 911 turbo behind . . . that's a fair bit of power for a testosterone-fuelled Tweenie's first car and provides a simple reason for why a fair few of them end up wrapped around trees or worse.

In the 90s, when Charlie and I were Scarfies in Dunedin, Boydog Racers were just coming onto the scene. There were bugger all around. Most young testosterone-filled Fullas drove Aussie icons of motoring such as Holdens, Falcons and Valiants. They were as big and slow as buses, were relatively forgiving when hitting solid objects, had large six- or eight-cylinder engines, were cheap as chips to buy and maintain, and were as cool as Arthur Fonzarelli.

The few Fullas that had small Japanese shopping baskets we called Rice Burners. (Their cars were called Rice Rockets and our big Aussie tanks Rice Eaters!) But good old Rogernomics dropped the tariffs on poxy little Jap imports which, coupled with finance companies providing easy cash, provided the perfect environment to breed a generation of Boydogs. All of a sudden the cheapest cars on the market were little four-cylinder papier-mâché lawnmower types. Nowadays they are like swarms of angry wasps pestering the public and festering away at society.

And it'll only be a matter of time until some feminist formally requests for the title Boydog Racer to be changed to Persondog Racer, given the surge in the numbers of female Boydogs. An alarming number of Boydogs are young Hoppers or Pandas too and they have embraced the Boydog culture fully and fervently.

Mitsubishi Evolutions, Subaru Imprezas and Nissan GTRs are the vehicles of choice for the modern-day Boydog Racer. These poxy little rockets are turbocharged, four wheel drive, have close-ratio gearboxes, have active differentials and can transfer torque between the wheels and also have all sorts of specs to add to the end goal of being noisy and peppy.

Charlie and I and a few of the Fullas went down one Friday afternoon to the Tron (Hamilton) to watch the fourth day of a test against the Aussies earlier this year. It was a beaut day in the sun, and it was great to see a crowd out watching test cricket. The highlight was watching the kids running around at lunch rolling the arm over — it took me back to the 80s, and my days of watching the great names of New Zealand cricket compete at the Basin Reserve.

Unfortunately, my experience that evening was not as morale-boosting. I was roped into taking my old Valiant to the Meremere Drags and experienced a nasty underbelly of Bogan Boydog Racers with far too much welfare money to spend on petrol and tyres in a display of primal, petrolhead, testosterone-filled madness. (Just for the record, the Val broke 18 seconds for the standing quarter-mile much to the chanting of the fume-intoxicated crowd.)

But the excitement was extraordinary and it was actually encouraging to see these young Boydogs letting out their aggression on the racetrack and in the burnout pit rather than on the road. The smell of burnt rubber and gas, the speed and the noise were quite spectacular. And a little observation of ours was that there was quite a tidy display of scrubbers wandering around, getting all frisky watching the Boydogs bury their hooves into the floor and ambling around with their choker chains and the button flies on the baggies half open. Those Boydogs that drove Mazda RX7s were particularly popular and it was a certain type of chick that was attracted to them — the Rotary Ho. An interesting side-note, though, is that the RX7 actually runs a *Wankel* engine.

There were a couple of older and shrewder Boydogs who clocked some of the fastest times in 'wolves in sheep's clothing' type cars. There were two shitty old 70s model Toyota Starlets that looked like they'd have trouble even getting going with the weight of a fully grown Fulla, but which bolted off the start line like a missile and broke 11 seconds for the standing quarter mile.

The event organisers left a grippy concoction which will pull the shoe off your foot should you walk over it, all to assist with off the line speed, and had a water puddle to help the burn-offs to warm the tyres just off the start line so that the Boydogs could smoke up their cars in preparation for their 12 seconds or so of acceleration and speed.

There was one silly Fulla who got so excited on the start line smoking the rear tyres of his Racer and kept it up for a good minute or so. The problem was that the smoke entered the cockpit and it filled up at quite an alarming rate. This problem was twofold. First of all, he couldn't see the start lights through the smoke and was left on the line when the lights went green while his adversary shot off like a sky-rocket. And, secondly, the burned rubber and oil vapours had overwhelmed him and when the haze had finally settled he was slumped over the steering wheel with his brain off in cuckoo land. The Fullas manning the ambulance were on to him in a shot and after they forced some Redbull and an intravenous drip into him he appeared to regain consciousness, but was advised not to operate machinery for at least 48 hours.

The Boydog takes on a different appearance in different parts of the country, wearing different clothes, listening to different music and driving different vehicles. Diametrically opposed to the aforementioned Auckland City, Taupo, Nelson, Wellington and Christchurch Boydog Racers, the **Rural Boydog**, or **Bulldog** as they are known, has a strong preference for large V8s of the Australian variety, usually passed down from the old man after years of faithful service as the family car.

The Bulldog is more reserved than his city counterpart and will adorn his car with the look of a nasty Offcut Bogan. Louvres, dice, Cragar mags, tints, twin trunks in front of either back wheel, and lowering of suspension are the most obvious of adornments. That said, the bulk of the modification will occur under the bonnet, making this thing like lightning on straight back roads but handling like a plate of soup on any corner.

The classy Bulldog will custom lie-flat bench seats that can slide forward and fold back into a double scratcher. This has two benefits, firstly, the ability to sleep off a party in the wops or at an outlying pub and the second is obvious to all. The music of choice will vary wildly from George Thorogood and ZZ Top when with the lads to Kenny Rogers (appropriately named) when with the local dusties. This choice of vehicle and style is most commonly seen in the Deep South from Invervegas to Timaru including Central Otago, Hawke's Bay, Northland and pockets of Hamiltit.

Some ordinary Fullas, sick of the Boydog Racer's bullyragging, have taken the law into their own hands and played havoc with Boydog Racers' cars. The most common and most vengeful reaction is to spray expanding builders' foam up the exhaust of a Boydog's car. A less vindictive variation is to stuff a potato with a hole drilled into it with a whistle sticking out the back to make a screeching sound as the car starts up. Others are: fresh dog turds under door handles, fish heads under the air filter, Vaseline on windscreen wipers, marbles in hubcaps, or patches of oil left under diffs to give the impression there is a leak. And of course the National Government has now brought in legislation allowing coppers to confiscate and crush Boydog-mobiles if they are caught being dickheads on the roads.

It's staggering that third-party insurance, at the very least, isn't compulsory in this country. But I imagine the premiums for Boydog Racers and their modified, street-legal go-karts would be prohibitive. The enhancing and maintenance of these machines must cost the Boydogs a bloody fortune, which is equally as staggering.

There are a number of smart Boydog Racers, though, many of whom have set up car clubs rolling under the guise of car enthusiasts. Some have even applied for charitable trust status and attempted to solicit local council support for drag strips and burn-out pads in the city centres to act as a control mechanism, removing Boydogs from suburban back streets. Sure, they are pissing firmly into the proverbial, but this is just the tip of the iceberg with numbers of Boydogs growing at a rapid rate. The car accessories business from stereos to mufflers has had a 300 per cent increase in the last four years in New Zealand. It's bloody hard not to make dollars hand over fist.

All this said, the hyped-up Boydog Racer is a good spender, contributing most of their combined earnings back into the local economy and is, nine times out of 10, a healthy specimen, spending a lot of time outdoors in the fresh air tinkering on their wagons, burning a bit of rubber and clogging up the streets and the odd court room. But I reckon they have a limited societal cost by comparison to those young Fullas who spend 18 hours a day inside on the PlayStations or playing multi-player computer games without any thought of the outside world. Or by comparison to the 56 per cent of obese kids waddling around the country, stuffing fast food into their chubby helmets. So what is worse? Boydog Racers are probably the best of the alternatives!

Don't confuse Boydog Racers with **Grommits**. Grommits are usually hard-core skaters, surfers or BMXers in their teens enjoying endless summers and a carefree lifestyle. They are not **Buckets** (the next-door neighbour type boogie-boarder or Fulla who has all the knee-pads and helmets and rollerblades along like a Sheila); they are gutsy little buggers, but are yet to gain their stripes among their clique, coterie or posse. Grommits often speak with a quasi Yankee accent and the word *like* is by far the most popular in their vocabulary. When telling a story it'll go similar to this: 'He was like . . . she was like . . . I was like . . . it was like . . . we were like . . .'. Acne seems to be an extremely popular facial embellishment for the Grommit.

Another close relative is the **Wangster**. The Wangster (Wannabe Gangster) saunters and loiters around the inner city and imitates hip-hop artists — surely there are better (and way cooler) role models than that.

There was a time when groups of Wangsters would cruise around Auckland city mugging other young Fullas and usually stealing their shoes. We have never witnessed this in person, but we did experience one wonderful run-in with some Wangsters a few years back. We had been invited to a mate's work drinks one Friday evening and had eased into a couple. With a slight glow on, someone made the suggestion we go out for a few more.

So a group of us were walking around the bottom of Queen Street looking for a watering hole when a group of Wangsters approached us. They singled out a Wodgewick in our group who was wearing a pair of Hi-top Converse All Star boots and a cocksure Wangster said to him, 'Hey Man, I'll bet you 20 bucks that I can tell you where you got them shoes.'

A brief period of silence followed as we looked at the Wodge and he, in turn, thought about it. It turns out that he'd bought them on a trip to Hawaii and was pretty sure there was no way this Wangster could have known that. So in an equally confident tone he said, 'You're on. In fact I'll raise you to 30!' The Wangster agreed then began to shoot all sorts of shit about what he was going to do with the money. The Wodge then asked, 'Well, where did I buy them then?' To which the Wangster replied, 'Buggered if I know, Bro. I said I could tell you where you got them shoes — and you got them right here on your feet. Now give me my 30 bucks!'

The Rugbyhead

The Rugbyhead (frequently more affectionately known as the **Footyhead**) is aged between 16 and 40, or within the range where he can play competitive rugger. He's a furrow-browed, cabbage-eared, gristle-haunched, mutton-fisted, Pro Magnum. He has a voracious thirst, the strength of a fully grown chimpanzee, and invariably suffers from juvenilitis — this guy has the uncanny ability to make or break any social event.

The young Footyhead learns early that life deals you a poker hand. Intelligence, looks, physicality, EQ, and x-factor being the categories. Footyhead holds a hand (3, 4, K, 6, and anything from 2 to Ace, respectively). Very occasionally, you can get as high as four picture cards but most hold only the one.

While not usually blessed with a quick thought processor, the Footyhead is very seldom daft. By dint of their name, they are experts in their field and as such tend not to stray too far into areas where they can be shown up. Interestingly, though, to the contrary, the Footyhead loves nothing more than inviting a non-Rugbyhead into their circle so that they can be educated on such things as tight and loosehead play, debate or listen to who was the best in which position (and during what tenure) and listen to the Rugbyhead bemoan the law changes adopted by the inferior Northern Unions in an attempt to peg back the advancement of the All Blacks. The Rugbyhead has an admiration (bordering on obsession) for some who have worn the Black Jersey, particularly those who have come from their home town, those who have represented their province, or those with whom they have played or drunk at their local club.

Footyheads tend to be tight forwards (although not exclusively). After years of locking horns and protecting one another from other packs of blighters with the specified intent to isolate and cripple their brethren, it is hardly surprising that they have such a resolute bond. This is not a game to the Rugbyhead — it's a lifestyle. There is no happier place for them than the post-match shower (aside from perhaps the bottom of a ruck). Here they will enjoy a well-earned soak comparing battle scars and stories — primarily relating to the damage they inflicted on their opponents, in particular celebrating the illegal acts of thuggery they got away with, always in retaliation for some thing that may or may not have occurred.

They will be the first in and the last out of the showers, ready for a beer at the exact same time as the backs who take an eternity shaving, sprucing, gelling and preening.

They will sit together and discuss at great lengths the team and in particular key personnel they will be playing against each week and come up with the exact same game plan every time — to keep it simple — 'Win the set piece and kick the shit out of the opposing pack.' Its simplicity is indeed its genius!

These chaps are, to a man, masochists, pure and simple. Only they can take pleasure from the array of tasks and duties that befall a tight forward. Broken noses, stitches by the dozen, missing teeth, cauliflower ears, cauliflower heads, clod eyes and dancing fingers (where they spring in any random direction similar to a Tasmanian's teeth) are par for the course, with the reward for the average club Footyhead being nothing more than the thrill of winning, earning a beer and thumping their opposition.

The greatest thug I ever played with or against was a chap called the 'White Pointer', named so for his pale skin and his warning of pointing at you before he administered whichever punishment he deemed necessary to ensure you did not become a recidivist offender. He had a reputation for filth and if you crossed him you could rest assured he would extract his revenge with interest. This often happened in new and unexpected ways, not always on the field and on occasion years after the alleged breach that put you offside. To be honest, you wanted him to get you as soon after the incident as possible, as the longer it took the more interest compiled by way of his inter-cranial Chinese whispers which convinced him your crime was worse than it was and that you were trying to avoid your punishment. (Add to that the anxiety of knowing that 'White Pointer' justice was accrued and it was near on unbearable.)

It was not unheard of for players to hang up their boots in the half-arsed hope that that would be the end of the matter. It wouldn't — as once they stepped back into the club as a supporter, Old Whitey would get his own back. He once followed a 'Mark' (as he referred to those who had been given the dreaded finger) into the toilets at a local Dunedin club, only to come charging out 30 seconds later, saying call an ambulance Rodney has slipped on a wet floor. Judging by the site of old Rodders, as he was carried from the ablutions, I think it would be fair to assume that he had slipped and landed on Old Whitey's fist, knee and shoe as he fell, the poor bugger.

During a game Old Whitey could get so focused on getting his man that what was going on around him became of only minor importance. When this happened his own team would start to panic, because when his eyes glazed he had a reputation of damaging his own players in cases of friendly fire. He gave one of his own locks 15 stitches, in an area that ensured he was on a liquid diet for 10 days, in a fury of sprigs, knees and elbows as he blindly ripped into a ruck after an opponent (who ended up far worse off than our lock!). He broke his halfback's nose, as he drew his arm back to deliver a right-handed biff to some hapless fool. He accidentally lopped the left ear off his fullback as he drove a ruck over from five yards out and got his boot tangled. The guy was a menace, full stop, and this was clearly why we became great mates (obviously, much safer than being enemies).

He would intimidate touch judges to such an extent that they would look away, so he could poke, snap, rip, break, ruck, kick, pull, punch, thump or knee someone, often without cause, but always with a reason — at least in his mind. You see, the way he saw it was that if you got them first and did the job properly they would no longer pose a threat, and not only that but the rest of their team would fall into line. The only tools of his trade outside his mitts were two sets of boots, one to show the ref during the inspection and one for the game, which had a new set of illegal 22-millimetre league studs that had been filed to a sharper point.

Rugbyheads' love of a social gathering and their desire to entertain can make them one of the most amusing males in the country. It can also make them one of the most offensive. When they get together they will invariably suffer group juvenilitis that is exacerbated by alcohol. In these circumstances it is best to step back and watch from a safe distance. Warning signs that things will take a nasty turn include: puffing of the chest, increased fluid consumption, huddling in close proximity, the presence of attractive women, the presence of another player they greatly admire, and comments such as 'unleash me' followed by group encouragement.

This will result in the Footyhead losing all inhibitions and attempting to impress all and sundry with acts of physical enormity and stupidity. At this stage it is clear that the Footyhead has reverted to his hard-wired, primal brain. Acts such as roof dives, house fires, car surfing, running through walls, wrestling, bottle breaking (often over each other's head), golf ball driving, urine skulling, tree climbing, naked singing, face planting, crate headbutting, hongi giving, arm wrestling, the 'Canterbury Next' drinking game and rioting are but a handful of what is to be expected.

On the upside, this is the best time to offer challenges and dares to the Footyhead! Peer pressure is something that very few Rugbyheads can resist, falling into the same head-space as lemmings as they follow each other off cliffs. All that is needed here is a perfectly timed enticement and all hell will break loose. Nothing short of a KFC or a McDonald's can stop a herd of deranged, booze-fuelled buffoons motivated by *one-upmanship*.

Post-game group rehydration or a court session is the Footyhead's finest couple of hours of the week. Having survived another war, they are now conditioned to reward themselves. This is a clear, real life, human example of Pavlov's dogs, where the ring of the bell and reward of food is replaced with a hot shower and the reward of liquid. The court session, despite its misinterpretation by academics writing thought-provoking behavioural theses marked by fellow academics who have never been invited to or understood court session etiquette, is all about discipline under pressure. It is indeed a brilliant way of subtly instilling group values and ensuring conformity to them by introducing a set of rules designed to instil discipline and respect to control errant characters, who, to be fair, without the team environment would potentially cause much greater damage as individuals.

One such Fulla, affectionately referred to as 'Carlton', is a constant form of entertainment, falling perfectly under the Rugbyhead umbrella. He is in his late thirties but still playing competitive footy (albeit held together by about 200 yards of strapping on game day — which his missus spends all of Friday night applying) and is undoubtedly the easiest chap to pressure into acts of bravado. He arrived at one of our great friend's farewell dinners (at his parents' home) and within minutes of the sit-down meal was out on the deck attempting to remove a cabbage tree that our friend's old man had mentioned in passing over dinner that he would prefer gone.

That was all the encouragement Carlton needed. By the time we sauntered out onto the porch he had stripped down to his underwear and had started his sprint from the far end of the deck, intent on launching himself off the deck into the cabbage tree just under the head in order to snap it as a favour to our host. Quite how Carlton's head works is a genuine wonder which never fails to amuse and stun. Before we had time to suggest that his respectful attempt at helping out our mate's old man was foolhardy at best, he dove at full speed off the platform in the superman position.

What followed was a slow-motion moment in time that has amused the gathered few for years since. Such was the passion that Carlton had for pruning this eyesore that he left the deck at about 90 per cent of full speed. Speed was not the problem, however; it was more a challenge with direction, as we watched in horror as he overshot the tree about two metres to the left and disappeared through the shrubbery with a sickening thud.

Poor Carlton had flown about six metres horizontally and about four metres vertically, landing in a belly-flop on the neighbours' driveway. We all tore down into the bushes only to find a near naked Carlton covered in scratches, cuts and bruises sitting chastising himself for missing the target! The impact would have killed most men, but believe it or not, we had to restrain Carlton later in the evening from another attempt. Such was his embarrassment that he returned the next day to this Fulla's house with a bottle of wine for the old lady and he sawed the tree for the old man.

The next story about Carlton needs to be prefaced with the statement that no matter how ridiculous it sounds — it actually happened! He was only 19 at the time and had been at an end-of-year ball with a girl he was keen to impress. The night had gone well — too well in fact. As they were leaving the fifth-floor ballroom at Alexandra Park Raceway, Carlton decided he would impress his date by sliding down the banister. Bad idea! He smiled, gave her a wink, got up to a jog and hopped up onto the banister . . . then over-rotated and promptly disappeared down the stairwell — five floors!

Now this Fulla without doubt has a cracker guardian angel on his shoulder and heavy bones, as he slammed his hip into the banister rail on the ground floor, shattering it into kindling and ending up in a heap with people running from all directions to assist. Now this is where it gets astonishing. After a minute trying to understand where he was, Carlton got up and dusted himself off and left arm in arm with his date.

Sure, he was in some discomfort, but he refused a medical once over, still preoccupied with his date, and managed to somehow make it home to her place where he slipped into bed in the embrace of his sweetheart.

He awoke at about 5 am as stiff as a board and black and blue from his left armpit to his calf. Worse still, he was in desperate need of going to the bathroom (number ones only, thank goodness). Too proud to ask for help by waking up his catch,

Carlton took nearly 30 minutes hauling himself in agony to a seated position on the side of the bed. By this stage he was feeling complete panic as he knew he could not reach the bathroom at the end of the corridor before his bladder popped.

Faced with such reality, Carlton had no choice but to take aim at a towel lying on the floor. His aim was perfect and he managed to unload a full bladder onto the towel, much to his enormous relief. The problem was, however, that the towel was covering a five-point electrical multiboard, which shorted with the moisture and burst into flames. Poor Carlton was sitting there near death having started a fire just out of arm's reach. Such was his pride that rather than waking his host, he sat there contemplating the alternatives for a few moments until the fire continued to burn itself out.

Eventually, it did so and a relieved Carlton fell back to sleep. Not for long, though, as he was woken by the scream of his date's mother who had smelt the burning towel and had come in to investigate. Somehow he'd managed to see a plastic bag near the charred towel and hot box and quick as a flash came up with a story about discarding a bag of ice that must have melted.

The Rugbyhead will seldom, if ever, be the captain, preferring to shy away from the limelight and focus on being a stand-up club man. Despite being by no means the sharpest or the bluntest knife in the draw, the Footyhead will make decisions ruled by his love of the game alone. A true Rugbyhead will wear his club 'number ones' out on the town, post match, as proud as punch for being a team man and with a genuine scorn for those who return home to get changed into jeans and a shirt before hitting the strip.

Ironically, if the Head did return home and change he would quickly learn he could get away with a few more tricks and scams with anonymity on the town. It is for this reason that a few Footyheads from most teams get labelled as buffoons. For a start their sheer size, and occasional clumsiness, make them hard to hide, but coupled with a blazer, tie and matching slacks the Footyhead can often be impossible to miss, thus creating an environment whereby their every indiscretion is noticed.

One of the Footyhead's proudest days is the day he earns his blazer. This is a sign you are an equal, having played the requisite number of games to earn your stripes. It is also time to partake in any number of traditional rites of passage. This will always involve a few beers as a lubricant to drop the guard of the victim and could be anything involving any array of nonsensical acts designed to humiliate. In our day, at university one had to sprint around the ground naked in full view of the patrons and then drop your plums into the freezing Leith River before re-entering the clubrooms. This is all part of the team environment whereby one's individuality is encouraged but never at the expense of the collective endeavour, hence the need for those being welcomed to make a right royal prick of themselves for the amusement of the team. It is a test to see that you value the team above your own pride. Very few ever fail these tests.

The Gym Dandy

The Rugbyhead should never be confused with the Gym Dandy. The Gym Dandy (frequently, but not exclusively a Muscle Mary of the Finkle variety) is obsessed with nothing else but sculpting his own body (physically that is, not mentally, emotionally or spiritually). All he talks, thinks and gets excited about is his gym routine and protein supplement-packed diet. The only place where he feels really at home is in a gymnasium working out in front of a full-length mirror. Anything else is outside his comfort zone.

His single-minded obsession of perfecting his body means he places no emphasis whatsoever on developing his interpersonal skills and, as such, unless he is talking about shifting tin or the latest body bulk formula, he has little to contribute to a conversation or social gathering. Rather than have a beer with some mates on a Friday after work he'll head to the gym for some bicep curls and sit-ups, then ease into a Brazilian berry-flavoured isotonic drink, followed by a double-chocolate protein shake made from whey. Why the hell he doesn't just have a beer and some steak and eggs is a mystery. They taste better, are a damn sight cheaper, and are surely better for you. And the flatulence and severe constipation those protein drinks cause is as horrific as it is malodorous and uncomfortable.

A Gym Dandy will choose to go for a jog along crowded streets, especially at busy times, preferring to beat the street and dodge pedestrians, the elderly, women and children, instead of running through the country's beautiful parks and reserves, in an attempt to attract attention to his physique. He'll mutter obscenities under his breath when he passes a chubby Fulla or one enjoying a beer or chugging on a ciggie.

Not only are they unable to undertake such simple pleasures as catching or throwing a ball, they miss out on the real joys of life that other Fullas indulge in. And nine times out of 10 they look absolutely bloody ridiculous anyway.

So they're good for nothings, really. They would be good for moving pianos, but actually don't do any practical 'weightlifting' outside of the gym for fear of injury. Some Gym Dandies are used in advertisements, where a Beefcake-looking Fulla is needed. Outside of that, they're tits on a bull.

The Fishhead

The Fishhead is an older rugby authoritarian, quite often a thriving Thrumpet, who has devoted a huge chunk of his (and his family's) life to the game he loves. They are charged with the hardest jobs, keeping the teams and club on track and most importantly upholding tradition in the face of the political correctness brigade's onslaught. They are therefore most often a former player who moves into one of several forms of management within or associated with the game.

They are intentionally conspicuous, clad head to toe in the full array of clothing and official insignia related to their club. Few of them can fit their blazers but they usually, upon growing out of them, will remove the honours pocket and graft it to the next. They are a real mixed bag, the old Fishhead, with some the salt of the earth and others running their particular responsibility with military pomposity. It is not unusual to see the Auckland Fishhead refuse entry to people not wearing ties or to serve beer first to those he knows are old boys of his school or club men — regardless of any logical order or standard bar etiquette.

The career progression for Fishheads starts at barman and moves into management and coaching, some even reaching as high as National Honours, although they need to be a real politician to do that as it's an *old boys* club, with strict criteria as to who is right to enter. These Fullas will spend the weekend either at the club or, out of the club footy season, watching every game and replay on Sky TV.

It's a thankless job, but one that provides the opportunity to ride the roller-coaster of emotions and influence the lives of many young men, something New Zealand desperately needs more of — with up to 50 per cent of marriages ending in divorce, the kids living with Mum and attending a school with mainly female teachers. So the Fishhead is, in many ways, a surrogate father or social worker, a guy who needs the social skill and desire to read young men from diverse backgrounds and to bring out their best both on and, more importantly, off the field.

So, in summary, Footyheads are the 20 of the 80:20 rule. They are good average Kiwi blokes, who are the extroverted pranksters of the team and who love the ups and downs of the roller-coaster ride. They are great team men who lift the spirits of the side when they sense things need to perk up, often with acts of sheer lunacy or tomfoolery. They are all, bar none, very social folk, having spent the best part of their lives playing with, and against, people from all walks of life and as such can usually hold their own. They are honest, hard-working and fair and subscribe to the motto 'everything in moderation, including moderation'.

So, if you're at a loose end and you want to rub shoulders with some great Kiwi jokers, head along to your local footy club, grab a beer and keep your eyes peeled for a big Fulla with a glint in his eye. He will likely be only too happy to shout you a beer and spin a few stories! It goes without saying they will all involve, or at the very least start with, rugby.

The Couch Kumara

The Couch Kumara is a less dapper and more idle, inert, inactive, indifferent and inattentive variety of Fishhead. His motto is 'Why do today what you can put off until tomorrow?' He's sifty and he's a prolific procrastinator. Built like beanbags, Couch Kumaras invariably have a large pot belly, and more chins than a Chinese telephone directory.

The Couch Kumara believes that time does not necessarily need to be kept. He does things without consequence of time or timing as food and beer is his focus, rather than a clock. A rather articulate Couch Kumara once told me that he believes in the spirit of the occasion regardless of the time required to soak up the atmosphere. 'Let the anal regimented blood lie,' he reckons. 'The insistence of timetable, the pursuit of what's around the corner in defiance of the now, is unnecessary,' he continues. 'Embrace the concept of time with the Fullas without the need to be cramped by the clock.'

You'll very rarely spot a Couch Kumara in public, except sometimes begrudgingly accompanying their wives at suburban shopping malls. You can, though, find them at sports stadiums. They're the ones that hold up 4 and 6 signs at the cricket and scream 'Show us your tits' when a bird walks past.

Really classy Fullas!

The Hopper

Hoppers are the Good Fullas who hail from North and East Asia and who've brought us bok choi, pork dumplings, fluffy toys and perfect forgeries.

Hoppers are a relatively recent addition to the Kiwi scene. In my school days we only had one in the whole school. His name was Murray Doo, and he was the son of the Aro Valley fruiterer, and a third-generation Kiwi. Handy little halfback too, I might add. Now they total 15 per cent of the country, but you could easily think that number a little on the low side if you were walking around central city Auckland. Gone are the days when they just ran fruit stores and takeaway bars. They're everywhere — adding to the rich smörgåsbord that is modern day New Zealand.

Having said that, though, this recent explosion of immigration, boosting the Hopper demographic, comes after a long history of Asian arrivals. Hoppers have been coming to these shores since the mid-1800s, when the search for precious gold nuggets was the draw-card. Yellow fever was a term that referred to folk as well as it did to nuggets and bullion. And it wasn't an easy beginning for the Hoppers here in New Zealand, where they had a tough introduction to the country who would later steal their native gooseberry and market it as its own to the world.

They had a prick of a time here in fact, found bugger all gold and were stranded with few rights and often not enough dough to get home. What was worse, they couldn't even indulge in every Fulla's favourite pastime, given the awful ratio of Hopper Fullas to Hopper Fullesses. In 1881, for example, there were only nine Chinese women to 4995 men. Those are tough odds, in anybody's book. And to make matters worse the Maori and Pakeha Fullas, themselves not getting as much action as they would have liked, spread malicious and unjustifiable rumours among their own women about the size of the Hoppers' wangers to further stymie and inhibit the Hoppers' chances with the ladies of the land. (Despite the effects of this rumour, the Hopper, to this day, will never wear board shorts, much preferring to wear speedos or the square tog.)

As a matter of fact, early Kiwi Fullas made it bloody hard for Hoppers to even get here in the first place. They imposed an entry tax on the poor buggers and even restricted Hoppers to one for every 200 tonnes of a ship's cargo. This was pretty damn unfair, particularly given that your average Hopper back then weighed 45 kilos fully clothed, including boots. Good job that the government said sorry in 2002 for the suffering these laws imposed on the Hoppers, even if it was about 120 years overdue.

An example of their early commercial savviness was the fact that Hopper settlers here in the 19th century scraped the fungus off felled logs that lay on land being cleared, dried it and sent it to China as 'Taranaki Wool', claiming it had amazing medicinal properties. It was then sold as a delicacy in Peking's finest restaurants. The Kiwi Hoppers were 'fleecing' their own kind with a dirty old toadstool!

Then, once all the gold had been ruthlessly pillaged and plundered until there was no more, the Hoppers needed to chance their arm at something else to make a crust. So they cheaply leased the land of many a Funny Whaka, and worked their gluteus maximuses off growing veggies and supplying markets around the country. They finally got on the good side of the rest of the stoic and prejudiced Kiwi Fullas after China's efforts in the Second World War, and their vegetable businesses then grew as quickly as their scarlet runner beans.

In the 2006 New Zealand census there were 146,000 people who identified themselves as Chinese (as well as 31,000 Koreans, 17,000 Filipinos, 12,000 Japanese, 7000 Cambodians, 6000 Thais, 5000 Vietnamese, 4000 Malays, 4000 Indonesians, and 2000 Laotians). This includes ethnic Chinese immigrants from other parts of Asia such as Malaysia, Singapore and, of course, Taiwan and Hong Kong.

It's hard to believe that, back in the 1970s, the majority of Chinese Fullas were assimilating into the New Zealand way of life and it was looking highly likely that their culture would become submerged completely. These days, only 30-odd years later, the Chinese New Year celebrations cause numerous traffic jams — and of course given the driving skills of the average Hopper, a large increase in minor traffic accidents — all over the country.

Lantern festivals and dragon boat races have just about become old hat. And

THE HOPPER

Hoppers throw a huge party in the guise of a sports tournie every Easter to celebrate the National Day of the People's Republic of China, which interestingly enough is actually about six months later on 10 October, not Eastertime at all. It goes without saying that sports which feature highly during this tournament are ping pong and badminton. In fact, I believe they are the only sports held at this particular tournament, which attracts Hoppers from Cape Reinga to Bluff.

The Hopper can cop a bit of stick from the locals, particularly in Auckland, and my theory is simply that they keep to themselves and most other New Zealand Fullas find that hard to understand. Undoubtedly, most Kiwis are very social and can't comprehend why anyone would not follow suit. Perhaps Hoppers, by nature, are a little shy or are just finding their feet in a country very different from their original home. Whatever the reason, I too hope they drop their guard, get out and about, and start sharing their flair, as, from my experience, the Hopper is one of New Zealand's funniest and most laid-back Fullas.

Take, for example, Captain Key, the owner of an incredibly generous Chinese restaurant in the South Island. This guy ran the joint with his wife and needed little to no excuse to cut loose! In our youth, we would celebrate at his restaurant anything that we knew could get a little sideways and for that loyalty we were richly rewarded. We would always get the top table which was raised off the ground by a couple of feet to add to the feeling of entitlement and excitement. Capt. Key would then welcome us with a shot of port and a round of beers and the nonsense would promptly start, not from us — but from him and his wife.

Within half an hour he would have one leg up on a chair and would be strumming a guitar (only capable of playing the note G — hence his name) belting out Kenny Rogers songs while his wife danced around the room like a whirling dervish. Within the hour he would be inciting rice fights (we all ordered sticky rice in preparation) and breaking his own chopsticks with crazy kung fu moves, and by the start of dessert he would be break-dancing with an unnerving focus on both the caterpillar and back spins, which he would insist we counted out loud.

One of the Fullas in our group once had a mushroom fried rice and insisted the mushrooms were of the 'blue meanie' variety. Mind you, he needed some excuse to explain his behaviour, as late in the evening, post dessert, we heard him swearing at someone at the top of his voice and then an unbelievable noise that shook the restaurant. The next thing we knew, this bloke was in a crumpled heap at the bottom of a spiral staircase with a large cupboard in pieces on top of him. He reckoned he had made his way to the toilet upstairs and had been attacked and thrown down the stairs by three identical dwarfs — definitely a case of mushroom fried rice-fuelled madness.

To this day I will always swing into Captain Key's restaurant and ask for a rendition of the 'Gambler', although, now in his sixties and full of aches and pains, he has abandoned the break-dancing routine! Captain Key is one of New Zealand's real characters and a damned Good Fulla.

Just for the record, however, here are several fictional Hoppers:

- The bashful Hopper — Shai Gai
- The Hopper publican — Ten Ding Ba
- The Hopper who harbours over-stayers — Hu Yu Hai Ding.
- The Hopper car cleaner — Wa Shing Ka
- The Hopper who has just returned from a holiday in Fiji — Wai Yu So Tan
- The Hopper trying to keep a low profile — Lai Lo
- The Hopper karaoke fanatic — Wai Yu Sing Dum Song
- The Hopper on a diet — Wai Yu Mun Ching
- The Hopper Cocky in summer — Bei Ling Hei

Not all, but the odd Hopper has a very different attitude to body waste and excrement than the rest of the Kiwi Fullas do. We all know of the practice in many Asian countries of using human manure or 'night-soil' as a fertiliser for vegetable crops. Well, thank Confucius that they have left that custom at home! But some have brought with them their willingness to excavate their nasal cavities in public and to hoik up big servings of phlegm then spit them out in the street.

At my local gym I have even seen some slashing in the showers, popping pimples in the mirror, washing their underwear in the hand-basins and even voraciously drying their cod bag and back passage with the hair dryer (despite the fact that hot seeds tend to sire girls) — each to their own I suppose, but you will never catch me leaving with dry hair! The same Hoppers will also eat a midday meal of pure MSG then spend the rest of the afternoon picking their teeth. Sometimes with the help of a toothpick. Sometimes not.

What is fascinating about the Hopper is that the main reason they come to New Zealand is to escape the hustle and bustle of the overcrowded cities of Shanghai, Seoul, Tokyo, Bangkok, Manila, Kuala Lumpur and Jakarta, seeking some wide open space. However, the paradox is that the bulk of the Hoppers here choose to live in inner-city apartments like sardines in a stack of tins, in New Zealand's most populous city. Apparently, 75 per cent of Kiwis born in North and East Asia live in Auckland. This puzzling behaviour is also demonstrated in their social habits.

Charlie and I caught up for a graze one Monday evening. We decided we wanted something plentiful and headed to a large Chinese restaurant in Greenlane for a big dish of beef chow mein, a decent helping of wontons and some Tsingtaos to wash it all down with. We sat down at the back of the restaurant and began to chew the fat, literally and figuratively. We were the only ones there and it was a bit like having supper alone in a large boarding school dining hall.

So in walked a group of young Hoppers, with their text books and laptops. They had the whole restaurant to choose from. And it was a big one at that. Well, they came and plunked themselves down at the table right next to us. I could have sworn (given their pointing while chattering away in Mandarin) they even discussed dragging the table over a couple of inches closer to us. Similar social etiquette is carried out on buses and trains, in banks and shops, and anywhere that they can get up close and cosy regardless of the amplitude of the room or space. Apparently, there is actually no direct translation for the word 'elbow room' in any of the Hopper languages or dialects.

Their fondness of group activity and resolute training to haggle over the price of anything from cauliflower heads to new two-door Lexus sportscars has been cunningly directed with the advent of social networking. The idea is very smart (a trait of the Hopper). It is to send out messages to like-minded purchasers of anything and then to descend en masse to the retailer and offer a large volume sale in return for a heavy discount. It's not unusual for dozens of Hoppers to turn up at electronics stores and demand 30 per cent off the sale price of electrical gadgetry.

Hoppers, particularly those of Korean extraction, are prevalent at Auckland's golf courses (apart from an extraordinary coincidence where there are none at certain Auckland golf clubs) and even more so at driving ranges. It is not uncommon for them to spend all weekend teeing off into a net. And, in fact, it is thanks to a couple of Hoppers that New Zealand golf is back on the map.

Hoppers have an enviable attention span, tenacity and discipline (there are only three unemployed Hoppers in the whole of New Zealand according to the latest census!) which can be applied to an extraordinary array of tasks from the meaningless to the genius, of which golf is a clear favourite. Indeed they love golf so much that they savour every single shot. Accordingly, they can be on the slow side on the course and tend to cop a fair berating from impatient locals, followed by a few well-hit balls dropping around their heads with the accompanying warning of FORE being whispered 150 metres back up the fairway.

Contrary to popular belief, the growing of long fingernails, particularly on the little fingers, is not for excavation but more as a sign that the individual sporting these holds a job that does not require manual labour. A small, visible status symbol for those in the know.

In our conversations with young Hopper student Fullas out here to study, they told us that obtaining a Kiwi passport increases their pull factor with young Hoppettes. Regardless of whether they choose to stay here or not, the ladies in their homeland find them more attractive if they have a New Zealand Certificate of Citizenship in their pockets. This has given rise to the forgery business in New Zealand, which has spawned a roaring trade in everything from monthly concession tickets for public transport to fully blown driver's licences, birth certificates and passports.

The Hopper, despite coming to New Zealand for a better life, often has real difficulty letting go of his old ways. It is now perfectly simple to live in Auckland and not speak a word of English. In fact, if I had the option of intentionally not understanding half the nonsense I hear it would make life a lot simpler. Indeed the Hopper, through the aforementioned propensity for convergence, has set up entire tightly populated towns, replicating their homeland, where the predominant language is Mandarin and the ability to selectively choose their language (or lack of) is a rare gift.

The Hopper has embraced the Kiwi café culture, not so much as participants, but as café owners. This has met with a modicum of success, as countering the

Hopper's undeniable work ethic is a relative inability to make a decent coffee. The fact that they prefer to down teas of all different colours (which are hard to screw up) hinders the ability to critique a good or ordinary cup of char. As cunning as they are smart, the Hopper will always opt for cash-flow businesses, where the ability to declare a percentage of actual revenue affords wholesale tax savings.

For this reason, average middle-aged Hoppers will carry a large amount of cash on their person and have large bundles in their homes. This fact has seen a rise in crime against Asians, as the criminal fraternity cotton on to the 'golden handbag' routine and the odd home invasion and extortion procedure. To counter this antisocial behaviour, all the Hopper needs do is jump into a Mr Miyagi crouch with a loud guttural scream and most ill-intended miscreants will scatter like dogs at a Tongan umu.

It is actually an extraordinary example of global marketing that the entire world considers every Asian capable of Bruce Lee-like feats of athleticism. This is in spite of the fact that, according to the latest medical research, the average weight for a fully grown Hopper is slightly above 50 kilograms, and the vast majority smoke like an Auckland city bus. Smoking is another status symbol to the Hopper, and different brands, styles and exhalation techniques have their own language and message.

The average Hopper has a lousy reputation when it comes to transport, despite their attempts to do everything to avert incidents. They have applied the 'Skunk' and 'Octopus' techniques to their driving. The Skunk offers any would-be assailant or neighbour a clear and visible warning, by way of their distinctive black and white markings. This warning has been replicated by the Hopper driving on New Zealand roads. They dress their cars up like love birds in a clear display that warns all other drivers into giving them a wide berth. Their decorations of choice are: neon lights, one-off paint jobs in unique colours, ridiculously oversized spoilers and tinted windows.

They also drive exclusively Jap imports and in order to ensure that they can be seen *and* heard they lob in the biggest stereo money can buy and huge mufflers to draw as much attention as possible. The net effect is that if you are smart you give them more of a berth than a fire engine or an ambulance. The older Hoppers are also aware of their driving challenges but being slightly more conservative offer warning in more subtle ways, the first of which is to drive either a Mercedes or

BMW exclusively, usually in abstract colours and in the smaller sizes. They also often wear white gloves which are very handy post accident to direct traffic around their victim's and their own vehicle.

However, be aware of the Octopus technique post accident. In much the same way as an octopus confuses his aggressor with a perfectly timed plume of ink, the Hopper is known to pile out of the car with all his friends and sprint around and around the car babbling away loudly only to stop after a few laps and blank-facedly deny any involvement with all of them claiming not to be the driver, making it nigh on impossible to finger the culprit.

Hoppers have set up driving schools and have been dishing out Kiwi licences for the right price to their countrymen, with no regard to passing the practical on-road test. The fact that the AA has a choice of five multi-choice written tests means that rote learning the test or remembering the first five and bringing in the answers ensures little need to actually understand the road rules they are getting a licence for.

That said, my personal opinion is that they are the most courteous drivers and pedestrians on the road, only too happy to be cut off and never walking out on to a busy road stopping cars as they dawdle with a feeling of self-entitlement, quite unlike many Anglo-Kiwis.

Most Hoppers work tirelessly on their hair with every imaginable product under the sun from clay to spray. Mind you, it's a hard road running a unique do when everyone's hair is straight and jet black.

They have the most skilled workers in the country, able to fix anything from Prada and Louis Vuitton bags and shoes, to electric motor mowers — you name it, they can fix it. Rumour has it the Americans took two years to build the smallest bolt in the world (much finer than a human hair) and sent it to the Chinese to gloat. It turned up eight weeks later with a nut on it!

In terms of food the Hopper will eat anything, literally, subscribing to the rule that anything that walks, sits or stands with its back to the sun is fair game! I am still scratching my head to find anything that does not fit within this guideline.

When it's all said and done, we have so much to thank the Hopper for: the two-dollar shops, sushi and spring rolls, Peking Duck, tai chi classes, karaoke, technological advancements, yum char, fireworks, green tea, leading-edge fashion, cheap knock-offs, half-price massage, compact design, work ethic, cultural learnings — you name it, New Zealand is much the richer for the Hopper making the pilgrimage, and long may they stay!

Mark my words, the next commercial generation will be led by diligent, savvy and focused Hoppers. In fact, the odds on a Hopper Prime Minister within the next 20 years are sitting at $2.30.

The Skinazi

The Skinazi is a white supremacist Fulla, found primarily in the South Island, in particular Canterbury, where there are too few Bros to kick some sense into them. They are the direct descendants of the 'Remittance Men' — despicable, degenerate and disreputable Pommy scum that were sent from England by their families, and supported financially to stay here, leaving behind them a shameful and sordid past, to start afresh here in New Zealand.

Ironically enough, the first Skinazis emulated the Jamaican Rude Boys and were both black and white Fullas. The English added the Nazi slant and got heavily into bad fashion, anti-establishment music and Paki bashing.

However, as anyone who has been to the Gold Coast will attest, we have a small percentage of Skinazis compared with Australia — a clear representation of the disparate IQ between the two countries.

The average Skinazi tends to be of sardine or whippet-like build and accordingly dresses in multiple layers to hide his physical frailty. Given the need to look larger than life, the Skinazi lives in cooler climates where our Maori and Polynesian brothers find it far too cold. And given his effeminate physique, the Skinazi will do one of three things to protect himself:

(1) Surround himself with at least half a dozen other Skinazis for any public outing — effectively resembling the pre-race traps at the greyhounds, or, if confronted, the post-race melee for the fake rabbit carcass. (2) Recruit a **WOLF** (White Oaf who Loves Fighting). A WOLF is, as the name suggests, a bloke who should at all costs be given a wide berth. They are of simple means and needs — seeking adoration and belonging by protecting their kin with acts of savagery. These guys can become so frenzied that they are not allowed to travel in pairs, as they have an uncanny knack of turning on one another halfway through a blue. Similar to knotted dogs they are nigh on impossible to prise apart, with tasers

and pepper spray merely acting as a stimulant. (3) The Skinazi will always carry an array of weaponry, from knuckle dusters to knives, batons and steel-cap boots.

Fortunately, they are easily spotted and universal in appearance, sporting a short back and sides with the accompanying short top and front, ranging from the zero to *plus three* in comb length. They have a love of denim in a variety of colours and will often be seen in the versatile jean-jacket with or without sleeves depending on season, and jean pants (otherwise know as the denim suit). This will almost always be accompanied by lace up steel-cap boots into which the jeans will be tucked. They will don a green, Army Surplus puffer jacket in extreme cold.

Skinazis have been here for a long time. The White New Zealand League has been around since the late 19th century. These days there is a Skinazi movement that is trying to instigate obligatory visas for anyone entering Canterbury in an attempt to restore full racial subordination in Canterbury life. Visa applicants will only be successful if they can prove they:

- are pure-breed Anglo-Saxons
- are Protestant by faith, but racist, xenophobic and anti-Semitic in doctrine
- have a net patrimony of over NZ$1 million
- are circumcised (but not, of course, Jewish)
- have a secret infatuation with Todd Blackadder, Reuben Thorne, Kieran Read or Robbie Deans
- and are sporting an array of meaningful tattoos and preferably have a Prince Albert as a tenuous tie to the old land

The Skinazis follow the Ku Klux Klan's greeting when trying to identify or recognise another Skinazi. One Skinazi will surreptitiously throw the acronym AYAS (Are you a Skinazi?) into a conversation. A fellow Skinazi will reply (rather ironically) ASIA (A Skinazi I am) to reveal his allegiance. A bitter and twisted conversation will follow.

There have been numerous communities concerned with the health of ethnic genealogy, from turn of the century Europe to marriage laws within the United States and the division until recently of South Africa. However, the Skinazi just loved the style with which the Huns asserted their myopic world view and as such are predisposed to wearing German Second World War uniforms and tattoos of Zie Reich.

If wishing to spot one of these Fullas, loiter around an Army Surplus store on the day of an advertised sale as they will undoubtedly turn up, often just to chew the fat with other Skins before heading home via several ethnic dairies to vent their spleen.

They set out to make large families for two reasons. Firstly, it is a damn sight easier for them to brainwash an idiot child than it is to successfully reason their views with a rational adult. And, secondly, because they hold the vain hope that they can breed themselves into a position of influence. For a Skinazi, the best night out with the kids is Halloween where they can don their Klu Klux Klan uniforms and pretend to be ghosts.

Not surprisingly, their children are easily identifiable. They are conspicuously white with shaven heads and most likely well freckled. They are often gap toothed, club eared and will always be simple — verging on mild retardation. This is due to both their parents' limited intellect and the fact that, as with the European royals, inbreeding often results in the inheritance of genetic flaws as opposed to strengths. As opposed to the Royals, however, they do not have undershot chins, flapping ears and bucked teeth. They are disobedient, raucous, disrespectful, hyperactive, and prone to outbursts — both verbal and physical.

If in the position to afford a holiday, they do not hesitate in booking lodgings on the Gold Coast where they blend in with numerous Anglo-Saxon mental deficients and where racist taunting, wolf whistling and booze swilling is encouraged. Ironically, their favourite politician is Hone Harawira, who they admire for his honesty and blinding intelligence. Like Hone, they also like to read Batman comics, drink Fanta, play hide and go seek, climb trees and build sandcastles. They also rate Willie Jackson as an aspirational intellect.

The Holy Grail for the Skinazi is a hidden grave containing bones that they allege to be proof of Anglo-Saxon settlements here, predating the Maori. These bones are located somewhere in the North Island and have (apparently) been carbon-dated to precede any other occupant of Aotearoa by more than a thousand years. These bones are moved often to ensure they do not fall into the wrong hands and anyone fortunate enough to see them will be sworn to secrecy. That said, the strange Skinazi Fulla who told us about them also said that they must have been Giants because they were the size (and, coincidentally, the shape) of cow bones. Another form of proof to the Skinazi that they are the indigenous people of New Zealand is the Kaimanawa wall in Taupo. This rock formation is apparently the tip of a massive pyramid, supposedly created by some Skinazi ancestors' lily-white mitts.

A small but vocal group of Cantabrians secretly aspire to be Skinazis, but refuse to because the current crop of Skinazi members are not from the *first four* boats which arrived in Lyttelton from Plymouth in England.

It's interesting that both Wellington and Dunedin had their very own *first four* boats, in Dunedin's case from Scotland, but neither of those cities nor their inhabitants make much mention of them. However, there is a vocal minority in Canterbury (much to the disdain of the majority of good, ordinary Canterbury folk), on the other hand, who claim to be a direct descendant of the 700 people aboard. There were two groups, on the *first four*: colonists, who travelled in the cabins, and planned to buy land in the new settlement; and emigrants, who were the working-class labourers and were jammed into the area below main deck.

These Fullas all believed that they could carve up two and a half million acres between themselves — two and a half million acres they all believed to be theirs by birth right. Tricked by the Canterbury Company into believing an idyllic Shangri-La existed, these muppets forgot about the Funny Whakas awaiting their arrival. . . . Over 150 years later, they still believe it's theirs by right. And these days, this minority give the rest of Canterbury (by and large bloody Good Fullas) a real bad rap.

I have spent a lot of time in Canterbury and it's a place that's hard not to like. My Tongan mate, however, will avoid it at all costs because he reckons every time he goes there he gets into a blue with a Skinazi or two. On a roadie, not so long ago, he was busy trying to convince a carload of us bound for Queenstown to stop either before or after Christchurch for the night, as it was, apparently as sure as night follows day that if we stayed there he would be involved in an altercation.

Given that the rest of us in the car had never had anything other than good experiences in Christchurch, and the next stop past it was Timaru, we told him he was being paranoid and settled in for the night in Christchurch. (To come clean we were also secretly licking our lips in anticipation.) Well, a long story will be cut short. We were in a bar enjoying a cleansing ale when a group of Skinazis turned up and started to make a spectacle of themselves. Our Tongan mate looked at us as if to tell us 'I told you so' and decided it was time to leave. As he stood up one of the Skinazis decided he would attempt to engage in a little bit of abuse towards our dear friend.

If you have ever seen a fully grown lion being heckled by a bunch of hyenas then you have painted half the picture. Eventually, the lion has enough and eats one or four of them. Well, now you have the full picture. So clean was the display, we didn't even need to put down our beers. Clearly, after this, our Tongan mate earned the nickname of '100 per cent' as a ratio of visits to scraps, and from what I understand he still has that percentage today. Perhaps he is just unlucky.

At any rate, unlike all the other Fullas outlined in this book, the Skinazi is one with whom it's best to have limited interaction, unless of course you are of a like mind, in which case a trip south is a must. Be sure to take in Timaru!

The Cocky

Cockies are the bread and butter (and meat and wool, and milk and honey) of the New Zealand economy. They ply their trade on New Zealand's fertile land, and frankly if it wasn't for them New Zealand would be a basket case of an economy. As it turns out, they help fill the grocery baskets of shoppers all over the globe, help dress some of the most fashionable babies and adults in the world and carpet the floors of some of the smartest buildings on the planet. In very broad terms, most Cockies are either Titpullers or Sheepshaggers. They are generally resourceful but understated Fullas — the lifeblood of the New Zealand heartland.

The High Country Cocky

High Country Cockies are classified as 'high' not so much in geographic terms, but more in socio-economic terms. They complain about how difficult it is to make a buck in farming, and they may well be dead right, but a fair few of them inherited a fairly large chunk of countryside at a pretty young age. And that's not a bad start to a working life to inherit a business and a residence all in one. In the 80s, Cockies lived well, sucking the hind tit and milking the system, through some very creative accounting. Cars were listed as farm vehicles, and all petrol was used for farm machinery. Income was distributed by family members, so all personal expenditure featured in the profit and loss account. This all came to an abrupt halt with the advent of Rogernomics. Since then Kiwi Cockies have become the most resourceful, efficient and innovative farmers on the planet and gave birth to the term Commercial Agritechnology.

A stroll through a Cocky's house is a warming experience. Not literally, because his house will be horribly damp, and smell extremely musty, and unless you are sitting in front of the blazing macrocarpa in the fireplace, sawn from the Forgotten (or similarly named) Paddock, his place is generally as cold as a mother-in-law's kiss. The living room will have a few trophies, a few taxidermatised animal heads (most will have a bit of the bog visible and will likely have a glass eye which is on a very peculiar angle or is, in fact, missing), and bookshelves full of *Footrot Flats* cartoons and Fred Dagg and Barry Crump books.

There will be an Elders or PGG Wrightson calendar in the kitchen which has been splattered with bacon fat, and every Cocky's kitchen will have a walk-in freezer which contains home-kill beasts, dinner scraps for the working dogs, and 10-litre tubs of Kiwi Ice Cream. To the side of the kitchen there is usually a shell packer to fill shotgun cartridges — much cheaper than buying them and you can pack in a few leftovers as experiments such as old AAA batteries and five-cent pieces to add to the joy of duck shooting.

Speaking of which, duck-shooting season is undoubtedly the highlight of the Cockies' social calendar. More dollars go into the top-shelf maimais than go into Cockies' weddings — and more piss goes through them over opening weekend than went through their weddings as well. The maimai is the rural equivalent of the urban dwelling Fulla's 'mancave', often housing the requisite barbecue, fridge, couches, card table and in some occasions Sky TV and stereos.

Obviously, the more degrees of water visible the better — which has led to the designer pond where Cockies bring in an excavator and dig a circle leaving the maimai in the middle and stepping stones a few inches beneath the water as the pathway. Suffice to say after a few Drambuies to warm the cockles prior to departure, and trying to find your way in the dark, can have some challenges — although, ironically, this is not as challenging as the post-shooting return for lunch, in broad daylight.

One opening weekend trip to Ranfurly, with a Cocky by the name of Big John, returned a very poor result indeed. The pond, which had 360-degree shooting, had returned over 120 ducks the previous year, so we were quietly confident of replicating the fortunes as we swigged on our first whisky in an attempt to warm ourselves up at 5 am. Well, to cut a long story short we were possibly a little over-enthusiastic as our haul later indicated. We managed to get a grand total of seven ducks, eight decoys, four plovers, two cars and a neighbour's maimai. We also had an unfortunate mishap involving a rental car, a fence and some harvesting equipment, which resulted in my inability to rent vehicles from Avis Queenstown for seven years.

Most High Country Cockies have some form of farm help, usually in the shape of a Funter (a Low Country Cocky), and will often have a second dwelling on the property which houses them. In the cottage in the Yards Paddock of a farm belonging to a Cocky out Raglan way lives a Salty old Seadog who has spent several years renovating it, but being a useless bastard has only tiled half the bathroom. He has, however, managed to build a beautiful rimu bar, where he serves his home-brew beer, which he usually drinks alone but occasionally skulls with a ragged bunch of other Salts while playing darts. Although poles apart culturally, socially and politically, this Cocky and the Salty Seadog seem to co-exist peacefully and, in fact, in an awkward and uncomfortable sort of a way, are actually mates.

I know another true blue, fair dinkum Cocky from the King Country called Sausage Digits Doug, known as such because of his unusually large and firm fingers which resemble Hellers London Pride pork snarlers and are estimated to be able to withstand up to one thousand PSI without bursting — the equivalent of dropping a shot put from three storeys (most Fullas' fingers will explode on impact with less than a swift hammer blow). I will just sidetrack here if I may — Fullas with these sorts of appendages are perfectly tailored to the conditions. They can withstand the bitter cold of a deep south winter without the need for gloves (or heated handlebars on the work bikes) and can also test the heat of tailing irons with the simple touch test, holding them for three to five seconds or until they smell their own fingers cooking.

Anyway, Sausage Digits Doug lives in his Swanndri, through all four seasons. It only gets washed if animal matter is splattered over it, but given it's generally the red and black gingham version, even then it's only in extreme cases. It must be said, though, that Sausage Digits Doug raised one of his very bushy eyebrows when Swanndri released a range by Karen Walker. Luckily, he had no idea who she was but he reckoned she may have been one of Wally Walker's daughters who worked as a rousie at shearing time during the varsity holidays. 'Bloody hard worker that Walker girl. And cooks a mean shearers' brekkie too. Had to fire her, when she was caught behind the shed with a young Maori Fulla gathering acorns so to speak,' Digits Doug told me.

Once a year he buys a pair of brand-spanking new gumboots (never call them wellingtons in front of a Cocky), which are hung upside down over a bit of four by two outside the back door of the farmhouse to keep the rain and the mice out of them, or in case one of the farm dogs lifts a leg and pees on them.

Sausage Digits Doug finishes every meal (which usually comprises meat and three veggies) with a strong cup of Dalghety Dust tea which he drinks with full cream milk and three teaspoons of sugar. When it comes to his musical interests, Doug once told me that he likes 'both' kinds of music: Country AND Western.

Sausage Digits Doug is unbeaten in the Piopio Gumboot Throwing Competition, and has represented Piopio at the Taihape National Gumboot Throwing Championships since its inception. He even entered the Fred Dagg lookalike competition a few years back and came a close runner-up (he's got a head like a cart pony). He's also a regular in the Hunterville Shepherds' Shemozzle, a gruelling and peculiar race with men and dogs and bizarre obstacles.

He takes extreme glee in shaking hands with a Townie, and will always judge them by their facial expression as he applies varying degrees of pressure to their mitt. If that doesn't solicit the requisite yelp then he will employ a ferocious ragdoll shake. He would never use those hand-mallets of his to hurt anybody seriously, though, but does punch hay bales with his bare fists when angry — usually in response to disagreement with government policy.

Old Sausage Digits Doug is an absolute chauvinist. It's not as if he is inherently pig-headed or sexist per se, or even believes that women are innately inferior to men, it's just that the role of the woman (to serve and obey the man) was drummed into him throughout his childhood. He is only just accepting the fact that women are asserting themselves in politics and business. But don't think for a second he's becoming more tolerant. When the Civil Union Act was passed in 2004, Doug retorted, 'Oh, for crying out loud! God made Adam and Eve, not bloody Adam and Steve!'

His wife doesn't think twice when she asks him if she can take the car into town to pick up some groceries, and his daughter knew she was shit out of luck when it came to inheriting the two and half thousand acres that Doug farms. She didn't even get a quarter-acre section. He loves her to bits, though; it's just that he made it clear from her school days that she needed to find a good man, get married and become somebody else's financial responsibility. And that's just what she did. She married young 'Biff' Williams, a stock agent from Onewhero, and Doug reckons she's pumping out kids like an old hay-baler. 'Four of them, she's got, and they're still going for it!'

His eldest son played 12 games for Manawatu while studying agricultural science at Massey. Right now he's share-milking in the 'Naki patiently waiting for Sausage Digits Doug to hang up his gumboots once and for all so he can move into the old homestead and take over the farm (which in turn will make him a much more attractive prospect with the ladies, meaning he'll be able to choose a suitable wife from the many willing candidates who will line up). His other son is a closet Finkle and lives in Mt Eden Village (but rather strangely has never been to Eden Park) with his partner, who he tells the Old Man is his flatmate.

Sausage Digits Doug drives a 1972 P6 Rover which is in the original condition he bought it in brand spanking new, but it's badly in need of a repaint and a reupholster of the seats. Wag and Smoke, his sheepdogs, and their predecessors have been running amuck inside it since it was new, climbing all over the seats. His second vehicle is a 1982 P38A Range Rover in British Racing Green, which he also bought new when times were good and farming was heavily subsidised. It is now rusty and stinks throughout.

There will be one or two occasions a year that a Cocky will go into the big smoke and, despite his best endeavours to blend in, in his number ones (RM Williams boots, moleskins and aertex short sleeve), you can pick him a mile off. Usually because he will be driving a Hilux that looks like it has been driven in and out of Rock Hudson; the exception is the FFBs (First Four Boats), the Christchurch farming fraternity, who will be in Range Rover Vogues. The usual reasons for a visit to town are to get a new Hilux, get the wife a few treats like new kitchen/washing appliances or threads, to attend a wedding or funeral or to visit any of the other kids, aside from the oldest son who is being primed to take over the farm.

There was a funny occasion I remember when a couple of Townies turned up at a rural barbecue in the Waikato bearing a few goodies for the lunch. They were Prankers from Auckland and brought an assortment of Babybel cheeses (the little gems covered with the red wax shell) and a large bag of pistachio nuts. Minutes later they were in shock and awe when they saw a local Cocky scoop a handful of pistachios and shovel them into his cakehole without removing the shell. Rather than spit them out, the Cocky continued chewing them until they were gone and then went for a second handful. He was seen later in the afternoon with red wax all through his teeth after hoovering several Babybels with no inclination to remove the shell of wax. You can only assume he's the type of Fulla who eats prawns, hard-boiled eggs and kiwifruit without peeling them either.

Like most Cockies, Doug is well informed on an array of matters from hours of listening to talk-back and sports-talk. But he actually intensely dislikes both as the buffoons who phone in raise his blood pressure with inane opinions that are bereft of any common sense or practicality. And when it comes to politics, he has staunchly voted National most of his life, but recently has flirted with NZ First and Act out of pure frustration. This backfired by opening the door for Uncle Helen, he now laments. (He should have known, he also voted for Bob Jones in the '84 elections, which was an indirect vote for the late David Lange.) As a result, he rues the day when Rogernomics took away the subsidies that helped him and his lambs get fat.

A more generous man than a High Country Cocky you won't find, though. Cockies, in general, are intrinsically kind-hearted and benevolent. Late one winter, years ago, I was driving a '64 Holden Special I picked up for 450 bucks from a Bogan in Taieri to go from Dunedin and meet Charlie and a few of the Fullas in Queenstown for bit of a shindig that we had heard had been organised there. Rumour had it that both the Swedish and Italian women's skiing teams were in town for some training during their off season and were coming along to the knees-up.

The very thought of this had got me a little over-excited and I may have pushed the old girl a bit too hard along some of the straights. Well, the Special decided to spring a hole in the radiator somewhere around Alexandra on State Highway 8 and before I knew it, I'd cooked the engine and blown the head gasket. The car came to rest in a huff of billowing smoke on the side of the road.

I waited about 20 minutes before a car came along. It was an old Triumph, and driving it was one of the finest examples of a High Country Cocky you will ever find. He took me back to his farmhouse in Muttontown, just out of Clyde, fed me and housed me and the next morning he offered to drive me through to Queenstown. He even said he had a special present for me and, with that, he came back with a merino lamb. Before I had a chance to be shocked, he had slit its chest open, reached in and stopped its little heart ('the most humane way' he told me), punched the skin off it, gutted it and bagged it up for the party that night in Queenstown. In addition to that, he said he'd get a local Bogan Grease Monkey to fix the radiator and the heads on the Holden for me at mate's rates, and that he'd personally ensure it'd be ready by the time I came back through. What a Good Fulla!

The do in Queenstown was a ripper, although the rumours about the women's ski teams were just that. There were certainly no Swedes or Ities there. In fact there were bugger all birds full stop — it was a bloody sausage sizzle! But it was a two day blow-out that was just what the doctor ordered towards the end of what had been a long and hard Dunedin winter.

I rang the Cocky in Muttontown on the party line that still operated there — long short long was the ring tone, I still remember. His booming voice answered on the other end, and he told me that the car was up and running and that his mate had replaced the engine with a fully reconditioned one and fixed the cooling system, all for a song. I told him that a mate of mine was going to drop me off in Muttontown later that day so I could pick it up and the Cocky quickly suggested we stayed a night on the way through. We actually hadn't intended to, but when we arrived the Cocky told us that his wife had stuck a side of home-kill beef in the oven and we were going to have that with some of the first of their home-grown Jersey Benne spuds of the season. Might even chase it down with a few brews, he reckoned.

So, we settled in for the night and had a superb meal, and a good night's kip. The next morning the Cocky had all his toys lined up for a morning of adventure. It was almost like a modern-day pentathlon. We did some clay pigeon shooting, rode horses and even did time-trials around a muddy track in an old three-wheeled Gnat that he had there. The highlight was when he let us go up in his microlight, which looked a bit like a cross between a go-kart and a hang-glider. The thing battled a bit with the weight of the two of us, which wasn't such a bad thing as we wouldn't have wanted to go too high up.

But as we should have known, it ended in disaster when we landed the thing in a large heap of silage. Luckily, there was no significant damage to either ourselves or the microlight but the stench stayed with us for days. The Cocky didn't mind too much though. He gave us a hose down and, as we were leaving, even told us a joke about his neighbour, who was holding a sheep in the front paddock when a bus-load of tourists pulled up on the roadside. One of them said, 'Are you shearing?'

The Cocky's neighbour yells back aggressively, 'No! Fuck off and find your own!'

Like this Fulla from Muttontown, High Country Cockies are a precious part of Kiwi culture and are generally just really Good Fullas. Have a weekend with one and find out for yourself.

The Funter (a Low Country Cocky)

Fishing, hunting, fighting and rooting is all that matters to the Funter, a low country farmer from a low socio-economic region. Funters are the milking mainstay of the low country farming fraternity. Early starts and early finishes offer sufficient time for an array of pastimes. Most of these involve guns, explosives, beer, mates and barbecues. Old club-rugby jerseys (with the collar up), dark blue jeans, and steel-capped Blundstone boots (or frequently a cheaper imitation) are the standard uniform for a Funter. The jersey will always be untucked, and the jeans always worn halfway down the arse cheeks, exposing far too much crack for most onlookers' liking. Some will wear shorts all year round and it's interesting to note that tight, short shorts are not considered offensive or fruity in Funter circles. When out about town, the Funter will often have both hands in his pockets, usually scratching away at himself furiously.

Funters working outside of share-milking are usually involved in seasonal agricultural work such as shearing, fruit picking, eeling, (illegal) whitebaiting or hay-making or they may branch out into more sophisticated roles such as ski-field grooming or forestry work. But never anywhere too close to a customer or any place where they will have the same boss for more than four months. Funters never contemplate responsibility.

The Funter doesn't mince his words (he's a Fulla of few words anyway). 'I kill possums,' a Funter called Phil from near Whangarei says frankly rather than use a euphemism like 'go possum harvesting'. And he does. Dozens every day, in fact. And he gets about $3 a skin too. The carcasses he then sends off to the freezing works to be made into dog tucker — although he keeps a couple a week for himself which he stews for his own personal consumption.

But possum isn't the only form of what most people would consider road-kill that the Funter eats. He delights in hunting pukeko — reckons they are trickier than ducks to shoot given their low flight trajectory and love of dense scrub cover. And he told me that if you soak them in brandy for a couple of days before roasting them they taste just like mutton. Serve them with a decent helping of boiled puha he reckons — and *Voilà!* A culinary delight! But it doesn't stop there. He joins the annual Kaimanawa wild horses cull, and lives off nothing but horse meat for the two months following. And his fridge will always have a huhu grub or two for a quick nutritious snack.

He knew the guy who snuck Calicivirus into New Zealand, although he gives no names. He hates rabbits and considers them vermin, particularly after his pet bulldog, Sid, choked on one trying not to lose his meal to his boss' farm dogs. He found Sid the next morning, stiff as a board, with two bloody ears hanging out of his gob after he'd tried to swallow the bunny — whole. His latest gig is trying to set up a commercial weka farm to breed the flightless native bird for meat. He reckons it tastes better than turkey.

He's a tough bastard is Phil the Funter. He played several years of senior reserve rugby, usually on a ferocious hangover, and suffered no injuries at all. He did, at the age of 16, pull a calf muscle, however, when he snuck into a public toilet to clear a pressure block after creeping into the local footy club wearing a fake beard to watch a few strippers in from town for a stag do.

There's another Funter out of the Hawke's Bay called Ray who is a real dag. He doesn't say much, either. But when he does it's pretty punchy. He doesn't speak in nuances at all. He gets his message across like a smack in the face with a fencepost. Anyway, given his love of weapons and killing he decided to join the army — as a soldier in the Regular Force. While the part-time Territorial Force would probably have been a better option for Ray, he was enticed by the good pay and low living costs the Regular army offered, and the possibilities to learn a trade through an apprenticeship — as well as the excitement of being surrounded by ammunition all day every day. So he dismantled his bivouac and headed down the road to Linton Camp, and signed up for the Army Recruitment course.

Things got off to a bad start when on the first morning he was forced to cut his mudflap off and get a short back and sides. Ray also thought having to make his bed (perfectly) every day was a little over the top, and having to shave every morning really got his goat. His non-conformist attitude started to show through immediately. He just couldn't help himself. He couldn't keep his hands out of his pockets, except when smoking, which he wasn't supposed to do in uniform anyway. He showed blatant insolence and disregard for rank. He refused to chip in to joint platoon chores or responsibilities. He used to skip the regular meals but then raid the mess hall kitchen when it was off limits. He never polished his boots. He just broke all the rules. His first report card read: *Technically sound but socially impossible. This soldier should go far and the sooner he does the better.*

But a couple of the generals tried to persevere with him. He was one of the most talented riflemen ever to enter the All Arms Recruit Course with an expert eye for the centre of any target. And he was so brilliant at the technical aspects of repairing armoury and ammunition that they also considered him for a weapon or ammunition technician. But he finally had to be turfed out of the army when he got a bit peckish in the middle of the night, broke into the kitchen and stole a whole frozen chook, took it across to the armoury, broke in (apparently the only person to ever have done so on Linton Base) and tried to char-grill the bloody thing using a flame-thrower.

All of this aside, Cockies need Funters, and New Zealand needs Cockies and Funters. Try to imagine New Zealand without them!

The Tulip Muncher

The Tulip Muncher is a New Zealand Fulla of Dutch origin. They are hard working yet frugal, and are often seen manhandling Friesian cows. Tulip Munchers have always liked New Zealand as an alternative to their rather sunken and overcrowded homeland. They like to be able to milk their cattle, knowing that they are, in fact, above sea-level and there are no dikes nearby. Curiously, though, their prime breeding bulls are often called Bulldyke.

Moving right along from the subject of dykes — New Zealand men have a lot to thank the Tulip Munchers for. Their daughters were always the cutest at primary school. Many of the belles of New Zealand school balls have a Van der Surname. Apparently, the most exciting event in New Zealand in 1953, according to some Fullas who were around at the time, was the arrival of a Royal Dutch Airlines flight from Amsterdam full of young Dutch birds coming out to settle in New Zealand.

Huge disappointment followed for all the Fullas, however — all but a handful of lucky Tulip Munchers that is, who had arranged the flight to bring out their brides to be.

And, of course, it was a Tulip Muncher who was the first non-Polynesian to discover New Zealand and report back to Europe on it in 1642. But it wasn't for about 300 years after Abel Tasman bolted from Murderers' Bay with a tail he'd grown between his legs that the Tulip Munchers started to leave their clogs, bikes and dikes and arrive here en masse.

In a WASP (White Anglo-Saxon Protestant) and Maori-dominated society a rather 'radical' recommendation was made at Cabinet level, at the end of the Second World War, that British immigration may not be sufficient and that Holland may be a solid source of Whites to bolster the population. After all they looked a bit like Poms, just a lot taller and a lot less pasty. And best of all they weren't Jerries. In fact it was the Jerries that drove many a Tulip Muncher to settle in New Zealand in the forties. That and the war-torn Dutch East Indies.

So the Dutch nationals needed a new home — and quickly. As a result, a limited number of Tulip Munchers were eligible for the New Zealand Assisted Passage Scheme — the very same arrangement that was responsible for bringing all those horrid Ten Pound Poms to our shores. However, even the Tulip Munchers were treated with suspicion in the New Zealand of the forties and fifties and they were fingerprinted and ordered to carry documentation at all times — hardly fair given what they had been through just prior to arriving here, thanks to Adolf's occupation.

They were also scattered around the country for fear that if they clustered in one place they may continue some of their Dutch customs. Heaven forbid! And they faced immediate deportation if they spoke ill of the Queen of England — although, ironically, they could say whatever the hell they liked about the Queen of the Netherlands without any risk of punishment whatsoever. With all due respect, though, it was probably not such a bad thing that many second-generation Tulip Munchers chose not to speak their native tongue given that Dutch sounds more like a gangrenous and infectious throat disease than a language.

Tulip Munchers soon became renowned for being assiduous workers — which in itself attracted the ire of their slightly less industrious and less conscientious WASP and Maori colleagues. As a result of feeling they were carrying the load for some of their less productive workmates, the Tulip Munchers were a little reluctant to ever shout the other Fullas a round of Lion Red after work, so they were labelled tight-arses to boot.

New Zealand cuisine had got off to a bad start by inheriting the dismal British cooking, and to be fair the Dutch dishes weren't much more chop either. But it is a Tulip Muncher that we have to thank for challenging the conservative and barbaric liquor laws that prohibited the sale of booze in restaurants, when in 1961 his restaurant was granted the first-ever licence to serve grog.

Poor old Otto the Tulip Muncher had been lobbying for years to have these archaic and draconian laws changed, and had even been convicted four times of the heinous crime of serving a glass of wine with a plate of meat and three veg. This was no ordinary Fulla, though. He even had a sense of humour (not common-place among Tulips) and was involved in a successful satirical skit about a mock police raid on a restaurant serving the sacred and forbidden sauce to its diners. His persistence paid off and common sense prevailed and some Cardycrat finally gave him a certificate to say he could pour some grog to those patrons eating in his restaurant.

These days, Tulip Munchers are fully integrated into New Zealand society. Many are still Cockies (and interestingly enough, unlike other Kiwi Cockies have hands as soft as a baby's bum — I can only think this can either be through excessive direct contact with the lanolin in sheep's wool or, perhaps more disturbingly, through self-manicuring given they spend so much time with their hands on tits), but some are now Prankers, CAVE Men, Cardycrats, Scarfies, Thrumpets, Salty Seadogs, Storytellers, Finkles and other Fullas, such as successful sportsmen.

Remember the old joke: How do you become the best middle distance runner in the country? You sit in the bath until you're Dick Quax. Well, Dick is a Tulip Muncher. In fact he is not Dick at all. He is Theodorus Jacobus Leonardus Quax. One of a number of proud Tulip Munching New Zealand sportsmen such as Eric Verdonk, Kees Meeuws and . . . Simon Poelman.

As Scarfies, Charlie and I hung out with a Tulip Munching Funter in Dunedin who was as rough as a bag of nails, but a hell of a Good Fulla. Buggered if I can remember his real name — it was unpronounceable and unrememberable. We just called him Van. Van was a second generation Tulip Muncher and like most Tulip Munchers was tighter than a snapper's arse. Also typical of most Tulips, he had two very cute sisters, but, given how fiercely protective he was of them, when anyone considered getting to know them a bit better, we called them the unDutchables.

Van's Old Boy grew tulips somewhere in the lower half of the South Island and, believe it or not, he actually exported the majority of them back to Holland! Anyway, Van had an eye for opportunity and quite an entrepreneurial streak. One February he came back to Dunedin, after having spent the Christmas break in Holland visiting relatives. He'd enjoyed his time there, particularly taking advantage of some of the looser laws pertaining to hash and whores. We fear he may have over-indulged in the former because he returned with a master plan to change his Old Man's tulip plantation into fields of poppies to harvest opium. God only knows what eventuated because shortly after telling us of his grand plan he disappeared and we never saw him or his sisters again, unfortunately.

But don't confuse a true Tulip Muncher with the recent wave of **Yarpies** to arrive here and establish themselves on the North Shore of Auckland. Yarpies are big slabs of South African beef who have left their homeland and brought their braais (barbecues), bakkies (utes) and biltong and boerewors (meats) to our great land to support the Boks and Saffa Super 14 teams when they play at Albany. In the 2006 census there were 42,000 South African-born New Zealand residents, and we reckon 40,000 of them live in North Harbour. Their gruff accents and direct way of talking can make them sound either arrogant or thick or both. But generally this can be a tad misleading, as your average Yarpie is a bloody Good Fulla.

Both Tulip Munchers and Yarpies have been valuable additions to the New Zealand social tapestry. And we have a feeling there'll be a steady stream of both coming here in the future.

The Waori

The Waori or 'White Maori' is about as brown as John Key, but if you shut your eyes and listen, he is as Maori as Billy T. In fact he's a dead ringer for Billy's character, you know, the Fulla who read the news with the yellow towel around his neck.

He is so absolutely gutted that his folks are white that he claims to be adopted and to not actually even know his real parents. Obviously, this holds little chop with his Maori mates with whom he so closely associates, which leaves the Waori in a position of forever trying to prove himself. Naturally, these Waori Fullas are predominantly located in the Maori strongholds of the East Coast and the Far North, although the odd Waori has been seen as far south as Wellington.

I have never seen one in the South Island, though, where any attempt by a white bloke to act like a Maori would be met with absolute ridicule in much the same way as would a Maori in Gizzy emulating a Toffer from Auckland.

That said, the Waori is one of the most fascinating buggers you are likely to come across, simply because he will do anything to earn the respect of his Maori mates. Of course his mates know this only too well and are constantly coming up with new ways of using this for their own amusement and benefit. It is a well-known fact that all Maori have a damn good sense of humour and to have a Waori mate willing to jump through 101 hoops to prove himself is a rare and treasured pleasure indeed.

Clearly, any Waori worth his salt is the master of anything cultural. He speaks Maori as fluently as his buddies, can prepare a hangi just as well, if not better (this is because his mates know he is willing to do it and take advantage of this fact, so he is well practised), is known for mad acts of bravery and for his unbelievable fitness and strength. His cobbers often refer to him as the 'ten guitar Pakeha'.

One Fulla I witnessed attending to a hangi on the East Coast was the perfect example of a Waori. As white as a sheet of paper with ash-blond hair and with a thick layer of bodily hair — this guy was a beauty. As if to remind him he wasn't Maori, his mates called him Pinky. He didn't say much, happy to be perceived as staunch. But when he did speak you kept looking behind his back for the real Maori Fulla doing the talking.

This particular night was freezing and would have been close to zero degrees and this bloke was wearing a tight pair of stubbies, a woollen singlet and some work boots and he stayed outside in that get-up for three hours attending to a hangi and hanging the kids' eels from the fishing contest.

During this time I was asking his mates about him and they were waxing lyrical about how they could not believe the lengths he would go to. Some regarded him as the direct opposite of Michael Jackson, and while Jackson had surgery to change his look, this Fulla changed his with mad acts of stupidity and bravery all related to earning his stripes. He was once trying to keep hold of a 180-pound Captain Cooker when he dropped the knife and two of the dogs copped a tusk to the torso and bolted. He not only hung onto it but he somehow grabbed the knife and finished the job. He then carried the thing for two hours out of the bush before getting patched up.

He was also remembered for jumping into a fight one night with a local gang to protect his mates and getting a slightly more indigenous look by way of a permanently flattened nose, which he was plainly stoked about! When he spoke he out-Maoried the Maori. When I asked him how the hangi was going he said, 'Sweet as, eh Cuz, but I get the first pig's head eh!'

Apparently, he once made a bet with his Maori mates that he could last for one hour in the hottest thermal pool they could find in Rotorua. They found it and he sat in it . . . for one hour. They reckoned old Pinky came out looking like a boiled crayfish and went straight to bed for about 18 hours, after skulling three big bots of blisteringly cold DB Draught.

The Waori, given his ancestry, is sadly behind the eight ball when it comes to dancing and singing. Lacking the mandatory Maori co-ordination and vocal abilities, the Waori dances like Paul Holmes and sings like a steer having its horns removed, which undoubtedly, when reminded of this, hurts his feelings. But he will give it 110 per cent, much to the chagrin of his mates.

The Waori is often a meatworker or in the fishing business and will be distinguishable at most bars by his white steel-capped work boots with a fresh splash of blood, tight shorts and woollen singlet. Naturally, he will be drinking Tui, DB Draught or Lion Red directly from a quart bottle and will likely have a face even his mother is not particularly fond of, earned by jumping into any altercation within a bull's roar . . . which is actually another reason he drinks from a quart bottle.

The Waori can tell you what most Maori place-names mean. My mate Willy the Waori (who also sometimes refers to himself as Wilemu, even though he knows well that no 'l' exists in the Maori alphabet) was down in Kaikoura fishing and shooting a while back. 'Appropriate name, Kaikoura,' he told me as he went on to explain that kai (tucker) and koura (crayfish) is what he was hunting and gathering all day during his stay. He's a smart Fulla, our Willy. And his pronunciation of Maori is so strong it can lead to confusion.

In fact, I was having a couple of beers with a group of mates one sunny afternoon in the garden bar of the Tatapouri Pub, just out of Gisborne, years ago. (Tragically, the Tatapouri Pub burned down in a similar and coincidental manner to that of several other iconic East Coast pubs shortly after the drink driving laws became more strictly enforced in the mid-nineties, costing the insurance industry a small fortune.)

Anyway, Willy the Waori walked in, said he needed to call an immediate hui, and with that announced he was leaving Poverty Bay and heading to the big smoke. There was a mix of happiness and sadness in his voice. It must have been a really tough decision. The Bay was his turangawaewae. He loved the area and knew nothing else, but he was excited by the opportunities the big city offered a talented sparky like him.

So he proceeded to shout a couple of jugs of Tui Pale Ale for the lads. When I asked Willy the Waori where he was going, I was a touch discombobulated by his answer.

'I've just paid a deposit on a whare in Monaco,' he replied.

'What?! Where?!' I asked even more befuddled.

'Not far from the City Centre in Monaco,' he said. Now I was totally baffled and bewildered — as were all the Fullas. But they all started to high-five and make jokes about how much sparkies rip people off — and how they hoped to go and visit him there one day. It wasn't till he said, 'It's a little brick and tile place, just off the Great South Road,' that we all realised he was actually talking about Manukau.

I saw Willy the Waori again for the first time in ages, six months or so back.

He's now married with four half-Waori half-Maori kids. These days he sports a koru tattoo on his arse and apparently had to be seriously talked out of getting a full moko. And his wife reckons he's the only man to have claimed to have recently sighted the taniwha down the Waikato River.

Another guy I spoke to up north, who was mates with a Waori called Joseph (he referred to himself as Hohepa), said that he reckoned that a Waori makes the greatest friend because they are 'so keen to please they are literally worth their weight in paua'. Sadly, because they are confined to the aforementioned Maori strongholds, Waori are as scarce as hens' teeth.

A more common specimen is the **Whro** (pronounced like Afro but without the 'a') or White Bro. This character is scattered all over New Zealand from North Cape to Bluff, and while nowhere near as rare or legit as the Waori, can be very amusing and bloody good value too. Characterised by his use of colloquial Maori terminology and mannerisms, the Whro will enter any public place with 'Gidday Bro' or 'Sup Cuz?' or the odd bit of Maori that he knows such as 'Kei te pēhea koe?' followed by a raising of the chin and lifting of the eyebrows to anyone paying him any attention. Unlike the Waori, the Whro is a poor and cowardly scrapper, working on the notion that if he acts Maori it will get most people to back off. If anyone, however, does call his bluff the Whro will stand his ground to the last minute trying to step them out and then bolt to the hills.

One Whro I once knew in Queenstown called 'Cuz' decided to never wear shoes, which in winter in Queenstown is relatively daft. He was the life of a party and always keen to hand out a hongi, sing, play the guitar, or spin a few yarns. One particular winter's night we had gathered for a knees-up at a cobber's joint and were having a whale of a time around a roaring fire when Cuz turned up with a 'Sup Fullas?' and a few hongis and monkey-grip handshakes with back slaps.

To cut a long story short, he had walked five kilometres through the snow and sleet on roads covered with black ice to get there — barefoot! To keep himself warm during the hike he had polished off the best part of a bottle of rum which would have made the trip more like eight kilometres, including all the weaving.

He had been at the party all of three minutes when one of the girls started screaming. Cuz's foot was on fire! Well, not literally, but there was an alarming amount of smoke coming from underneath his paw, and the unmistakeable smell of meat cooking. He was standing on a huge ember that had been shot out of the fire. When alerted, Cuz kicked it off and loudly offered to do a bit of fire walking as a party trick. Obviously, such an act of bravery was not to be sneezed at, and the requisite embers were thrown on the floor. (It is worth noting that the house was rented and the floor was polished concrete.)

The next couple of minutes stimulated the full spectrum of emotions from glee and hilarity to fear, revulsion and anger as he traipsed back and forth over the embers. It was the last night Cuz walked anywhere barefoot, as he spent the next two weeks in bed — with his feet getting dressed twice daily.

Last we heard of him he was seen working for DOC tramping around the bush doing work on the huts. His employment contract stipulated that he needed to wear appropriate safety footwear at all times, so I assume his feet have never been better. The contract, however, said nothing about clothing, so on a nice day in the bush he doesn't wear any at all.

The Whro is a character that most Pakeha Fullas actually have in them just waiting for the right circumstance to burst free. Check yourself next time you stand on the sideline of a rural footy match in a Maori area or slip into the Ruatoria pub for a cleanser. Everything will change. Your movements will slow down and be more purposeful, your gait will alter and you will find your knees have a new-found spring which allows them to bend deeper.

One leg might appear shorter as if to make you drag the other slightly like you have a noticeably stronger leg. Your armpits might feel like they have a suitcase shoved into them, raising them from your body, like John Wayne pre-gunfight. You will likely start to sniff a fair bit, will have a new-found peripheral vision and a grin will undoubtedly accompany your slightly squintier eyes. With this, your language will change, as will your topic of conversation. If you have half a brain, you will put some Robert Nesta Marley on the jukebox and hope to get a subtle eye inviting you to chance your arm at a game of darts or pool. From there you will be in for one hell of a night because local Maori hospitality, as any Kiwi bloke worth his weight in kina will tell you, is the best in the world.

Don't overdo it, though, as the locals can tell an imposter and for God's sake don't go near any of the local wahine, as no matter how well you have done, the line in the sand is there for a reason.

The Carny

A Carny is a Fulla who runs or works at a stand, booth, ride or game at a circus, carnival or fair. Born into a life of trickery, mysticism, animal husbandry, gun-barrel tampering, tent erecting, Ferris-wheel fiddling, hot dog frying and trapeze dangling, the Carny can, despite having zero formal training, turn his hand to the most remarkable array of tasks with a modicum of success. Coupled with very light fingers, this is quite a profitable combo.

Despising the idea of being held in one place for too long, the Carny is an itinerant. Drawn to the adrenaline of live performance, his is a life of freedom and uncertainty.

Carnies live off the smell of an oily rag and are life-stylers who will stop wherever the feeling of optimism exists. They expertly avoid the everyday challenges of the outside world, living by their own rules within their own walls, similar to the Romans' sense of law behind closed doors (but without the exclusiveness).

Carnies will invariably set up camp on the outskirts of town in vacant lots, parking their miniature circus, including: an array of degenerate animals, umpteen caravans, a collapsible big top tent, and neon signs, running off either a generator or an unwitting neighbour's supply. By the time the councils get around to issuing a trespass notice, the show will have moved town (called 'Jumping') leaving in its wake hundreds of thrilled children and a rise in petty crime of about 50 per cent. In any event, by this time a number of the Carny's tricks and scams will be starting to attract unwanted attention.

Once that 'show time' adrenaline kicks in, Carnies put on the poker face and become masters at extracting dough from people. The odds of a big win at the casino look generous by comparison to your chances at the fairground. Well-rehearsed routines, where fellow Carnies win big from the top shelf in front of gathering crowds in order to coax punters into trying their arm, are seen as par for the course and once a big spender is earmarked they have numerous techniques (from marking the person with chalk to shadowing them) to ensure the other vendors know who to target. They will fix their games so people can't win, and will then change the rules in retrospect if they do.

I recall one unsavoury incident a few years back where I came across a circus in Courtenay Place in Wellington which had sprung up in a vacant lot. After a beer or two, I decided to try my hand at a shooting stall and, given my inability to hit anything, was convinced the barrels had been bent. As repayment for this underhand trick I started to fire a few indiscriminate slugs into the top shelf stuffed toys. Feathers were flying and I was definitely getting my money's worth, when 'ka-bam'. I got blindsided by the stall operator. . . . Silly really! I still had the gun. So after a short stand-off with a few words exchanged, I took to my heels.

That was just the start of it, as the Carny Fulla took chase and then roped a few mates into the pursuit. I had about five whippets chasing me down Courtenay Place. After about two kilometres they were still in pursuit and I was starting to get a bit knackered. After five kilometres, as we approached the railway station, I was getting a bit panicky, as the tank was starting to run empty. Thankfully, they also were running out of puff and finally gave up the chase. But let me tell you — they are fit and fast and unless you are feeling bloody energetic, follow the rules of the fair.

One Carny (or Trixter as he referred to himself) interviewed for this book spoke in depth of numerous ways of 'borrowing a little from Peter to pay Paul and the ponies'. He spoke of a well-known clown, known as 'Fingers' (until a nasty accident with the collapsible tent removed most of them), who made a living 'removing sugar from pockets' while pretending to be drunk and bumping into patrons. It was not until after the accident that 'Pincer', as he has since been renamed, was eventually caught and his scam exposed.

When it comes to food, Carnies can and will eat anything, although there is always a frenzy of excitement when the fat vats get up to sufficient heat and the first battered sausage comes out of production. It is customary that this first sausage is given to the oldest member of the crew — in the case of 'Trixter's travelling circus' this is a chap called Simmo, who at the age of 46 has no teeth and has a hell of a time gumming through it, but who to this day has never given one away.

The Carny's job, family and social life are all rolled into one. Predictably enough, this closeness leads to numerous in-house challenges to test each other's mettle and attempts at outdoing one another. One story we caught wind of was of a young Fulla who was dared to jump off the bridge heading out of Taupo and was washed over the Huka Falls. As fortune had it, he not only survived but this showmanship won the heart of a young pony-trainer and they were married on the Ferris wheel shortly thereafter. The Ferris wheel is the heart of any circus, holding a mystical allure to wee children and Carnies alike. It is usually run by the boss and is where many romances blossom, proposals occur and children are conceived (second only to the ghost train).

As sure as Carny women have piercings, and the blokes tattoos, without fail all Carnies drink heavily. Every night is a party. Intoxicated scraps over women abound. Bozo the Clown still has four air gun pellets in his chest, neck, arm and groin and Old Man Dennis has a bald patch on the back of his head from wrestling over a Sheila a little too close to a gas heater (although he claims he was hit by a badly thrown fire stick from a Czechoslovakian ring-in juggler). And poor old Jacko the Joker (who ran the gun stand) bolted after the wedding of a Carny woman, who he had always fancied, to the resident strongman — and to this day it's rumoured he lives in the bush above Opotiki. He never even said farewell and left a large debt owing on his stall.

The Carny tends not to age well and has a relatively short life expectancy. Booze, cigarettes, high fat food, appalling living conditions, hard manual labour and stress all contribute to this premature ageing.

One horrible example of such side-effects halted the career of Jimmy Juggles as he was known in Carny circles. We met Jimmy researching this chapter and to call his story a sorry one is a gross understatement. Jimmy had been in the circus since 1965 when, aged seven, he started as a trapeze child, being tossed and hurled from artist to artist, 10 metres above the crowd. The 60s, when Jimmy started in the circus, was a time of trial and error. OSH was only a dream to a very limited number and safety nets were an unnecessary expense (which had they been installed would have had a negative effect on attendance — as crowds flocked to see mishaps).

A series of slips and falls curtailed Jimmy's trapeze career at the age of 13, by which time he was proving nearly impossible to catch, having broken his right leg numerous times, resulting in it being some three inches shorter than the left. These falls, coupled with a weekly thick ear from his old man, meant that poor Jimmy Juggles was on the lower half of the bottom half for IQ. He was also suffering blurred vision, deafness in his left lug and pins and needles in both hands. This led, quite logically, to Jimmy diversifying his skills portfolio and entering into many different roles from sword swallowing to snake charming, which ironically left him with a pierced lip (two decades before it was trendy), after the company anaconda latched onto his face when he accidentally stood on its tail with his thick-heeled right boot.

It was, however, the juggling arena where he earnt his reputation and it was well justified according to Jimmy! If you ever visited the circus from 1972 to 1993 and saw a juggler with a club foot, a hearing aid and horn-rimmed milk-bottle glasses, it was probably Jimmy Juggles.

Jimmy was a real performer (and still is) and he devoted thousands of hours to learning to juggle everything from pick-axes to fire balls, and at his peak in the 80s he was the best in Australasia. By this stage his eyes were shot and his hearing was impaired, and he was starting to mumble a few decibels louder than required. His pins and needles had progressed to full numbness in both hands, which Jimmy turned into a positive by juggling naked flame.

He started with fire sticks which he would pretend to over-rotate in front of the crowd so that the fire was being handled and not the stick. He would then start yelping and hopping all over the stage while continuing to juggle, much to the huge delight of all who were there to witness. This routine was what propelled him to the top of his game and into a life of temptation in the fast lane. The next few years were all about upgrading house-trucks, top-shelf booze, jewellery and loose women. Jimmy was making hay!

This ended abruptly in September of 1993, when Jimmy was the draw-card for a large Russian Circus that had secured his services as they travelled the country. The sight of a deaf, blind, club-footed, numbskull juggling fire had wowed the crowds from Kaitaia to Invercargill and the troupe had offered Jimmy a sweet deal to travel with them for the Australian leg of the tour.

Jimmy was ecstatic to be travelling out of New Zealand for the very first time and hit the ground running (or hobbling) in Australia, with the first four shows receiving rave reviews and Jimmy basking in the spotlight, after having his photo taken mid act with his new sponge-juggling routine. The sponge juggling involved Jimmy dousing sponges in methylated spirits, lighting them and hurriedly juggling wearing a pair of safety goggles as the fire droplets rained all over him and the stage.

THE CARNY

On the night in question, Jimmy strode onto stage to the vigorous applause of the assembled mass ready in anticipation for his brave routine. As he tells the story, he was running a little bit late and had forgotten his sponge bucket so just before starting he told the announcer to buy him some time and he raced around to his room and grabbed the tin bucket and tore back to start things off.

The routine was going perfectly. He juggled swords and chainsaws, balls and bats — but he knew what the crowd wanted. The moment he pulled the safety goggles out of his bag you could have heard a pin drop! He then poured a generous amount of meths into the bucket and flicked in a match. The crowd was on the edge of their seats as Jimmy reached in and grabbed the five sponges, one after the other, and began to hurl them skyward.

Seconds into the act Jimmy dropped one sponge and then all five and as he lent over to pick them up they all started running in opposite directions. . . . Jimmy had mistakenly grabbed the Ringmaster's daughter's pet guinea pigs, which she had put in an unused bucket to carry around. The crowd lost the plot as the smell of hair and the squeaks of the pigs filled the tent. The Russian Circus were labelled barbarians by the media and future venues cancelled bookings and refunded advanced bookings. Jimmy Juggles had brought the biggest travelling circus to its knees.

Jimmy had one cracker story about a young acrobat from the Russian Circus, called Nada, who had been travelling through Russia for years before she managed to travel to our fine shores. She was something of a straighty-180, who chose to live clean and wanted to better herself so she could leave the Motherland. She didn't drink, smoke, party or cause any trouble and her main friend was a pet cat called 'Tinki'.

Well, to cut a long story short, she was travelling and performing just south of Siberia and the winter had hit hard with everyone being confined to their trailers. About three o'clock one morning the circus strongman stumbled home after a few too many vodkas and went to her room by accident. He opened the door and realised he was in the wrong caravan and stumbled off trying every other door until he found his. Problem was that he had opened the door wide enough for Tinki to bolt out to have a wizz.

When Nada awoke and called Tinki, she was gone. She panicked, rushed to the door and found the poor thing on the doorstep — purple and hard as a rock. Somehow it was clinging to life and she lifted it inside and hurriedly started to rub it with a towel . . . big mistake! There was a sickening cracking noise and both of

Tinki's ears snapped off. In a major panic flap, Nada grabbed the cat to hug it and snap — off came its tail about halfway up. With no more fleshy appendages to snap the cat made a relatively quick recovery, but was battling in the looks and balance department from that unsavoury moment forth.

Jimmy Juggle's brother Danny was another natural. He was a dwarf, born looking like an 80-year-old man. Any physical oddity is a real cash spinner, and Danny put it to good effect. By the time he was 15, far from his appearance naturally correcting, it had progressively worsened, leading to him being marked as 'Half Man Dan' and the 'Sawn-Off Pensioner'. His job was to dress as a clown and to abuse and mock fairground attendees as he sat above a tank of water. He'd then coax them into taking pot shots at a target which, if hit, would dunk his abusive frame into the drink.

Dan was the best in the business and could pick a target from 50 paces, starting with a gentle bit of ribbing to engage the punter and working into a full venting of his spleen, complete with expletives and all, until the poor prick dropped $10 to have three throws at the target. Every time he missed, the pressure would increase — as too would Dan's abuse. He would target the punter's girlfriend or wife, even kids, calling him an 'effeminate custard-armed f#ck face of a disgrace' and an 'embarrassment to his family'.

Children would cry, wives would also take shots and Dan would keep yapping until it seemed like half the fairground was gathered around willing the schmuck to dunk the dwarf. Professional through and through, Half Man Dan would target new punters and rip into their clothing, hairstyle, general appearance, you name it, anything to get a rise. He was literally worth his weight in gold and would easily pull more loot than any other stall. It was not unusual for kids to come back 20 years later with their own children, looking to redeem and exact revenge on behalf of their fathers.

There are numerous types of Carny in the New Zealand scene:

The Harvester

The Harvester is so named for his comparative ability to entice dollars from pockets by any means, legal or otherwise. One Harvester called Peter has a file on him as thick as a brick and has earned the affectionate name of Pe-noose within

New Zealand policing circles for his ability to slip the noose or long arm of the law. A master of imitation, face paint, contortion and cheap magic tricks, Peter has been an embarrassment to the New Zealand police for the past 15 years, and has left a trail of destruction in all the small towns his show has visited.

His crimes are all (as he would say) 'victimless', although there could be some arguing this fact given his crime of choice is theft. From harvesting pockets, letterbox trawling (the Carny equivalent of a lucky dip), trading car parts and his favourite, beach house sitting — where he moves into beach houses during the winter months when the Circus takes a few months break and rewards himself with a few big ticket items by way of payment for looking after the house.

Pe-noose is pretty stoked that the long arm of the law has always been one or four behind. He was born in Dublin and grew up with the itinerant Tinkers & Knackers (think Brad Pitt in *Snatch* . . .) as they are known. The Tinkers have devised a very shrewd scheme which pays handsomely. What they do is set up camp in a neighbourhood and start flogging everything from car mirrors to fruit off trees which they then sell back to the locals. This results in the locals coming to a financial arrangement, settled out of court, with the Tinkers & Knackers who then move off to the next affluent suburb to apply their ruse over again. So, after a misspent youth of growing up under the sophisticated Tinkers & Knackers syndicate in Dublin, Pete headed to our fine shores with his stepmother to visit a crook relative and has never left. Apparently, we have years to go to catch up to our Irish counterparts, but Pete is not so keen to divulge too many secrets because he still has a few tricks to play.

The Roller

The Rollers are more like Gypsies who have left the circus for a more sedate lifestyle as they age or get injured. They will blow glass, read palms, sell kites and dream catchers, make tin flowers and sell magic beans to children.

One hilarious story we heard of a Roller, who was romancing one of the glass blowers, occurred when, post a flagon of Rich Ruby, the bloke went outside to pick a tin flower for the lovely. Well, it was a cracking Wellington southerly and the tin flower was whizzing like a DC3 propeller and this rosy-cheeked Lothario knelt down in a mock sniff of the six-inch flower prior to picking it. Bobbing and weaving like a prize fighter the unfortunate twit drove his pickled bugle straight into the mini prop and was rushed to hospital with a flap of conk needing to be reattached.

The Flipper

Most motivated of all in the cut-throat Carny line of work, having run away from the trade fair circuit to join the circus, is the Flipper, named for his 'act before thinking' attitude and his bouncing from trade to trade and job to job. One Fulla called 'Racin' Roy' was conceived in the ghost train when his parents attended the 1978 trade fair in Newtown, Wellington. He found his way back to a life in the fair 13 years later and has tried his hand at everything on offer, from the hotdog stand to the motorbike 'cage of death'. Roy can rip anything apart and put it back together, usually with a few additional bolts and nuts, but to this day this has never been a major issue.

The Flipper is motivated by money and money alone. Roy had so many scams and tricks, from selling tap water in reused plastic Evian bottles, fishing goldfish out of local creeks for prizes, to making his own battered hotdogs out of sausage meat, sawdust and pork lard. He would only sell food which could land over a 300 per cent mark-up. Candyfloss was the margin winner hands down given it was essentially spun sugar sold at $2 a stick.

The only time he lost money on candyfloss was the time his girlfriend (of the time) poured his stash of speed (used to pull long night shifts) into the vending machine after a savage, relationship-ending argument. He had no idea until the fairground came under siege from 200 kids climbing the fences and shooting the guns at each other and throwing the sort of tantrums one might expect after feeding them two litres of lime cordial, three raspberry fingers and a family bag of jelly beans as a chaser. By the time he figured out what was happening, there was a queue of 20 adults asking for candyfloss and the spinner was nearly chopped. He quickly shut up shop, finished the last three sticks of floss himself and flew into the fairground like a crazed baboon.

Charlie and I visited the Royal Easter Show this year, and we are proud to report that the Carny is alive and thriving. There is a burgeoning class of icky young

Carnies, taking over the mantle. They give the impression of being so totally dishonest that we weren't quite sure what to believe. But a couple of them told us that the Hurricane (a spinning up and down ride) was so badly in need of some maintenance that one of the carriages was likely to come flying off and end up landing in the Haunted House.

Another foul Fulla told us that the bloke who operates the Gravitron lives on a sole diet of baked beans, targets punters who have just eaten an unhealthy helping of junk food, then, once they are in, the doors are closed and the centrifugal force takes over, he emancipates some methane from his gastrointestinal tract and watches the unlucky participants suffer as they spin out of control, and gravity and inertia prevent them from being able to cover their eyes and nose (and they often lose their lunch).

This new generation of Carny does quite nicely thank you very much. A hefty fee for entering the park, then the old trick of charging coupons for rides so nobody knows quite how much they are spending. They pressure kids into pressuring their parents to pay for rides, or have a crack at the laughing clowns, or can-skittle games, then give away crap prizes and cackle their Carnyselves as they fill their pockets with cash.

But while Carnies may rub some Fullas up the wrong way, they do keep them on their toes, and they bring delight to children all over the country, even if these same kids' parents are a little wary of them. Not only that, and despite the appearance of most of the rides, there have been very few safety incidents at fair sites in New Zealand (and most have involved the Carnies themselves). And let's face it, when they take your money they do so with a smile and give you a fair bit more in return than a casino, the TAB or your Lotto ticket.

Finally, I have it on good authority that a local circus will pay top dollar for a troupe of midgets and miniature ponies, so keep your eyes peeled!

THE STORYTELLER

Storytellers are Fullas who hate the sound of silence but love the sound of their own voice and were born to entertain, yarn, yak, utter, chatter, babble, gabble, ramble and prattle.

A good Storyteller will be able to spin a beautiful yarn out of a mundane or routine procedure. For me, a great indicator of a Storyteller is the tale a person tells of their trip to the longdrop dunny at my bach. A non-Storyteller will return from using the facility and avoid any mention of it, but a real Storyteller will come back with a truly dramatic account of his round trip. This will usually involve staggering around in the dark, encounters with giant wetas or unidentified biting objects, all number of strange noises, silhouettes and shadows, misadventures with the dunnypaper, accidents, misplacements and misfires, bumps, bruises and cuts, and a general array of toilet humour.

THE DIVIDE-BY-TENNER

The Divide-by-Tenner is a beautifully colourful character. One of life's great charlatans. A master raconteur. The 'I've been everywhere' man. Most social sets have one. In my personal case it's Will or 'William tell' the Divide-by-Tenner. He gets his colouring pencils out whenever anyone is keen to listen and paints a masterpiece of a story which most of us now know how to interpret as it really happened — that is by dividing all facts, figures and superlatives recounted . . . by ten.

You see, the Divide-by-Tenner works on the theory that if you say anything with sufficient confidence and authority, people will believe it. He's a great socialiser with a vast array of stories banked that are in need of new sets of ears. It is as though the whole list needs to be told (and added to) every month for fear that it will be lost, leaving the Divide-by-Tenner like Muhammad Ali without arms. As a result, the Divide-by-Tenner is a very social animal, always working a room to find a new person to regale with the same stories.

Will the Divide-by-Tenner is a walking, breathing sports encyclopaedia. He can tell you the batting average of every test cricketer from 1970 to the present day, and knows exactly how many first-class balls Sir Richard had to bowl to claim 400 test wickets ('A lot less than Kapil Dev,' he'll add). He claims to have played for the Kapiti-Horowhenua secondary school cricket side which beat a Canterbury side that boasted such names as Chris Cairns and Nathan Astle. No one in either team seems to remember Will at all.

In spite of the fact that Will the Divide-by-Tenner talks incessantly, he never cares to involve himself in gossip or slander. As a matter of fact, he often quotes Leviticus, Chapter 19, Verse 16: 'Thou shalt not spread slanderous gossip among thy people.' What he often does do, though, after listening to a good story, is to recount it with himself as the main character. In fact, if you added up all the things he says he's done and all the places he says he's been to, he'd have received a letter from Buckingham Palace for turning 100 years old, twice!

But he's the man to have on hand at weddings, funerals, parties or wherever a pre-rehearsed or impromptu speech is needed. He'll leap to his feet and jump behind the pulpit at even a glimpse of an opportunity, and usually do himself proud, even if perhaps someone has to give him a not so subtle sign or two that he should bring his discourse to a close.

Divide-by-Tenners also have an uncanny knack of getting away with snide remarks and cheeky gestures, or telling rude jokes in inappropriate circumstances or in front of the wrong people. Yet they always come through unscathed. Whereas Fullas like you or me would be bashed or beaten for saying some of the things they do, or thrown out of the house, office or party for overstepping the mark, people just seem to shrug their shoulders and say, 'That's just how a Divide-by-Tenner is.'

The Divide-by-Tenner is the perfect social lubricant. The 'go to' man when the Fullas are entering foreign ground. Quite literally — he has raconteured all over the world and is the perfect bloke to cut the ice. Given his ability to spin a yarn and talk incessantly, he is a hit with the ladies (fact: women speak at a ratio of 2:1 to men), although once he starts replaying the same story bank, the birds tend to head for the hills. Also, he can only tell women half the stories, which means he can be seen as selfish, given his need to tell the other 50 per cent of his stories to the Fullas, because of some offensive or confidential content.

Clearly, nine times out of 10, the Divide-by-Tenner has drinking issues. This is a classic case of conditioning. Put simply: the pub is the ideal environment for the Divide-by-Tenner to ply his trade. He may also have a predisposition to cannabis, which makes everyone laugh — the perfect setting for any Storyteller. The other benefit of cannabis is that it pokes the short-term memory, so that the same story can be told again soon thereafter.

They will often be smokers, as the act of drawing on a cigarette allows them a pause through which they can read the mood and gather their thoughts. It goes without saying that the best place to see these characters is in the courts, both as lawyers (defence and prosecution) and occasionally on the stand. The best Storytellers enter the advertising and sales and marketing fields, where their ability to bullshit clients, consumers and each other is best rewarded. Occasionally, dull and ordinary Divide-by-Tenners enter the world of politics for short tenures until their fabrications become public at the hands of news writers still smarting from having their only interesting story stolen by a Divide-by-Tenner many years earlier.

Waffle, a Fulla we knew at uni, was the most incredible Divide-by-Tenner, although, astoundingly, he is in denial. (This is also a common occurrence when a Tenner is confronted about his addiction to telling *porkie pies*.) Anyway, we have studied the behaviour of this guy Waffle and noted the following observations consistent with all Divide-by-Tenners.

A mere fraction of the stories they tell directly involved them yet, over time, such is their intoxication with being the communicator (ancient tribes all held in high esteem the Storyteller who talked of history passed down through the generations, chosen for his ability to remove the colouring crayons from his yarn) that they will recount the same tale in the first person by claiming that they were there to witness the incident. If this goes down without recognition they will slip themselves into a more prominent position in the story and from there into the central role.

With the passing of time, they will start to believe their rendition, which will have been overinflated and will now have them in the starring role as the protagonist, and they start telling the overglossed story back to the original character who told them in the first place. Further, if you confront them they will actually fiercely argue that you are wrong, such is their tie and investment in the yarn that they have commandeered.

The New Zealand record for spinning a yarn (and I'm happy to be corrected) was reputedly in 1993 when the notorious aforementioned Divide-by-Tenner, aptly named Waffle, told a story that lasted the length of the road trip from Dunedin to Queenstown (normally three and a half hours without stops). The fact was, however, that Waffle was so intoxicated with his story that on every given opportunity to stop for a beer we did. The trip eventually clocked in at just under seven hours by the time we hit the lake in QT.

Now, obviously, we were not sitting still listening the whole way. There were side conversations and background music, but Waffle was only too happy, when one zoned back into the 'anecdote', to go back to the point where we last zoned out and repeat himself.

As with all Divide-by-Tenners, Waffle was very patient, as he wanted to ensure every last detail was outlined. There were stories within stories, tangents and garden paths with dead-ends during his marathonversation. Sadly, for the life of me, I can't remember the guts of the bloody yarn (see previous comments on cannabis) which will mean that when we next ramble on a road-trip with Waffle, I will no doubt have to endure the damn thing all over again.

The **Old Master** is a veteran version of the Storyteller who has begun to show a few lines, wrinkles and grey streaks in the hair. His stories of the past keep getting bigger and better. The Old Master still cuts the mustard, though, as he has the guile, cunning and street smarts to bury his younger counterparts when it comes to holding the floor. You know exactly the type of Fulla we're talking about!

THE WIDEBOY

Another slightly less likeable version of the Storyteller is the Wideboy. Where the Divide-by-Tenner generally tells stories for the pure entertainment of others, the Wideboy unashamedly spins yarns in an attempt to boost his own massive, yet rather brittle, ego. And Wideboys are all fixated with money, even though every one I've ever met has been as tight as a nun's nasty.

Wideboys think they are as cool as Elvis but are actually about as much fun as a ruck to an unprotected scrotum. Here's a story about a real wanker called Wade the Wideboy. A few of the Fullas and I were sitting in this flash bar in Parnell, when in walked Wade. Now there just happened to be a table of fine-looking young lasses sitting close to the bar, and Wade quickly wasted no time as he spotted his chance to impress them. After ordering a DB Export Dry, he pulled his cell phone out of his pinstriped suit and started talking at the top of his voice about a huge deal he was just about to pull off.

'Mate, once we bank the cheque I'm straight down to the BMW dealer to get myself a Seven Series,' he crapped on. 'And I can't decide if I'm going to buy a bach at Queenstown or Wanaka. You know what? Fuck it! I'll buy one at both.'

And on and on he went with the whole pub listening to the fact that he was just about to broker a deal giving him 'seven figures' until . . . his cover was well and truly blown. His cell phone started to ring, demonstrating that his entire supposed two-way conversation was in fact a one-way farcical charade.

The table of babes were expecting a bottle of champagne I reckon (they should have known better — Wade, like most Wideboys, is so mean he wouldn't shout if he slipped off a cliff). Instead they laughed poor old Wade the Wideboy right out of the bar. No doubt the pub down the road heard the same conversation later that evening — I just hope Wade remembered to turn his phone off this time around.

Unfortunately, where the Divide-by-Tenner's mouth often gets him out of trouble, the Wideboy just can't help putting his foot right in it, winkle-picker shoe and all. This is the principal trait that sets them apart. A few years ago, I was heading up to Waikanae with a Wideboy from Wadestown, whose name eludes me, to do a Master of Ceremonies job that he had asked me to do up there. I had asked my old mate, Trev the Battler, to drive me up there as he had a nasty infection as a result of an unfortunate accident and was on strong antibiotics and so unable to drink and therefore the perfect taxi.

As we got on the main road, a cop coming the other way decided to screw a 'U'ie right in front of us to take off in hot pursuit of a speeding motorist. We were travelling in the outside lane with the Wideboy riding shotgun and as the fuzz came along-side us the Wideboy wound down the window and yelled out, 'Write yourself a fucking ticket!'

Well, this cop had an ego as big and as bold as the siren squealing from under the bonnet of his Falcon, and his attention had now suddenly turned from the speedster to us. And with that, the blue and red lights started flashing and Trev the Battler was signalled to pull over. Once he had approached us, the cop stuck his moustached melon in the window and copped a face full of the Wideboy's smart-arse, barbed attitude. All number of contemptuous questions and caustic comments were fired facetiously at the copper, about our rights, his rights and then in a sarcastic tone he asked, 'What exactly have you pulled us over for — to check the rego and warrant?' And that's exactly what the bluecoat did — and as (bad) luck would have it, Trev the Battler had forgotten that they had both expired the week before and he was promptly fined $360.

For all their misgivings, though, Wideboys are very loyal and devoted to their friends and particularly to their family members. There was a Wideboy, known by us as 'Poppa' — God only knows why as his name was Giorgio, who formed part of the extended Italian community in Wellington. He was spending a brief stint in the slammer as a result of a range of minor indiscretions and run-ins with the law, the latest of which was selling and receiving stolen goods — a gig which had been bringing in a handy little cash-flow, he had told everyone in town, including an off-duty policeman who happened to be at the TAB one afternoon when the Wideboy popped in to put $2 each way on a greyhound that was racing at the Manawatu Raceway. He, like most good Italians, had still been living with his parents, and his Old Boy wrote to him in jail:

Dear Giorgio,

I hope things are good for you in there, Son. I really miss you, I have to say. I'm not going to be able to plant my tomatoes and zucchinis in the veggie garden this year. I am getting too old to dig up the garden. I wish you were here to do it for me as you have the last couple of years.

Love Pops.

After a couple of days, his father received a letter back in the mail early one morning which read:

> Hi Dad,
>
> Whatever you do, don't dig up that garden. That's where the bodies are buried.
>
> I love you, Giorgio.

Later that afternoon several policemen and forensic scientists turned up at Giorgio's Old Fulla's house and dug up the entire back lawn. They found no bodies. They apologised to Giorgio's dad and left. The next day Giorgio's father received another letter saying:

> Hi again, Dad.
>
> You can plant your tomatoes and zucchinis now. This is the best I could do given my current circumstances.
>
> Love as always, Giorgio.

You can instantly tell a Wideboy by his greetings, salutations and particularly his parting farewells. 'See you round like you're bowl-cut', is what he tends to say to a Whippersnapper or a Hopper, 'See you when you're older' is his usual toodle-oo to a Grommit. To other Fullas it'll be 'Smell you later.' And for Fullesses he pulls out 'Taste you later' which goes down like a cup of cold sick, nines times out of 10. Make like a fanny and split, make like Tom and cruise, make like a tree and leave, make like a bird and flock off, make like (the late, great) Michael Jackson and beat it, make like diarrhoea and run, make like a dog and flee, make like a bowel and move, make like Father Christmas and leave our presence, make like a donkey's dick and hit the road, and make like a nut and bolt are all standard swansongs for the Wideboy. And being a dreadful judge of character he will invariably misread his audience and offend all and sundry with his choice of adieu.

The Wideboy delights in smoking where it is plainly prohibited, such as bars restaurants, shops, banks and the like, then expresses surprise and indignation when asked to refrain. He does the same at large public gatherings such as grandstands at sporting events or whenever a crowd draws and where he knows chuffing away on a gasper will get up the noses, literally and figuratively, of the punters. He then unleashes a barrage of abuse at anyone who dares to protest. When feeling particularly vexatious, or in a really crowded area, the Wideboy will spark up a strong-smelling cigar or a potently pungent pipe, just to really cause a furore.

Wideboys are far too tight to buy and maintain a dog, but if they did they'd definitely own a yappy type like a small terrier or an angry corgi.

It's a very smart idea to keep the telephone numbers of the Wideboys you know recorded in your mobile phone. That way you'll know not to answer when they ring. This can save you time and pain. Even when speaking by phone with a Wideboy you can sense he is not listening to a word you are saying and is only waiting for you to shut up so he can talk about himself, which he believes to be far more interesting.

Charlie was talking to a Wideboy the other day who was dropping names willy-nilly and started asking Charlie who he knew. After he'd rattled off a few of Charlie's mates, he said, 'I suppose you know Charlie Haddrell too, do you?' And before Charlie could say a word he'd continued, 'Funny sort of a Fulla, our Charlie, yeah, yeah, nah, we're great mates Charlie and me.' Charlie hadn't even had a chance to probe any further when the Wideboy had ploughed into the next name he could think of.

The Wideboys' fake claims of university degrees and positions they've held which litter their CVs are absolutely classic. With a bit of doctoring of some emblems, coats of arms and certificates that they've found on the internet, they complete an honours degree in about half an hour. A quick flick through some corporate websites and all of a sudden they have held a high-powered position in a blue-chip company.

With the recent trend of potential employers ringing referees for a character check, a Wideboy acquaintance of mine, who I'd love to name and shame, but deep down I admire his gall and balls so won't, even looked up Fullas with the same name (he was blessed with a rather common one) and included some of their education and experience in his own CV. He is now working as a lecturer at a university in Australia in a field that one of his namesakes back here in New Zealand has a degree and a reputation in. Given his gift of the gab and ability to baffle with bullshit, he will have all number of students hanging on his every word, I'm sure.

The CAVE Man

Contrary to what images their title may conjure up, and what you have learned in history classes, CAVE Men are alive and well in New Zealand. If you are a masochist and want to encounter CAVE Fullas (Citizens Against Virtually Everything), all you need to do is try to undertake something seemingly positive in your local community, like opening a low-key eatery in a popular holiday destination, and they will come crawling out like cockroaches from every possible nook and cranny.

My suggestion, though, if you want to save yourselves pain and misery, is to just listen to talk-back — it attracts them like dog-shit does flies — and you can always turn talk-back off once you've suffered through enough bitterness and twistedness being transmitted through the airwaves. If you spot a Fulla with a Green Party supporters' badge or a Greens bumper sticker, it's a pretty good bet you are looking at a CAVE Man. They support the Greens not because they have conservationist values, or a true concern for the planet or humanity, but because it's a great avenue to protest any form of human progress in the name of guardianship.

The CAVE folk seldom, if ever, live in central city areas, preferring to inhabit the outskirts of larger cities with lots of native bush, where they can delight in: bird fancying, tramping, fossil scrounging, growing body hair, scroggin eating and lamenting the imminent carbon and climate-fuelled Armageddon. A large number tend to be itinerant and are attracted to sparsely populated areas where their voice can better be heard, such as the West Coast of the South Island, where the existence of giant wetas, prehistoric snails and big business offer a mouth-watering opportunity to run amuck.

Contrary to popular misconception, they are lazy buggers and prefer to wait for a cause and then gravitate towards it. They tend to be needy folk of frail self-confidence and as such will never act alone — furthermore, doing so would contravene clause 12.A11 of their constitution, stating: *'All decisions will be made by consensus of a group of no fewer in number than three individuals.'* Surprisingly, in a grave oversight in this document, no age limit is imposed on the individuals, giving rise to numerous examples of pre-pubescent children being registered as members of X, Y or Z societies and dragged along to secret meetings with the sole purpose of making up the numbers.

CAVE Fullas take great pleasure in setting up societies and self-proclaimed protectionist organisations, always purporting to represent a much larger portion of society than is the reality and allocating each other overblown titles which allow a feeling of self-importance.

These people exist for one simple reason: as a small country, New Zealand has insufficient news of note and, as such, desperate reporters often accept the free hit of reporting the errant musings of the bell curve's peripheral tenants. This creates a predictable situation where the media seeks to report anything controversial enough to solicit interest among bored and curious citizens who fit within one standard deviation of the mean.

Fortunately, despite their best endeavours to hide behind their society and retain their anonymity, their appearance is so frightfully ghastly as to ensure they offer the average Kiwi Fulla a visual warning to stay clear as obvious as the red stripe on the back of a katipo spider.

In fact, their very appearance summarises them. They are inherently gloomy and will dress, no matter what the weather, to provide safety in case of a shift to inclement weather. By way of example, a typical summer outfit will consist, from bottom up, as follows: knitted, knee-high walk socks; brand-less, nondescript but hard-wearing cross trainers in brown/tan (although they bemoan the short life of their favoured zip-side shoes), or sandals; above the knee walk shorts (often far too tight for comfort); and undoubtedly and invariably with both coin pocket and key clip.

It is worth noting that CAVE Folk, upon meeting one another, make an instant judgement as to the other's importance based on the number of keys hanging from their belts. They will often go to ludicrous lengths to outdo one another.

This peer pressure has led to some overladen CAVE Fullas dragging one leg like a lame farm animal, such is their drive for self-importance. They are likely not to wear a belt as this may inhibit a clear view of their keys. Their shirt will always be short-sleeved and a tie or bow tie will be worn to work, and to any other gathering of perceived importance. All CAVE Men will wear beards (as too do an alarming number of CAVE Women), regardless of how full or wispy their facial follicle growth.

CAVE Men will hate this book. They hate to be stereotyped or pigeonholed. 'Labels are for lentil packets, not people!' they decree. Their mission is to meddle in the lives of normal Fullas to protect these Fullas from themselves. This serves to give CAVE Men purpose, as without us Average Joes to protect their otherwise sterile life would be quite directionless and without cause. While outwardly detesting self-assuredness or ego of any kind, the CAVE Man will religiously snip, cut and record every mention of his name and cause in a scrapbook to be referred to for strength in times of trouble (so this is often daily).

They are also controversially contradictory in their thoughts and behaviour. Charlie and I knew a finicky, nit-picking CAVE Man at varsity, who we won't name so he can't be awarded the satisfaction of appearing in print, who staunchly opposed some of the pubs extending their licences beyond 10 pm. Not only that, he voraciously opposed smoking in public places and used to put up anti-smoking posters throughout the pubs of Dunedin. Well, bugger us! We then saw him at a Values Party demonstration one day, protesting down the main street of Dunedin in a public march to legalise cannabis!

Still, challenges make one stronger, as they say, and that is probably why God scattered CAVE Fullas around the country. Here are a few other pesky nitwits and bothersome buffoons that I've come across that can be classed under the CAVE Men umbrella of Fulla.

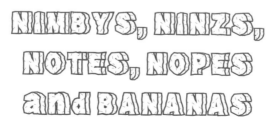

NIMBYS, NINZS, NOTES, NOPES and BANANAS

Several unfortunate species of CAVE critters proliferated under the Labour Government of the late 90s and early 2000s, the NIMBY (Not In My Back Yard) being the most common of them. NIMBYs object to anything that may be of benefit to anyone else but themselves, happening anywhere near them and will poop a party at every given opportunity. Their narrow, myopic views are the bane of property developers, telecommunications companies, utility companies and average Toms, Dicks and Harrys the length and breadth of New Zealand. NIMBYs can become so meddling they become NOTEs (Not Over There Either), NINZs (Not in New Zealand) or even NOPEs (Not On Planet Earth). And an extremist NIMBY graduates into a BANANA (Build Absolutely Nothing Anywhere Near Anything). A BANANA's motive to block any project whatsoever is not one of conservation or the preservation of nature as we are led to believe — but one of an abhorrence of seeing anybody achieve anything, especially something that might be a financially fruitful venture.

Now it's important to note that not all NIMBYs are NINZs, NOTEs, NOPEs or BANANAs, but all NIMBYs, NINZs, NOPEs, NOTEs and BANANAs are CAVE Men.

A meddlesome NIMBY called Nathan, who lives in Central Otago, specialises in objecting to any object or building, whether on private or public land, that does not fit within the natural colour palate of the native flora and fauna, or the dimensional shape of the prevalent geographic forms.

In layman's terms, Nigel spends his time and a considerable amount of the taxpayers' money stopping the public erecting sculptures, buildings or public amenities on any land, especially their own, unless it is painted a certain colour and is of a certain shape.

Just how Nathan reached such a low point begs speculation. It would, I suggest, be not too far from the mark to surmise that Nathan is an English immigrant (they are born whinging) who was the youngest child of a dominant mother and an effeminate father, and who, as a direct result of being bottle fed, has craved attention from a young age.

Sadly, his father was so brow-beaten by his mother, who among other undesirable traits had been in a hidden lesbian relationship before the accident that brought Nathan into this world, that he divorced himself, figuratively, from the family and spent most of Nathan's young life locked up downstairs playing with model trains and tunnels and toy soldiers — which he enviously admired for their tie to a masculinity he had not so secretly longed for.

Malnourished in much the same manner as the runt of the animal litter, Nathan the NIMBY spent his youth day-dreaming and fantasising about being a Sergeant-Major in the army, which given his frail disposition was patently absurd. He found an affinity with the impractical sciences such as astrology and genealogy and always liked the outdoors, which for about 10 days over the English summer could actually be enjoyed. When he talked, no one listened. When he liked someone, the feeling was not mutual. And when he was told that the family were moving to New Zealand, he felt nothing.

His twenties in New Zealand were non-eventful. So, too, his thirties. His social highlight consisted of visiting the public library where he studied, among other things, the migratory patterns of the monarch butterfly and the breeding challenges of the South Island high country tahr. He loved reading community papers and this is where he found a number of not-for-profit organisations advertising for assistance. He headed along to an interview with a like-minded NIMBY, who actually could have passed for his brother, such was the resemblance both physically and attitudinally, and was offered what appeared to be his dream job.

And so started the working life of Nathan. It did not start as he had envisaged, though, because given his lust for attention he raised the ire of this NPO by offering to hire a function room, where they might run a dinner with guest speaker and a silent (so that people could retain their anonymity rather than bid publicly) auction to raise funds for the 'COTTPS' (Central Otago Tom Tit Protection Society). This big-headed attempt at grandstanding in his first three years was preposterous and he was asked to leave.

He did so begrudgingly and went into a deep depression, having lost those who he quite correctly thought were his only friends. A year or so later, still smarting with bitterness towards the group that disowned him, he set about carving his own nettlesome niche and decided upon colours and dimensions of native flora and fauna being as good a reason as any to protest development. Motivated by column inches, taxpayer dollars spent and the number of citizens hamstrung by his intrusive provocation, Nathan the NIMBY has at last found an opportunity to be remembered. (It is interesting to note that although he fronts as a Kakapo

Cuddler he is, in fact, botanically and ecologically illiterate.)

Nathan's case is typical of the 'drawbridge effect', in which people migrate to an area and then campaign against any change whatsoever — including accepting other inward migrants. It's rather extraordinary to hear Nathan, in his broad Geordie accent, lament the effects of immigration on New Zealand's culture and environment. Even more staggering is listening to him get stuck into Poms, who he blames for all the world's wrongs. (He may be on the money there actually — it's just that it's a bit rich coming from someone who hails from Newcastle upon Tyne.) He is an active member of Neighbourhood Watch, reporting anyone looking suspicious or not from the area to the Fuzz, and was a strong proponent of recycling all waste. Yet, discrepantly, he refuses to allow any new prisons or rubbish dumps in Central Otago. In fact he doesn't want any further development at all.

A group of CAVE Men from a left-wing university that I won't name, but I'm sure you can guess which it is, even tried to ban Christmas, such was their loathing of seeing people enjoy themselves. Their reason was that it may offend atheists, pagans, Jews, Muslims, Hindus, Buddhists and other non-Christians, who they say, as a combined group, are actually a majority. But, even the people whose views they were supposedly fighting to have heard took offence and disagreed with their plan, saying that it was a time to spend with family and was of particular enjoyment for children.

So the bloody CAVE Men turned on parents as a group and even had a crack at children, calling them irresponsible for leaving brandy and biscuits for Father Christmas. The CAVE Men claimed that Santa would then drive pissed, if he had a tipple at the bottom of every chimney, and that the parents were promoting obesity by filling him full of cookies. They didn't stop there — they went after Father Christmas too, claiming he was cruel to animals. 'Treats his deer like shit,' they reckoned, 'setting a bad example for those who are responsible for the welfare of animals. And doesn't give them sufficient bio-breaks or pay them time and a half on their route around the world on Christmas Eve.' Thank God common sense prevailed.

But CAVE Men have their place here in New Zealand. They can give lost souls a feeling of inclusion. They keep hundreds of lawyers, who would otherwise be out of work, employed. They also keep Cardycrats occupied by lobbying and petitioning for all number of issues of 'public' interest. And when they finally track down the last moa, which all CAVE Men believe is out there, it will be them laughing last and loudest with a daft, bothersome, snorting chortle.

The Scarfie

The Scarfie is a scruffy, silly, scallywaggy student, usually living in self-chosen squalor in the suburbs of the North East Valley or North Dunedin. Despite spending six years completing a three-year degree, showering only a handful of times during that period, and living on a sole diet of Speight's, Huttons Cheese Sizzlers, tea and toast, the Scarfie will invariably become a very successful entrepreneur.

Responsibility is shirked by the Scarfie and study takes a back seat to having as much fun as is humanly possible in an effort to create as many stories as one possibly can to then share with those who also experienced them or who can share similar stories, during the rest of the Fulla's lifetime.

Dressing down is the best way to describe the Scarfie's fashion sense and generally acting (and complaining about being) poor best explains their demeanour — although interestingly enough they always seem to have enough beer money.

A true Scarfie will drive a Holden or Falcon of at least 25 years of age and if he wants *real* street cred his mode of vehicular transport will be Valiant. The logic behind this is simple. Despite the increase in petrol costs, any of the aforementioned vehicles will fit six grown men for a roadtrip and can sleep three comfortably — one on each bench seat and the lucky one in the boot.

The Scarfies who probably best fit the stereotype were my old mate Sam and the six Scarfie flatmates he lived with at Sifterosa, a condemned five-bedroomed flat in Castle Street. Sam and the Fullas used to undertake some downright grotesque acts, in an attempt to outdo Sam's older cousins' stories from Lincoln and Massey. I can't for the life of me remember the real names of his flatmates but they went by the handles: Crusty, Sniff, Slippery, Skank, Digger and Sifty. Seven boys into five bedrooms may sound like quite a mess but it was like musical beds in there and Sam joked he spent most nights playing 'away games' anyway.

Crusty's favourite party trick was the pelican, and he preferred to receive rather than give, because it was the more shocking of the two components of the routine. (Ask a Scarfie if you are not aware of the pelican.)

Skank used his own pubic hair, or some he would randomly find in the shower, as dental floss. He was often seen consuming the contents of a full ashtray of butts, gum and gunk as a bet for a free jug of piss at the Gardie's Tavern midweek.

Digger was a master of spadework and claimed to have laid over 50 girls in his first year in Otago. He achieved his Hocken wings several times over and rumour has it he even had a root in the professors' dining room. But his boldest claim is to have got one away in the Clock Tower, so that every time he sees a picture of Otago University he has fond memories. Now that's good foresight!

Sifty smoked obscene amounts of weed, but was blessed with an exceptionally high IQ and, even though he wagged most lectures and tutorials, with one day's swot managed to get B+s in all subjects and act as tutor to the rest of the flat in all subjects, even those he was not sitting.

Sniff was a quieter Fulla and I'm not sure if his moniker came about from the fact that he always had a runny nose or because of his rather odd habit of sneaking into girls' flats and rummaging through their drawers and dirty laundry baskets.

Slippery was something of a criminal, but made shed-loads of friends due to his monthly 'bacon heist' where he would steal an entire industrial fridge worth of meat from some unsuspecting local Dunedin butcher and sell it to his mates at heavily discounted prices. Sam and the boys learned from Slippery that to get free bacon you just slip a couple of packs into the kleensacks at the supermarket so the checkout girl misses them on the way through. (This stunt became a little trickier with the introduction of bar codes and scanners in the nineties.)

Slippery also supplemented his income nicking books from the varsity library and selling them to the campus Norks. He flogged bottles of milk from letterboxes soon after it was delivered, siphoned his petrol from the good folk up on Maori Hill, fleeced tools from unlocked garden sheds, pinched pies from pie-warmers, pick-pocketed cigarettes (and lighters) from unsuspecting patrons at pubs, and as far as I am aware never paid for anything, ever. But his greatest heist actually happened quite by accident. As he walked home from south of the Octagon he came across a butcher's truck filling up a store at 4 am loaded with mutton and beef sides. Slippery, Sam and some mates fleeced two sheep and the bulk of a cattle-beast and managed to drag them into an alley behind the Speight's Brewery. The boys then bolted home and grabbed Sam's Kingswood station wagon and loaded up. Predictably, the heist made the news so the boys promptly had a pretty big barbecue, with everyone invited, to get rid of any incriminating evidence.

Slippery, the lucky bugger, also once stumbled across a brewery truck delivering kegs while on a weekend mission in Christchurch with Sam and managed to pilfer two kegs of Carlsberg eight per cent Elephant beer. He raced back to his mates' (Lincoln students) flat and hid them in the garage. There were two problems with this score. Firstly, they had been seen and, secondly, they had not grabbed a keg pump. News travelled fast and the local constabulary rang the house after being tipped off to Sam's orange Kingswood station wagon parked outside, which fitted the description of the one seen fleeing the scene. Clearly, they denied any knowledge and were then left with the need to destroy the evidence before the boys in blue paid them a visit — and quickly. Their plan was brilliant and simple. They raced out and bought two small trees and buried the kegs in the back yard with the bushes as markers. A few months later when the coast was clear they dug them up for a knees-up. The second problem of the pump was overcome with an axe and they all lived happily ever after. As Sam often said, 'Adversity breeds genius and the sun shines on the righteous.'

However, Sam the Scarfie is a rather injury-prone Fulla. One of the more memorable examples of this unfortunate characteristic, which is indelibly etched into my memory, was when Sam, attempting to do a Luke Duke of Hazard slide across the bonnet of his HQ Holden in an effort to impress the ladies, misjudged his dismount and impaled himself sphincter first onto the rusty windscreen wiper, which pierced his anus and caused some severe bleeding.

He refused to go to Accident & Emergency that evening and, my word, his rissole was a terribly sorry sight the next day, when Sniff, who was studying medicine, examined the aftermath of the nasty incident combined with the effect that eight litres of Speight's has on the texture of one's stool. Sam, the poor rooster, once attempted to karate kick a fence paling down after a few other Fullas had successfully done so, only to have the paling snap in two halfway through the act and to land on the sharp edge of the snapped piece, which slid right up his inner thigh and came to an abrupt halt in his groin as he pole-vaulted on it. The resultant splinters in the most uncomfortable of places rendered him useless for the best part of a week. The common thread again was that he was three-quarters to the wind and refused any medical treatment until the next morning.

To add to his propensity for self-harm, Sam the Scarfie also has a slight speech impediment, caused indirectly as a result of his six or seven years of hard binge drinking at such infamous establishments as the Garden's Sports Tavern, the Captain Cook, the Oriental, The Bowling Green and other such iconic Otago institutions. His impediment is not caused, however, by an excessive intake of alcohol and the effects this has on one's brain, but instead from the callousy scar tissue formed on the tip of his tongue and the roof of his mouth from years of biting into piping hot steak and cheese pies from the Regent Street 24-hour dairy or Georgie Pie when pissed as a parrot at 3 am and sizzling his palate.

A Scarfie's flat runs short of all food and household supplies on a regular basis, everything, that is, except tea and toast bread — of which there is always an abundance. It was estimated, in a study undertaken by some students at the Otago Polytechnic, I believe, that an average of over 350 cups of tea are prepared each month in each of the flats of North Dunedin. And the same study suggests that only about 200 of these are actually drunk. Tiger Tea is the brand of choice, and every marketing student worth his salt has worked through the 'What? No Tiger?' case study — the moral of the story being the worse the advertisement, the more it sticks in consumers' minds.

Scarfies' pyromaniac antics have been well highlighted in the press. Most people in New Zealand have seen footage of a burning sofa at Carisbrook and a bunch of Scarfies with a can of Speight's in one hand and a can of petrol in the other. Everyone who's studied in Dunedin will have a funny fire story or two. Here's one of mine: As I mentioned, Sifterosa was condemned and deemed unfit for residential use. Part of the report stated that the floor structure of the second storey was so unstable that filling the bath in the upstairs bathroom could mean that it would come crashing down into the kitchen below. So rather than waste a good enamelled cast iron bath, one Saturday morning Sam the Scarfie and the Fullas dragged it downstairs, out through the hallway and into the garden out the back.

It was no coincidence that they had organised a cold start dinner for that evening and I had kindly been asked to participate. And I didn't need a second invitation. A cold start dinner consists of inviting a member of the opposite sex, with whom you have never spoken in your life, to dinner. To break the ice, silly games such as pass the ice (by mouth) or (sometimes nude) twister are played. Well, the Fullas had a little plan to warm up the cold Otago evening and keep things up-vibe and interesting. They lit a small bonfire under the bath, and once the beer and the wine had loosened everybody up, they suggested that random couples take turns in the bath.

The timing was impeccable. The evening had gone a little flat and the Fullas were wondering if they were going to get any action or whether the evening might peter out and everyone was to go to bed empty-handed. Digger confidently announced, 'For an occasion [pronouncing it in his Gore accent 'fornication'] like this, we need to keep warm and clean. Everyone in the bath!' One of the girls generously took it upon herself to peel off her clothes, get starkers and jump into the bath first, which I estimate to have been a steamy 60 degrees hot. Digger wasted no time, and within 10 seconds flat was wearing nothing but a smile and climbing in to join the rosy-cheeked lass in the tub.

Within a flash Slippery and Sniff had got cosy with a couple of the Scarfesses they had taken a shine to and were undressing themselves and the girls as fast as they could. Skank and Sifty realised that not everyone was going to be able to bathe at the same time so they knocked a few wooden palings out of the picket fence at the front of Sifterosa and started a bonza of a bonfire to stop the night's nippy air playing havoc with everyone's nipples. Before you knew it there were knickers, knackers and knockers everywhere and a beautiful night of peace, love and warmth ensued. It was finally ended when the Good Fullas from the Dunedin Fire Brigade turned up to put the fire out. It wasn't a problem; we had all let off a bit of steam by then. And I feel obliged to add that on this particular occasion, we were careful not to throw the babes out with the bathwater.

Of course, the other serious half to being a Scarfie, as any Otago student will attest — is study. When finals (exams) roll around, and it's time to get the head down and the books out, the best place to study is at the university libraries where you are close to text books and other students who have notes that can be borrowed. The hardest challenge in this environment, however, is to find a quiet seat where you can study, as every available seat is already taken at some ungodly hour every morning by the resident Norks and other cramming swotters. This usually leads to some creative thinking, the best example of which was pulled off by a Fulla called the 'Ginger Camel'.

Now this guy was a thinker who hated to play by the rules. I nicknamed him the Evil Genius. He had noticed that there were special rooms dedicated to handicapped students which had their own cubicles, good lighting, sponged seating and a locked door to ensure no interruptions. They were superbly quiet and were usually half full at best. Having witnessed this, the Ginger Camel could not get it out of his mind that the best room in the library was half empty, close to everything and that you could be guaranteed a seat at any time of day, which met well with his sleeping habits.

All he needed to do was find out the punch code to the lock. This was easily achieved, as he just sat outside the door pretending to read a book and waited for one of the disabled students to come to the door. He then wrote down the code and cunningly shot off to a printer to get some business cards printed. The next day and for days after that, he was in the best seat in the house in preparation for his end of year exams. Of course, all good things should come to an end, and one day a staff member came into the room, having been tipped off by an internal nark (who happened, of course, to also be a Nork). He asked the Ginger Camel for his ID and was ignored. He asked louder and was again ignored. He then grabbed him by the shoulder, to which he was met with a very loud *uuuuggggggghhhhhh* noise and a blank stare. The staff member again asked for his ID and the Camel reached into his wallet and pulled out a business card and handed it to the bloke, who upon reading it apologised and left the room never to bother him again. 'What did the card say?' I hear you ask:

'I am hearing impaired, please speak loudly and directly at my face. Thank you.'

I told you he was an evil genius! Last I heard he was working for one of the world's leading banks somewhere in Europe.

At the other end of the scale was a Scarfie called 'Mud', named as such because everything he touched turned into it. Mud was a Battler of the finest order. He once bought a car from Turners Auctions and went round the corner to the pub to show it to the lads and had three beers in quick succession before driving 500 metres home. He got pulled over and blew 408 micrograms and lost his licence for six months. He reckoned that the car he had bought was so cool, he was going to wait it out without selling it, only to then have it borrowed by some passers-by one

Friday night and for it to turn up a few days later in the Leith River. What's worse, he didn't find it for a whole day and night and all the while it had been raining and the river had been rising.

When he found it, the thing was two-thirds under water. He had it pulled out of the drink by a local towie and tried to start it which had the effect of sucking a huge amount of water, with what little petrol was left, through the motor. He left it sitting outside his flat and after six months the motor had rusted on the inside and was shot to bits. A wrecker agreed to give him $20 for it, but then charged him $50 to tow it away!

He had a girlfriend who came over one night and fell for his flatmate. He missed every exam in his first year by no more than three per cent, yet did not know that if he had applied for impairment they would give him a three per cent margin to play with, which would have got him through all six subjects that year. He sent a look-alike in to sit his exam and got busted. His room got knocked off by some Bogan when he was back doing specials (catch-up exams in January) and he broke his leg after slipping on black ice while showing off to some bird he fancied after class. Last I heard of him he was selling Japanese imports on the Gold Coast. I only hope his luck is changing.

Sam, on the other hand, has fallen on his feet. I caught up with him again recently, and after we shared a few old Scarfie war stories, he told me what he'd been up to since we had last had a beer together about 15 years prior. He had headed over to the UK and via the network of the Scarfie Mafia resident in London had landed a job in banking where he did Sweet Fanny Adams but got paid silly amounts. He then got a transfer to Shanghai (not a bad move apparently as his health had deteriorated as a result of the poor English weather and poor English food and his habit of over-indulging in disco biscuits and depriving himself of sleep) and again did bugger all but made a mint doing it.

He freighted his belongings back here a few years ago and bought a nice house, flash car and a successful little importing business and lives a great Kiwi life. He's taking an active interest in politics and I wouldn't be at all surprised if he makes a good fist of it, in the not too distant future (I only hope they don't go digging for dirt, because there are some silly stories about him that some may not find that amusing . . .).

Like Sam, there are many ex-Scarfies all over the country and they are much the better Fulla for having been through the Scarfie experience. And we are all the luckier to have them around.

THE NORK

A Nork is a general term for a class of Kiwi Fulla who is peculiar, socially challenged and overly obsessed or fascinated with technology, science, electronics, gaming or other such intellectual pursuits or narrowly focused areas of knowledge or expertise. Quite often these interests can be purely and wholly imaginary or virtual.

The sub-groups of Nork are the Geek, the Nerd, the Dweeb, the Twerp and the Dork (with respective IQs of 140, 120, 100, 80 and 60), and most Norks can be pigeonholed as one of the aforementioned, with varying degrees of the other category traits mixed in to their persona. They are always pasty and pale and either extremely skinny or conversely very fat, sometimes even verging on obese and often with unfortunately placed feminine body-fat deposits — a bit like a 3 am hourglass. They are always desperately unathletic and frightfully uncoordinated. Many even have an allergy to the sun. Invariably, they wear glasses which are usually as thick as the base of a 750 ml bottle of Speight's. They have such limited social skills, due to their isolated existence, that having left home (often in their mid thirties), and Mum's cooking, they live exclusively on a diet that can be ordered online.

If you want to wind up any of the above group of Norks to the edge of sanity, a very cruel trick to play is to destroy their fuse box. It is not uncommon for the Nork to become physical when his power supply is interrupted. This is a high-risk strategy, as if you got planted by an irate Nork, it could be incredibly embarrassing, as clearly one cannot retaliate, governed by the same rules that apply to women or children.

Norks can be found all over New Zealand, but given their rather reclusive lifestyle they can best be found in cyberspace or at any electronics store (which often happen to be their employers of choice). Though normally loners, outside of the virtual world, Norks' big events on the social calendars revolve around gaming and, in particular, mass gaming challenges. These usually involve world record sleepovers for bespectacled pimply teens participating in mass participation record attempts usually for games such as Age of Empires.

Gone are the days of a pinball challenge with the winner worthy of a crown most would aspire to. These arrow-witted youths are at the forefront of man's development and will undoubtedly be responsible for keeping up with the expansion of China and India, who have an extraordinarily high number of Norks wearing their fingers to nubs in the pursuit of first-world Nork status.

You can identify a Nork by the multicoloured biro pen he carries in the top pocket of his nondescript shirt, enabling him to multi-task. But the Nork is not at all interested in his physical appearance, because: (a) the Nork is not at all interested in his physical appearance, and (b) because he has many different avatars which are the most amazing physical specimens — monuments of athleticism and aesthetic beauty. In layman's terms, an avatar is an imaginary representation of the Nork's alter ego in his pseudo cyber-world.

Most of the more advanced massively multiplayer online role-playing games (or MAMMORPGs in Norkspeak) come with sophisticated software that allows the avatar to be created with unique facial structures, body types, hairstyles, skin colours, tattoos, dress, skill-sets and even personality traits. The latest rage in MAMMORPGs is the World of Warcraft (WoW), a highly addictive game in which the highest-ranked Norks receive massive credibility among the wider Nork community. WoW Norks can be easily spotted by their long, dark trench-coats, which they wear religiously, regardless of the time of day, or time of year, and by their clear signs of sleep deprivation as a direct result of all-night sessions of WoW 'questing'.

Philosophically speaking (in Nork vernacular lexicon), a Nork is an archetypal designation referring to *Homo sapiens* with a prolonged pursuit of cerebral and esoteric concernments, particularly in the fields of written matter, both fictional and non-fictional and both printed and digital.

But not all Norks are created equal:

- **Nerds** are totally preoccupied with trivial academic pursuit.

- **Geeks** (these days quite a compliment denoting an extraordinary technical skill) are Nerds who have honed their Norkiness to their advantage.
- **Dweebs** are Nerds who have managed to attract a phenomenally beautiful female partner by being extremely well endowed in the pelvic girdle, or Geeks who have managed the same feat by making silly amounts of money utilising their Geekiness.
- **Dork** is really the only true derogatory classification of Nork. Dorks are socially inept, physically and intellectually challenged, and only interested in comic books and *Star Trek*. They often carry a nasty, complex chip around on their sloping shoulders.
- A **Twerp** is a cumbersome, gawky, ungainly, maladroit and awkward Nork (but decidedly more pleasant than a Dork).

In my schooldays the Nork sub-genuses hadn't split to form five scientifically separate species. However, with the advent of the PC, and in later years the internet and rapid progression of telecommunications, the Nork and its taxonomic categories have really found their niche place in the world. When it comes to 'hireability', Norks with a larger percentage of Geek in them are often highly sought after for their technical prowess.

Norks with a higher Nerd ratio in them have the technical skills but lack the ability to communicate with anyone other than a fellow Nork. Those Norks with a Dork- or Twerp-dominant personality are usually just shit out of luck when it comes to jobs, and resort to pounding the pavements as metre-maids, parking wardens or other professions where little or no social interaction is required (or desired) by the employee.

This is quite a curious situation as obviously the respective city councils, from experience, have a 50–50 split of Norks and Neanderthals. This is quite genius, as both have a diametrically opposed technique of negotiating with frustrated drivers, with the Nork clearly referring to the letter of the law and corresponding clauses of illegality, and the Neanderthal negotiating in silence with an impersonation of Lou Ferrigno. (As any Cocky will tell you, this is similar, in fact, to the eye dog and huntaway styles of sheepdog mustering.)

A guy I went to varsity with, Neville the Nork, has the special ability to drift off and disappear into his own special dreamy world in cyberspace, far from the rigours of reality in the real world. He feels much more at home in Second Life than he does in his first life. Harry Potter, Dungeons and Dragons and increasingly the World of Warcraft offer so much more adventure, and a feeling of being, than Wellington does. When Charlie and I caught up for a beer or three to discuss the Nork, we were remembering how Neville the Nork used to take academic theory and apply it to the simplest daily chores. Rumour has it he used multivariate calculus to work out how to maximise the set out of his bedroom for optimum productive studying.

A few of our mates in Dunedin flatted with another unfortunate Nork by the name of Julius. Julius had a phenomenally high IQ and while he was quite antisocial, his EQ was remarkably high too. Without ever showing too much emotion, he would readily help the rest of the boys (four Rugbyheads with little interest in academic pursuit or, to be fair, anything which required effort outside of rugby) with their study, essays and other homework. Poor little Julius was the only one who did any sort of housework too, and he lost out substantially when it came to paying the bills. He was half the size (and I mean that literally because he would have been, at a stretch, 50 kilos) and yet went fifths in the enormous food bills the other Fullas would rack up. They constantly had dirty rugby gear in the washing machine and dryer and so used all of the electricity too.

What was worse was that Julius was one of the first Fullas in Dunedin to have his own computer — and it came equipped with one of the early versions of Microsoft Office. Julius generously taught his flatmates how to use the computer and let them use it when he was not. His generosity was repaid by some sloppy computer etiquette. One of the Fullas spilt a full bottle of Speight's over the keyboard (he had been using the CD drive as a drink holder!). The others served up some serious mistreatment to his PC too.

Julius' patience finally wore thin. He set up an 'auto-correct function' in Word, changing the words *what* and *that* to *twot* and *twat*, ruining a couple of the Fullas' essays in the process. He then took a screenshot of his desktop, and saved it as his screensaver, meanwhile removing all the icons. The Footyhead Fullas nearly went mad when nothing they clicked on worked.

Given their strong preference for staying indoors, Norks suffer quite seriously from vitamin D deficiency, through a lack of direct contact with sunlight. This should not be a problem for them for much longer, however. A highly ambitious group of Norks plan to work closely with the University of Canterbury (UC) and the Institute of Environmental Science and Research (ERS), a Crown Research Institute (CRI), to develop a system of emitting ultraviolet B (UVB) radiation from the liquid crystal displays screens (LCDs) of personal computers (PCs). The UVB radiation is emitted at wavelengths of approximately 265 nanometres, which penetrates the epidermal strata of the skin, engendering vitamin D in both the stratum basale and the stratum spinosum which in turn promotes phagocytosis, a food vacuole or pteroid form of endocytosis, involving the vesicular internalisation of particles and liquids in those that have been exposed to the radiation. In technical terms what this means is that Norks will be able to get a screen tan from their computers.

Hackers are a rather nasty form of Nork, wreaking havoc with servers around the country and abroad. New Zealand is blessed (or otherwise) to be famed for one of the world's most infamous hackers, Akill. As a testament to the 'hireability' of the more geeky of the Norks, Akill, who devised and developed a virus which beat all anti-virus software and destroyed the bot codes of well over a million computers worldwide, has recently been hired by one of New Zealand's biggest telecommunications utilities to formulate security software for the company.

Another annoying form of Nork is the **Spammer**. Once again New Zealand has one of the best known Spammers on the planet. In fact this Kiwi Spammer, called Lance, holds the world record for the largest ever fine, when he was ordered to pay NZ$25 million by the US Federal Trade Commission for advertising bogus penis enlargement drugs by email. What a horrible Fulla! Little wonder he targeted the Americans, really. They must be making up for some deficiency with the trillions they allocate to rockets, war heads, battle ships and fighter planes.

Most Norks have the displeasure of being virgins until well into their twenties. This is a direct result of their unsightly and disagreeable physical aspect, severe problems with acne, antisocial behaviour and often just a general lack of interest in the fairer sex. Of course there are a few who buck this trend — almost exclusively Dweebs — and manage to attract only the most beautiful of the opposite gender, leading to the well documented 'Babe with Dweeb' syndromic phenomenon.

In latter years, however, the Geekier of the Norks have managed to attain a phenomenal success rate with the ladies. This is directly correlated to their earning power and in the digital age this has skyrocketed exponentially. You see, the Dorkier and Twerpier of the Norks play and read pointless trivia like games and comics. And the Geekier, Nerdier and (surprisingly often) Dweebier of the Norks invent and develop pointless trivia like games and comics. And then get rich on the profits. In some industries Geek is now a title of honour, and with that comes power. Norks are very aware that power is only second to money when it comes to pulling skirt and some of them have used both of these to great effect, and managed to pull some enviable trophies.

The Nork is a very useful ally to several of the Fullas as well. Scarfies rely on Norks to help them with assignments and examinations. Prankers get them to prepare over-the-top presentations solely to impress a target audience (and although they will never, ever publicly acknowledge that a Nork prepared the presentation, they'll reimburse him generously). Cardycrats enlist their help to flesh out worthless reports, which are then never read by anybody. And Finkles just plain fantasise over the magnitude of their intellectual grunt.

If and when befriending a Nork, always attempt to ascertain their field of expertise — and if possible learn the Latin term for it. That'll really open them up, and they'll let their defences down and warm to you. Geeks and Nerds, and even a few Dweebs, will be fluent in Leet, which is an indecipherable language known only to Norks and used in the virtual realms of Norkdom. But don't attempt to speak it with them. They are even more defensive than the French when it comes to others butchering their language and will only scoff even at an honest attempt to speak it.

The beauty of a Nork is that they usually take great pride in exactly what they are and what they represent and are not the slightest bit tied up with superficial worries or hang ups. There's no ambition to climb up the social ladder and no ego to be bruised in everyday life (barring of course the Dweeb whose sole focus is scoring pussy, and the only way he can do that is by reaching the top).

A Nork is a mother-in-law's dream, because they are generally very polite and always remember birthdays and anniversaries. That, and the fact they can always act as the ambulance at the bottom of the hill when you lose that precious document, or want the annoying tracked changes in a Word document to disappear but don't know how to do it. It's also totally staggering what a Nork can do with some raw data and an Excel spreadsheet.

Ever had the feeling that your computer thinks it knows better than you do and insists on formatting a programme against your will? Well, Geeks (and a large percentage of Nerds also) actually know even better than the computer. Use them. They're good.

THE ADRENALINE JUNKY

Adrenaline Junkies (AJs) are those Fullas who have an addiction to the fight or flight response that the body produces as a reaction to situations of extreme fear. They enjoy being on the edge at all times and actively seek activities that create a spike of epinephrine release from the adrenal glands — activities which usually involve extreme heights or extreme speeds or both. Jumping, climbing, diving, sliding, flying, riding, driving, it doesn't matter; as long as the heart is pumping, the chest is tight, the bladder relaxed, the colon evacuated, the forehead a bit sweaty and they get the odd facial twitch — then the AJ is a happy Fulla.

Most Adrenaline Junkies are mountain men. And they just love mountin' women. So it's only natural that the majority of AJs are found in or around Queenstown. It attracts them like bees to honey. The mountains in Queenstown seem to create a sensation of closing in on them and this tends to make the AJ go a tad mad. And the adventure tourism buses (or Vagina Liners as most AJs refer to them as) bring a steady flow of excitable young women into the valleys of Wakatipu for the AJ to hunt and conquer.

The original and most internationally well-known Adrenaline Junky is AJ Hackett. He's called AJ, not because (coincidentally) his Christian names are Alan John, but because he's a 24-carat, authentic, true blue, pure-bred Adrenaline Junkie. He brought bungee jumping to the world. But, for him, just plummeting towards the earth tied to a rubber band wasn't enough. He needed more thrill. Initially, he had to add some extra anxiety into the equation to heighten the experience. First of all he bungeed at night, plunging 320 or so feet into the darkness from a disused rail bridge. Then he decided to leap off the Eiffel Tower and hightail away from the Froggie Gendarmes just for added excitement and entertainment. Next, he leapt from a helicopter with the extra challenge of dodging the rotor blades so as not to get minced like meat in a blender. Then he decided, like a Good Fulla, to commercialise it so we could all test our mettle and leap like lunatics.

There are quite a few Adrenaline Junkies going around, but none as authentic as the AJ from Glenorchy that Charlie and I got to know in Dunedin who went by the pseudonym Mad-dog. Mad-dog was into anything that got the butterflies in the stomach fluttering. Basically, all of his pastimes brought him face to face with the possibility of some serious maiming or, God forbid, a fatal end. 'You've gotta die of something,' he reckoned, 'so it oughtta be something exciting.' Like all good AJs, Mad-dog wore a 'pussy tickler' tuft under his bottom lip and seemed to have a backpack sewn into his back.

Mad-dog had to always be on the edge. Always. His behaviour and attitude could be described as furious, feverish, fervent, frantic, frenzied and frenetic. For example, after a weekend of sky-diving or parapenting back in Queenstown, he'd fill his boot up with a couple of sacks of weed, not just to make some money by flogging it off to Scarfies, but more for the exhilaration of driving back to Dunnos knowing that if he were stopped by the Fuzz, he'd be fucked.

However, I'm sure the cash-flow did help finance his motor racing interests and other extreme sports activities. And he certainly didn't need the weed for his own personal consumption, because every time he'd fling himself out of a plane, or run off the edge of a cliff, he'd trigger a rush of natural hormones and chemicals which gave him a far better hit than any recreational drug possibly could. To heighten the angst of the trip, he'd disconnect the sender unit on the petrol gauge so he'd never know how much petrol he'd have in the tank then play 'chicken' with himself and take a gamble on which petrol station he needed to stop at.

To get himself through the mundane Dunedin winter of studying, in an attempt to get his adrenaline fix and halt the craving for exhilaration, he'd volunteer as a fireman just to have the chance to enter a flaming building and experience back-draught, he'd clean the windows of the highest buildings or dredge the deepest drains in the city, he'd gamble, play paint-ball warfare or do anything palpitating, solely to get charged and maintain a tumultuous lifestyle.

Mad-dog also brought hyper-arousal into his relationships. He'd always start arguments with his girlfriends just for the stimulation of the conflict and the drama. And for extreme titillation, he'd often be running two or three girlfriends at a time, not because he was addicted to women or rooting, as such, but more for the buzz of playing one off against the other with the danger of getting busted while juggling dates. When not moving at extreme pace, he'd be hanging in cafés, drinking two shots of coffee an hour just to spike the caffeine rushes, and flicking through photos of fellow AJs in action, looking for ideas and inspiration for his next adventure.

It's hardly surprising that Mad-dog was fully bald by the time he held his twenty-first party — which was quite a roarer, I can tell you!

It'd be fair to say that most Kiwi Fullas have a fair pinch of Bogan and most too have a good portion of AJitis. In particular the rural set, who have an array of boys' toys from motor/quad bikes to jet boats. It's not entirely unusual to see a car doing paddock work after a hoar frost, dragging a rural AJ clad only in sacks. Or a quad bike dragging a skier down an irrigation canal.

One rural AJ game, created by 'Honk' Rogers from around Central Otago, is a vehicular version of curling called 'quadling', whereby four blokes grab their quad bikes and head to an iced-over lake. It's best not to listen to Honk, who insists on doing this with a skinful of single malt (which is understandable for curling as it's so bloody boring).

The aim of the game is to get the bike up to speed, drive onto the ice, lock the brakes before the start line and slide towards the bulls-eye some 50 to 60 metres away. The bikes go one after the other and more often than not make contact in the attempt to knock each other out of the way.

This ended in tears one afternoon a few winters ago, when Honk, on the fourth bike down, slammed into 'Nipper' Smith and the combined weight of all four vehicles was too much for the ice shell which broke and the four quads sank and all four Fullas ended up in the soup. As you can imagine, trying to haul yourself out of freezing water, fully clothed, onto ice is nigh on impossible so they all bobbed there until they were mercifully saved by a passing four-wheel-drive vehicle. Sadly, though, 'Ox' Morgan, who had a hole in his Blundstone boots, needed to have three of his toes removed because of frostbite.

Charlie and I tracked down another AJ from Arrowtown, who we also knew from Dunedin days, called Crazy Craig. Crazy Craig was a gun skier and general loose cannon. We laughed remembering him trying to teach himself the backward flip while ski-jumping at Treble Cone. He broke two sets of vertebrae on two separate occasions until he mastered it.

Anyway, when we found him again recently he told us of his adventures as a cameraman for a crazy bunch of AJs called Storm Surfers. Just this year he has travelled to Samoa, Tahiti and Russia in search of massive waves. He told us how they'd been out to a couple of places called Barn Bay and Yates Point, out from Milford Sound, and surfed 20 foot!

That wasn't enough for them, he reckoned, so they got towed on surfboards behind a helicopter on Lake Wakatipu at 45 knots. The next day they took the snowmobiles up into the back country and let off some avalanches thanks to the help of some gelignite. Then they headed down to Port Craig right at the bottom of the South Island and surfed a ferocious storm there, battling snow and hail and riding 30-foot waves. Conditions were so bad that the helicopter pilot bolted on them, so no filming could actually take place, and the two crayfish boats they had on standby couldn't get back in to port until after the storm had passed so stayed out at sea. All the while, apparently, these lunatics were being towed by jet-skis into 30-foot, very fat walls of freezing cold water, which white pointers lurked under.

One of my good mates, called Jerrad, was an AJ from an early age. He was the youngest pilot in New Zealand aviation history and, at the age of 15, would hire planes after school for training. One of his tricks to get the pump moving good volume fast was to take a single-engined Cessna up to its maximum altitude at night before the air becomes too thin for the engine (12,000–14,000 feet). When the motor, starved of oxygen, conked out he would switch off all the instrumentation in the cockpit (aptly named in this circumstance) to ensure he was in complete darkness and would then enjoy 60 seconds of ground rush as the plane plummeted towards the town lights below. He would then repeat the routine until he had his fix. He is still involved in high-risk activity working as a leading banker in Europe, but this time the risk is to other people's money.

The AJ is remarkably energetic in his business dabblings. He'll always have a number of 'projects' on the go and always seems to have 'just sold his business', which often proves confusing as nobody ever knew what his business was or did.

The AJ is always up for another 'project', however, especially if it involves assisting on a film set and requires him to be hanging from his omnipresent carabiner.

The AJ would never dream of being shackled by a *nine to five* job and would prefer to bounce from one project to the next. Having to do business with Prankers or city-slickers who don't know a crampon from a tampon is his worst nightmare. The AJ takes great pleasure in mocking these city slickers, Prankers or JAFAs as he refers to anyone not a 'local', and their ineptitude in the elements, while often overstating his ability in an attempt to impress (Fullas) or undress (Fullesses).

But AJs are a valuable and key part of our wonderful world. They are the 'Crazy Kiwis' that millions of tourists flock to visit. They push the boundaries and push back on the structured system. Some may call them 'nuts', but it must be recognised that they are also the very proud owners of a fairly massive set of nuts.

The Wodgewick

The Wodgewick or Wodger or Wodge is a Thespian and self-professed intellectual. He is a confused capitalist conservationist who eats alfalfa shoots and drinks fair trade coffee, but will fly business class to an exotic destination to help out a third world charity before spending a week in a resort recuperating after the stress of it all. While professing to care for the planet and humanity (in that order) Wodgewicks inadvertently leave their significant carbon footprints all over the show without sweeping them up, and have a habit of being extremely condescending towards anyone not sharing their views. A reformed Wodgewick recently described Wodges as 'the sand in the gears of modern civilisation'.

He judges all books exclusively on their cover first and foremost and if it does not appeal will never bother to look at the pages. Despite portraying an inclusive demeanour, he is a relative shut-shop if you don't hit an 8+ on the cool scale.

In every generation there are great thinkers and in ours it is not the Wodgewick, despite him considering himself as such. The reason is that, sadly, most of the thinking Wodgewicks do is about themselves — more specifically how their actions and attitudes might influence how others perceive them. Outwardly egalitarian and laissez-faire, inwardly conflicted and a mite contrived, the Wodgewick lives in the 'next to be trendy' suburbs and does everything for appearance.

Externally, they are concerned with leading-edge issues such as the supposed hordes of Kiwis who live below the poverty line, a lack of funding for fine arts and dance, and the government's inactivity on global warming. All this despite being capitalist at heart and prolific consumers. These are the guys whose desire to look intelligent and bohemian drove the prices on op-shop clothing out of reach of the poor buggers who could afford nothing else. To match the bohemian look they often run old-school rides leading to half-decent Kingswoods, Regals and Falcon Deluxes going for around 20 grand. They do, however, drive these sparingly so as to reduce their petrol bills (often engaging in 'neutral cruising' — sticking the car in neutral when going downhill) and tend to ride single-speed bicycles the remainder of the time, or until they can afford Hybrids — which a Wodgewick will be so proud of that he will drive it absolutely everywhere, negating any environmental benefit.

A Wodgewick will ferociously social climb — and will befriend many a Pranker and Finkle. They will berate John Banks as an out of touch capitalist and will call John Key 'just a banker' while secretly aspiring to meet them both. Should they be fortunate enough to have the opportunity they would blow it by clinging to them like a needy child and developing an awkward stutter.

They have driven the prices of houses in Ponsonby, Grey Lynn, Point Chevalier and Kingsland through the roof in Auckland. In the capital city, Mt Vic, Newtown and Island Bay are full of them and there are a fair few down south in the hip (or soon to be) areas like Sumner in Christchurch and the lake regions. On the upside, they are responsible for bringing down the prices of solar energy, organic foods, eco-products and for the increase in backyard veggie gardening.

Wodgers have names like Simon Harrington-Smith (always Anglo-Saxon and usually double-barrelled). One mate of Charlie's and mine, Nathaniel Monstuart-Willoughby, a Wodgewick of the highest order, is so pissed that we have cottoned on to his little charade that he no longer invites us, his old varsity mates, to his house for fear that we will collectively take the mickey in front of his new girlfriend — who thinks he is such a deep thinker.

Charlie and I were in Nathaniel's Falcon Futura recently going to buy some music (which incidentally Nathaniel insists on buying in LP — despite the fact that plastic is one of the Wodgewick's many evils), and Nathaniel was ranting on about the horrific inequity in New Zealand society and the fact we were heading for wide-scale civil unrest due to the widening gap between the rich and the poor, when a guy sidled up with a pump bottle of soapy water and a window brush and squirted it on the front window and began to give it a super clean.

Well, this Wodge lost the plot and let go a tirade of abuse at the poor prick, who was so shocked he walked off without asking for a dime. We felt so bad we called him back and gave him a couple of dollars and then told Wodge he was a contradictory arse and needed to sponsor a starving child to clear his name. Believe it or not, he did — and even carries the photo in his wallet as proof, or as we suspect, a conversation starter with like-minded souls. To be honest I am pretty sure I have seen this same photo in other wallets.

Nathaniel is the same Wodgewick who, after leaving school, worked on a kibbutz in Israel for three months and came back with a Euro accent! All of a sudden he was a self-proclaimed expert on the Middle East situation and had supposedly devised a foolproof process for peace in the region.

Nathaniel has recently marched against mining and the harvesting of native trees and quite vocally voices his opinion against both. What he doesn't realise, of course, is that all the materials for his latest renovation (adding a new kitchen and another bathroom to his Grey Lynn villa) including the wood, the matai floorboards, the slate, the marble and the appliances — all come from said activities.

Another example of his contradictory behaviour is his constant bemoaning of the inequalities between some of New Zealand's racial minorities. However, he recently moved house because his five-year-old son was about to start school and was in zone for a decile 2 school. In his very own words he said, 'I will just feel more comfortable with Geldof in a school where the kids look the same as him [i.e. vanilla].'

The Wodge is by nature a little flowery and sensitive. I would suspect it must be very tiring being a Wodgewick, as you are in a constant state of unrest with 101 things that one needs to be up to speed on to keep up with the trends and numerous things that need fixing for the next generation. Looking after the next generations' interests is the stated raison d'être for the Wodge and they will claim to be doing all they can to make it reality.

The anti-smacking rule is a classic example of a Wodgewick-supported betterment going too far and backfiring. However, the irony is that the Wodgeling (or Wodge's child), who has never even been sent to his or her room for fear of the parents being ostracised from the cool club, is quite possibly the most ill-disciplined, loud, obnoxious, opinionated child brought onto the planet. It is not unusual for the Wodgeling to be so demanding that nannies, grandparents and uncles and aunties curiously always find things to do when the Wodge calls up in need of a babysitter.

Wodgelings do not subscribe to the rule that children of a certain age should be seen and not heard, oft precociously parroting their delusional prepubescent thoughts on everything from mining our natural resources to race relations and always doing so with gay theatrical abandon — with encouragement from their parents who just love their unbridled 'free spirits'.

Wodgewicks ride the wave ahead of trends and as such are usually employed in creative fields, academia or those related to consumer behaviours, and thus are well informed about the next issue of significance that they can be seen to be promoting to the ill-informed masses. For this reason, most people think the Wodge is a cool sort of character — and indeed, in his own way, he is.

Wodgewicks lead a number of industries and their focus on portraying the right image means fashion plays a huge part in day-to-day life with the time they spend choosing an outfit rivalling teenage girls on a school mufti day. The outfit needs to look like it's just been thrown together, but in reality has been thoroughly thought through — from hats, glasses to braces, pocket watches, ripped jeans and chucks taylors, the Wodge is a walking billboard of all that is slick. Nathaniel recently paid $250 for a Docle & Gabbana cotton T-shirt bearing the slogan 'Let's Make Poverty History', which, of course, begs the question: does the slogan mean eradicate poverty, or take poverty to historic levels?

They are responsible for defining what is cool in the music business from locations, live acts to entire genres. They often pay absurdly inflated prices for art pieces from those they collectively suspect to be the next big thing and are responsible for keeping some of the dreadful comedians and theatre companies in the market.

In fact, the Wodgewick is invariably the critic who writes reviews of everything from movies to live comedy, music, theatre and restaurants. This job really appeals to the Wodgewick as it allows him a feeling of superiority in his chosen field. These unquantifiable opinion pieces are not to be believed at any cost as most of the general public will attest! For comedy, and theatre in particular, the reviewer is nine times out of 10 assisting the promotion of a middle-aged thespian mate on the bones of his arse, who no one has had the decency to tell: 'It's nice to have an interest, but you are in fact on an absolute hiding to nothing. Quit while you are behind.'

Many are the lost kids of the 60s, 70s and early 80s who have found a united voice in thought provoking the status quo with an underground revolution of intellect or, more accurately, interest. They believe knowledge is power — something they desperately crave despite outward appearances, yet they seldom appreciate that a little knowledge is a dangerous thing.

Be warned, if challenged on a specialist topic (always emotive and usually with no definable right or wrong answer) they can get fully bitchy, calling names and offering weak comments like 'You will simply never understand' before leaving and sulking for days. The fact is that they are so passionate about all they stand for, that they are easily wound up by conflicting views, meaning they are easily baited, which is a fun sport when there is little else on offer as can sometimes be the case. One need know little about the topic and can usually engage with a simple open-ended comment like 'Are you genuine about that?' This will give them the long-awaited opportunity to deliver their well-rehearsed diatribe on the subject during which anyone can find holes sizable enough to exploit at will.

Despite the irony, most Wodgewicks aspire to be philanthropic, neo-burlesque thespians or musicians. Those with no musical or theatrical talent turn their hand to debating, vegetable gardening, interior decorating and even home brewing — usually with a fair bit of success. A number of speakeasies have been popping up over the emerging suburbs of New Zealand, where the Wodgewick can chew the fat with his colleagues and cement new trains of thought and query the entrenched thinking of the establishment, encouraging a feeling of self-worth above reality.

With sufficient encouragement the Wodgewick will genuinely start to believe his own hype. This transformation runs many parallels to a caterpillar's transformation into a butterfly, with the Wodgewick turning from a 20-something philosophical drifter into a 30-something opinionated specialist. Wodgewicks would be horrified to know that they are sometimes seen as a little stuck up and arrogant, as this would mean that people have seen through their impenetrable front. These guys are aware from the day they decide to become a Wodgewick, with all the kudos such a position of social standing holds, that they will have to live a little white lie. As a result of this, they are often lacking in self-belief and need to group with other Wodges to bolster fragile self-opinion.

A small number never make it past being a dinner party bore and within 10 years will become bitter middle-aged men, sufficiently aggrieved that sensible society has not identified with their superior intellect and made the vital changes that they have long known we need.

Most Wodgewicks are, in fact, the remnants of the 90s SNAGs (Sensitive New Age Guys), an extinct form of Pranker, who delighted in reversing traditional role playing.

They are prolific talk-back callers, letter to the editor writers and secret meeting holders and a big part of the knocking system clobbering everyone that does not agree with their beliefs rather than celebrating difference.

A rather mean variety of Wodgewick is the **Chiwi** (sometimes spelt Cheawi). He's quite a Good Fulla, and one who knows how to get the great pleasures of life on the cheap. But he's as tight as a gnat's chuff — frugal, thrifty, penurious and parsimonious. The Chiwi brews his own beer (often using rimu leaves and manuka gum he gets from public parks or stands of native bush), distils his own spirits, grows his own vegetables, hooks his power up to the neighbour's line, goes to the pub to watch the rugby (because he doesn't subscribe to Sky) with a hip-flask in his jacket, bites his batteries (apparently that makes them last longer) and picks goodies off the inorganic rubbish collection for his missus' birthday present.

He is in many ways the only pure form of Wodgewick left and is a lovely remnant of a bygone era. This is a Wodgewick who has not yet, and will never, transform from down and out thespian and who, through necessity, is pinching his pennies while spending any spare loot supporting other Wodges in a similar situation. A lot of these Wodgewicks head to Waiheke Island and turn into **Wingers** (Waiheke Swingers). Similar communities exist on the Kapiti Coast in Wellington, Farewell Spit in Nelson and around the Wanaka lakes.

Wodgewicks are interesting characters and despite taking themselves a little on the serious side on occasions add a huge amount of culture and cool to the cities we live in.

THE WODGEWICK

Just beware of the guy looking too cool for school and carrying himself with a little too much of a spring in his step with more front than a 48-wheeler Mack truck. He is undoubtedly a Wodgewick and will be making judgements on you well before you have even noticed him hanging out in an up and coming café having a macchiato and holding a copy of the latest gig guide.

The Henanigan

Oh my word, the Henanigan! A real prankster (not to be confused with a Pranker). Always up to all sorts of tricks, antics, horseplay, high-jinks, stunts, gags and other inane and harebrained escapades. Typical Henanigan capers include:

- Boarding-school tricks like super-gluing some Nork's alarm-clock to the floor, with the switch glued 'on', then setting it for 3 am so the Nork gets an absolute hiding from the rest of the dormitory when the alarm rings and he can't turn it off.
- Pouring water on a fellow boarding school boy's bed during the night then making him think he is wetting his bed — soiling it is an even dirtier trick.
- Dropping a sleeping mate's finger into a cup of warm water to relax their bladder and urinary tract.
- Bananas in exhaust pipes, dead fish in air filters or under back seats, and other innocent yet annoying and painful manhandling of another man's vehicle is also typical Henanigan behaviour.

The Henanigan also crashes weddings, makes prank calls, slips red hot chillies into an unsuspecting sandwich, booby-traps the beach, precariously places wetas, blows a ref's whistle from the sideline, fills chicks' hair-dryers with powder and always has a pen and Post-it note handy for backslapping fun. His car will always have a whoopee cushion, and fancy dress in the boot, just in case there's a chance for a party trick to play on some poor, unsuspecting Fulla. The Henanigan's shenanigans would be redundant were it not for the unsuspecting victim, of which the Henanigan needs plenty.

The vehicle is the mobile office of tomfoolery for the Henanigan. One such chap, called Chad, ran a car full of every conceivable prop to victimise any unfortunate passer-by. He used to work in cahoots with another Henanigan (this is not uncommon) called Russ. Victims came in all shapes, sizes and personality types dependent on the trick he wished to play. (Chad spared very young children and the extremely elderly, but anyone in between was fair game.)

For example, the old ruler trick was best played on a bloke who had a fighting spirit — that way he would hopefully give chase, thus dragging out the amusement. This trick involved a 40-centimetre hard wooden ruler and a cyclist riding up a hill of moderate incline. Chad could spot this well before anyone else and would be rummaging under his floor mat for the ruler which he would pass to Russ sitting shotgun. Within the blink of an eyelid Russ would have the window down and be hanging out the side like a dog on a ute. I don't know how they timed it, but they always arrived just after the cyclist had risen up off the seat to get into his work on the hill and would place a perfectly timed backhand cuff around the back of the victim's hamstrings!

They would then slow down and take a photo of the cyclist screaming and yelping like a third former who had just received his first cane in the headmaster's office. Their ways of ensuring they were never fingered was to don balaclavas for any car tricks and to drive gravel roads to make the number plate illegible. Post trick, they would wash the car and wait a few weeks before the next assault.

They would drive past people at crossings and unload two-litre pre-pumped super soaker water cannons at their shorts, they would turn the car's ignition off and time the motor's backfire while they pointed plastic guns at pedestrians and cyclists, and Chad's car came equipped with a loud speaker that he'd use to extract the urine from people on the footpaths and roadside cafés about their choice of clothing, canine or their general aspect.

They once bought a locomotive horn and strapped it onto the back of Chad's ute under a tarpaulin. They then cruised around awaiting the slightest indiscretion from either drivers or pedestrians before raising them off the ground with a train horn three feet from their ear. They only did this a few times before they chucked the horn into the Clutha River to hide the evidence, as they felt they were close to being whistle-blown themselves!

The advent of the speed camera gave these guys a new lease of life. They stitched up a chap who had stolen Russ' girlfriend by taking his number plates off his car and borrowing a similar one for a test drive from Turners Auctions and racing past a camera 14 times. The poor bugger got fingered with $1500 worth of fines while he was sleeping (possibly with Russ' ex-missus) and had his licence disqualified.

They even pulled off a legendary scam where the pair of them pulled up and started a conversation with a revenue gathering constable sitting in a speed camera van and as one distracted the constable, the other unscrewed the back number plate of the speed camera van and attached it to another Turners van and then proceeded to speed past the van which was giving the tickets, effectively catching the very copper operating the camera speeding during his own patrol.

They once stole road cones and set up a detour on George Street in Dunedin beside the Alhambra grounds, directing traffic around the ground and creating a looped circle with no exit. They then sat on the roof of a nearby flat with a beer and saluted one another until the snail-paced traffic jam was eventually sorted out by the authorities.

These two Fullas were renowned for testing the boundaries of taste and even got into funeral crashing. All they needed was an op shop suit, which at $15 offered a good return on investment. They would then slip into the funeral and more specifically the wake and ply themselves with food and booze until they felt they had had their fill. As an escape play they carried two eye-drop containers: one with plain water for imitation tears, and the other with Listerine mouthwash.

As fortune had it, they never needed to pull out the Listerine escape but the script called for this to be administered to anyone who sniffed a rat by saying 'My! Your eyes must be sore. They are bright red. Here have an eye drop.' As you can imagine (and as I can tell you first hand having seen them pull this off at the pub), an escape without detection would be guaranteed as the victim bolts around knocking things for six in the search for a cold tap!

Chad and Russ once made a trip to Christchurch and, while stumbling home quite disoriented in a new city and feeling the bite of a sub-zero winter's night, after having humiliated some locals with inane pranks and gags, they made the decision — they needed to find a room fast for fear of exposure. They staggered to the nearest house and found a sliding window which they crept through, finding two single beds which they quickly helped themselves to.

Suffice to say, they had obviously taken a few shots of confidence on their night out and woke the next morning scratching their heads as to where and how they had got there. In fact, as bad luck would have it, they were awoken by an older woman bursting into the room and saying, 'Oh, you must be some of Johnny's mates! Breakfast is served.'

Well. Anyone but the Henanigan would slip out the window they had entered and beat a hasty retreat, particularly if one of them had fire-trucked (wet) the bed, or worse — dumptrucked. But not these two. No, they strode into the lounge and downed some bacon, eggs, toast and tea all the while being very general and nondescript about their relationship to Johnny who was out of town, helping his old man on business.

Apparently, the younger brother, who smelt a rat, given his interrogative questioning, needed a firm boot under the table. . . . The brazen confidence of a Henanigan, fuelled by the knowledge that they have a great story to tell, is something quite extraordinary.

Pinkies, charlies, dead-arms, dead-legs, nipple-pinching, ear-flicking (knob-flicking for the more sadistic Henanigan), arse-cheek whipping, wedgies, shin-kicks, chinese burn, cup cakes, and other such painful yet relatively harmless tactics are part of a Henanigan's artillery. And you need to always be on alert when eating with a Henanigan. They can play havoc with Masterfoods Hot English mustard or Kaitaia Fire chilli pepper sauce. And shit I've seen some Fullas suffer greatly when a Henanigan has lobbed large doses of wicked wasabi into a bowl of guacamole.

A very cheeky Henanigan Charlie and I know, called Henry, got wind one day that a good mate of his had hired a stick movie from a store in central Auckland. A few days later Henry gave this mate, Christian, a call sounding all concerned, asking Christian if he was watching the TV3 News. Henry then proceeded to tell him that they were running a story about adult video stores in Auckland and there was a clip where Christian was seen, clear as day, in the footage, walking out of the porn store with a brown paper bag.

The poor prick freaked right out, thinking of all the possible people who might have seen him on TV. Henry could only chuckle, knowing that Christian was going to exacerbate the problem trying to 'rectify' his non-existing predicament.

Henanigans can be a bloody nuisance at times (as a note of warning, the more risqué and immoral Henanigan will often contemplate a relationship with mates' mothers). A Wise-Guy Henanigan I knew, called Hayden, once put an ad in the paper advertising my car for sale, which I had absolutely no intention of selling. That little gag cost me a weekend of hassle and a change of telephone number. Hayden was as welcome as a fart in a phone-box at my place for a month or so after that episode.

And it can backfire for them at times too. This same Fulla Hayden, shortly after starting his first corporate cadetship job, walked past his boss Ross' office, who'd ducked out to get a coffee, saw his PC logged on, jumped on the email, and wrote to all of his boss' Outlook contacts (including the whole organisation and various important clients):

Dear All,

I root chickens.

Love Ross.

It didn't take long to identify Hayden as the culprit and he was fired immediately. Apparently, his boss Ross lasted only a week longer, and left of his own accord, sick to death of all the chicken jokes from his colleagues.

However, they can also be bloody useful. Henry the Henanigan used to take great delight in being the sober driver — partly because he found everything so amusing he didn't need to drink soup to have a good time, but mainly because of the amusement he'd get from the following caper.

What he'd do is drive ahead of all of us, swerving and weaving all over the road, so as to attract the attention of any Fuzz waiting out at checkpoints. The Boys in Blue wouldn't hesitate to wave him to one side and get the bag out for him to blow into. Slurring and spitting, he'd ask if he could blow up a condom he had in his pocket for practice, then he'd get out a bugle and blow on that, he'd blow a whistle, he'd blow them kisses — you name it he'd blow it, just to distract the cops for long enough so we could all drive past the checkpoint safely.

Many a mystified copper was totally bluffed when he finally blew negative on the tester, and was able to carry on his merry way. Good Old Henry, he's a bloody good puck. We still see a lot of him these days. His nickname is General Motors, 'cause he's always 'Holden' his whizzer. But some actually reckon the nickname came about due to his inability to keep his motor-mouth disengaged.

Another well-known local Dunedin Henanigan called Sweed suffered, as all Henanigans do, from a very short attention span leading to his being easily bored. This, coupled with his love of motorbikes, had him alleviating his boredom by phoning the local constabulary and complaining that a madman was doing burnouts and pulling wheelies in the Octagon in central Dunedin and had nearly run a few passing-by pedestrians flat.

He would then jump on his bike and go to the Octagon and behave like a buffoon until the cop cars arrived. This would then provide as many minutes of entertainment as Sweed wanted as he led the coppers on a wild goose chase all over Dunedin until he decided to put them out of their misery and burn off, leaving the cops to eat his dust. On occasion he would alert the Fullas to his ruse and we would gather to witness the pandemonium. This added to the adrenaline in much the same way as petrol adds to any good barbecue.

Sweed once told me he knew a Fulla who had had a few too many sherbets and attempted to cook a sausage in his bare hand. Suffice to say, he would have been better off eating his fingers which received third-degree burns and left him with a permanent claw/nub and the nickname of 'Hook'.

During my Scarfie days, I was doing a roadie from Dunedin to Auckland with a good mate of mine, Bangers (named so for his extremely large man boobs). We stopped in near Bulls, where I dropped off Bangers to stay with three Henanigan brothers whose olds had a farm there. The Overlander Transcenic train passes through their farm, and after a few beers over lunch, the brothers and Bangers decided to go down and play a wee game with the tourists travelling from Auckland to Wellington on the 'Silver Bullet' train as it was then known.

The train passed directly by the hay paddock and Scum, the funniest and also dirtiest of the brothers, decided it would be a good idea to get nude and get down on all fours to eat grass like the sheep. Well! The look on the faces of the passengers as they saw these naked blokes eating grass like farm animals was one of total and sheer amazement. Scum, by this stage, was hanging out of a tree by one hand and feeding himself a big handful of grass from the other. I think the poor tourists were particularly taken aback with Bangers, though, whose moobs looked like giant udders swinging in the breeze. (I feel obliged to note that although they pretended to eat grass that silly afternoon they claim they had, in fact, not smoked any prior.)

These same brothers, collectively known as 'the Brothers Scum' would amuse themselves in numerous ways. One of the most memorable of which was to go 'pheasanting'. This involved a disassembled shotgun, a kid's tricycle and an element of high risk. The objective of the game was to have one brother ride the trike as fast as he could up their gravel driveway wearing four rugby jerseys and a bike helmet, while the other brother assembled the gun as fast as he could and loaded it with shot and fired at his sibling.

Clearly, the slower you were on the bike or the faster on the assembly the more painful the welt. The game went a step too far one day when Bruiser, the eldest of the brothers, hid a pre-assembled shotgun in the grass and shot Scum from about 30 metres. It took the doctor two hours to pick shot out of his brother's back and arse-cheeks. From that day on, they decided to play with less risky ammunition like double-happies and sky-rockets and slingshots.

Henry the Henanigan tells of a similar story of when he and several Scamps (an Imp, a Puck, a Rogue, a Rascal, a Trickster, a Picaroon, a Scallywag and a Rapscallion) many years ago decided they'd head up to Auckland from Dunedin so they could make the twenty-first birthday party of a good mate and fellow Henanigan.

They were short of Pat Cash so needed to be creative on how to get there for very little cost. Someone had told them that a good gig was to relocate a couple of camper-vans which the rental companies always needed back in Auckland after tourists left them at the bottom of the South Island.

Well, what followed was a trip full of tricks and traps and genius ways of doing things on the sly. Christchurch was the first stop, and they had heard through

Reuben the Rapscallion's older brother that there was a 10-year school reunion on. Even though the Fullas were only about three years out of school they turned up after it had kicked off and pinned on the remaining name tags and hung out as a group eating and drinking to their hearts' content. When someone would approach them, one of the group would launch forward to cut them off and spin some yarn so as not to have their skulduggery foiled.

The next day, when it came to crossing Cook Strait, they only paid for two people while the other seven hid in the dunnies of the camper-van, in wardrobes, under mattresses — little Rick the Rascal even closed himself in a suitcase. But it was in Wellington where they really caused havoc. The night they arrived they headed straight to a top restaurant and set about ordering from the menu. When they were close to finishing their meal (but not quite) they asked the waiter if he could show them on the map where the Southern Cross Tavern was. While he did that, Scott the Scallywag tucked the corner of the tablecloth into the waiter's belt and as he left he dragged the cloth off and plates and glasses and condiments went flying.

The Fullas kicked up such a fuss the maître d' came over to sort out the kerfuffle and refused to let them pay. They then headed to the pub and Roger the Rogue began challenging all-comers to an arm wrestle with the loser shouting beer. As they faced off over a bar leaner, he'd give them a wink and gently lift his hoof into the groin of his adversary and caress his crutch. The challenger would instantly lose concentration and with it the wrestle. This little gig paid for most of their beers. They were on the prowl all that night and the next morning.

When fatigue crept in, they looked up the addresses of some large furniture stores, and tested the beds by having a little siesta on them for a couple of hours. Once rested, they then set about terrorising the city. They'd all sit in a bus-stop pretending not to know each other, then when there was a critical mass of punters at the stop, on the cue of a cough from Patrick the Puck, they'd all scream and run off leaving some startled and rattled travellers.

They'd found an old pram and didn't need any encouraging to get Rick the Rascal, who was knee high to a weta and had a face like a bashed-in crab, to crouch under it and stick his head through a hole they had cut, while they covered the sides with a blanket from the camper-van and put a pillow case on the top covering Rick completely. They then left the pram abandoned on a busy footpath with Rick making baby noises and when concerned passsers-by pulled the pillow case off they'd see Rick's foul face which would bark at them and send them scampering.

They'd do all the usual tricks like pretend to trip over a non-existent wire, then watch others 'step over' it. They'd all point to the sky and others would follow suit or look up in wonder, but they overstepped the mark and had to scarper when, after a road-worker had headed into a portaloo to take care of his business, they set up a large family tent, which they had in the camper-van, over the front door of the dunny, and whipped up a collapsible table and all sat around it pretending to play cards. This poor bugger walked straight out of the portaloo into a tent full of Fullas playing poker! He panicked and ran straight through the tent wall, making a new door for it in the process.

But not long after the event, his shock had turned to rage and he returned with some of his fellow roadies to inflict a little trick of his own on the lads. Luckily, they had loaded everything back into the camper-vans and when they saw the Ministry of Works boys heading towards them at pace they high-tailed it out of the capital city.

They made the twenty-first in Auckland only to relate their adventures to all at the party — and I am told their present was a jar full of farts they had collectively contributed to and trapped in a glass jar with a sealed lid and the accompanying sound track that Paul the Picaroon had recorded while the Fullas had their arses in the jar with his dictaphone (which they then played on the PA while the guy was doing his yard glass to put him off!).

Charlie and I met a few of the Fullas for a beer just the other day at the Paddington Pub in Parnell (the old Nag's Head). We were meeting there for a couple of quiet cold ones before heading up to the Oh Calcutta curry-house for a fiery vindaloo, some poppadoms and a few Kingfishers. Henry the Henanigan was there as was Bevan the Battler. Now, that's always going to be a win/lose situation. The Fullas were getting hungry and we were about to head up the hill for dinner when Henry came back with two pints of Speight's.

He bet Bev that he couldn't balance the two pints, one each, on the backs of his hands with his palms facing down. If he could — the two pints were his. Bev stretched out his hands, his face a picture of concentration, and Henry carefully placed the pints. A smile came over Bev the Battler as he stood there with two pints beautifully balanced on the backs of his hands. With that Henry the Henanigan said, 'Well done, Son. They're yours. Now bottoms up everyone we're off for a cuzza.' And so hapless old Bev was left standing there like a spare prick at a wedding, unable to move and a little too entangled and embarrassed to ask for help.

One year in Dunedin I flatted with a couple of really good Fullas, one of whom was a somewhat hairy Henanigan from Hawera called Herbert, and another called Pete who was a 300-pound prop who played for the Pirates footy club. The first day we moved into the flat, Herbert the Henanigan played a cruel trick on his poor mum. He rang collect and said, 'Mum, whatever you do, don't hang up; the police have said I can only make one call. I want you to know that in spite of what I've just done, I love you very much . . .' His mum went into a tail-spin and the joke actually backfired a little as his mother suffered a bad knock to the head from the fall she took when she fainted.

Anyway, one Sunday morning after a long evening on the jars the night before, Herbert, Pete and I decided to head down to some tea rooms on George Street for a cuppa and a feed for breakfast. Now, Pete could eat food like nobody else. To this day, I've never met a man with a bigger appetite or capacity for consumption. And that particular morning he ordered three Jimmy's Roxburgh Steak and Cheese Pies and launched into them, then finished with a serving of Devonshire tea.

Now, as you would expect the tea, the steak, the cheese, the pastry, the tomato sauce, the whipped cream, the jam and the hangover got Pete's metabolism moving at pace, and Herbert, quick as a wink and sneaky as a snake, disappeared off to booby-trap his victim. Nonchalantly, he came back to the table a minute or two later and poured himself a fresh brew of tea. To throw Pete off the scent he proceeded to change the salt and sugar shakers around so the next diners would end up with sugar on their chips and salt in their tea (a standard Henanigan prank).

Sure as God made little apples, Pete excused himself and said he was off to shorten his spine. He disappeared for an endlessly long time, and came back as white as a ghost with a terrified look of horror and dismay across his hairy, chiselled dial. What Herbert the Henanigan had done was extremely juvenile yet, at the same time, quite genius. He'd strategically placed four tomato sauce sachets under the pads of the dunny seat with small pin pricks at one end. Each side had